Extraordinary! I was totally hooked on the privacy topics covered. Personal information is part of every ministry. It's time for churches to think smart! This timeless classic offers relevant and comprehensive data privacy knowledge that every church needs at its fingertips. Grace covers almost all ministry and church operational concerns in the most delightful and supportive way. As a church you'll quickly discover processes that were not on your radar whether you're small, large, expanding, or a new church. Grace's analogies are unforgettable and true to life. The average church member or worker would have no idea how extremely important it is to protect privacy or what goes on behind the scenes/office administration in a church. Every church needs to understand privacy and how to apply its principles across ministries, activities, and church business functions. Grace goes deep to show why privacy needs should be addressed and warns against potential legal and regulatory consequences, which should be avoided at all costs. Her message is relatable, urgent, and life-changing to churchgoers, employees, volunteers, and leadership alike.

Lisa Banks, Retired Information Technology Specialist,
US Department of Homeland Security

What Others Are Saying about Grace and Her Strategies

What a great resource! You're going to continue to open the eyes of church leaders and members to a whole new world that they need to consider. There has been a flippant attitude in most circles (oftentimes mine included) when it comes to how we handle people's information. You create a strong argument for the danger of this and give some great practical guidance on what action steps to take.

As a pastor, I know that I am called to care for the people in my congregation. Part of that includes providing biblical teaching and godly counsel when requested, helping to facilitate the meeting of physical needs of members, and safeguarding the overall work and mission of the church. As we step further into a new age of technological advancement, part of that pastoring role must include making sure that the church does not harm its members by mishandling their information. This book provides a great challenge to be responsible in this area. As someone who was also in an adjunct role at a seminary, I think this information must be presented to students who feel called to the ministry so that all churches are able to be responsible and further the kingdom of God without unintentionally harming anyone.

Grace does a great job of providing a resource for every pastor, Christian institution head, and ministry leader. The misuse of the information of people in Christian circles can cause great harm, even though it may be unintentional. It can also weaken the credibility of churches and trust in the church community, hindering people from effectively receiving the gospel of Christ. Grace presents the need for responsibly handling the information of those we minister to as well as steps on how to do this. She takes the time to speak to churches of different sizes and touches on everything from content that churches should and shouldn't put in their bulletins to ensuring that counseling information and social media are handled responsibly. She makes the complicated seem more understandable and achievable. We are truly in a new era of ministry, and we need more resources like this.

Dr. Joshua Powell, Pastor and former Adjunct Professor of Evangelism,
New Orleans Baptist Theological Seminary

Grace's passion comes off the pages. I was completely blown away. God has given her the gift of storytelling and instruction. She keeps us thirsty. I can't tell you enough how on-point she is. Grace will help us train our volunteers and employees. This book highlights the value of privacy, safety, and peace in the church. She is a true beacon to people. When I finished Chapter 2, I was ready to order 100 copies of this book and give them away. We need this book and we need the entire series in seminaries. We need privacy like we need communion! This is an important book and a long overdue masterpiece of wise counsel for church administration. Grace has truly taken the concept of caring for people to the next level. She gives practical help and hope. She's a great communicator with a kind, warm, and nurturing spirit. She's a church privacy nanny!

Rev. Ann Bilbrew, Head Pastor, Living Springs Community Church,
Riverdale, Illinois

Well-articulated. This book is a critical and comprehensive privacy guide for faith leaders. Grace does a phenomenal job! You've been a great privacy subject matter expert supporting critical national, local, and international news stories with your vast knowledge on topics ranging from spy planes to drones to privacy concerns on capitol hill to hacking to identity protection, and now this. If anyone was going to write the first-ever operational church privacy book and render this much depth and compassion, it had to be you. Amazing! Grace, you're more than a quiet and skillful authority in intel, you're a strong woman of faith.

Hamil Harris, Former Veteran Staff Writer for the Washington Post;
Chaplain, Baltimore Police Department; and Adjunct Professor,
University of Maryland School of Journalism

CHURCH PRIVACY TEAM

Church Privacy Team

Copyright © 2024 by Grace Buckler. All rights reserved.

First Edition: Published in Washington, DC, by NAD Publishing, Washington, DC 20044.

www.NadPublishing.com.

Request for information should be sent to info@nadpublishing.com.

All rights reserved. No part of this book may be reproduced, amended, stored in a retrieval system, used, distributed, sold, or transmitted in any form or by any means—digital, electronic, mechanical, recordings, photocopy, or other—except quotations in printed reviews or articles, without prior written permission of the author or publisher.

All Scripture quotations, unless otherwise stated, are taken from the Holy Bible, New International Version® NIV®. Copyright © 1973, 1978, 1984, 2011 by Biblica Inc.™ Used by permission of Zondervan. All rights reserved worldwide. www.zondervan.com. The "NIV" And "New International Version" are trademarks registered in the United States Patent and Trademark office by Biblica, Inc.™

Scripture quotations marked (NLT) are taken from the *Holy Bible, New Living Translation*, copyright © 1996, 2004, 2007, 2013 by Tyndale House Foundation. Used by permission of Tyndale House Publishers, Inc., Carol Stream, Illinois 60188. All rights reserved.

Scripture quotations marked (ESV) are taken from The Holy Bible, English Standard Version® (ESV®), copyright © 2001 by Crossway, a publishing ministry of Good News Publishers. Used by permission. All rights reserved.

Illustration by Anna Trubina

Author's Photo by Teron James

Publisher's Cataloging-in-Publication Data

Names: Buckler, Grace, author.

Title: Church privacy team: building a trust-centered church by protecting members' privacy and complying with privacy laws and regulations / Grace Buckler.

Description: Includes bibliographical references. | Washington, D.C.: NAD Publishing, 2024.

Identifiers: LCCN: 2023952587 | ISBN: 978-1-7369478-8-3 (hardcover) | 978-1-7369478-1-4 (softcover) | 978-1-7369478-5-2 (ebook)

Subjects: LCSH Privacy, Right of. | Privacy--Moral and ethical aspects. | Christian leadership. | Church work. | United States--Religious life and customs. | Confidential communications--Clergy. | Data privacy--United States. | Christian life. | BISAC SELF-HELP / Safety & Security / General | RELIGION / Christian Living / General | FAMILY & RELATIONSHIPS / General

Classification: LCC BV652.1 .B83 2024 | DDC 253--dc23

Library of Congress Control Number: 2023952587

Printed in the United States of America

CHURCH PRIVACY TEAM

BUILDING A TRUST-CENTERED CHURCH BY PROTECTING MEMBERS' PRIVACY AND COMPLYING WITH PRIVACY LAWS AND REGULATIONS

GRACE BUCKLER

Resources By Grace Buckler

Church Privacy 101

Church Privacy Team

Church Privacy: Who Cares? You!

Motivate and Inspire Leaders!

Share These Books

Special Quantity or Bulk Orders

Buy 10 or more books for a 30–40% discount.

To place an order, visit NADPublishing.com.

Scan the QR code for discounts.

NAD Publishing titles may be purchased in bulk at a discount for educational, business, fundraising, event, or promotional use. Custom imprinting or excepting is available to fit special event or branding needs. For general information, please reach us at NADPublishing.com.

LEGAL NOTICE AND DISCLAIMER

Please note that the information in this book offers a broad application of privacy best practices, implementation, and goals. You are responsible for your own choices and actions either directly or indirectly. Your results will be highly dependent on your efforts, the scope of your data collection activities, and your legal and regulatory obligations. Individual church environments and applicable laws are different and require consultation with a licensed professional for assessment and insights. You acknowledge that the information contained within this book is for educational and awareness purposes only. Please consult a licensed professional for more customized guidance and advice that is tailored to your specific church and your needs. All effort has been made to present general, accurate, reliable, up-to-date, and relevant information. No warranties of any kind are declared or implied. Note that the author is not engaging in the rendering of legal, financial, medical, IT, security, or professional advice. Therefore, the reader acknowledges that under no circumstances is the author or publisher responsible for any direct or indirect losses incurred as a result of the use of the information contained within this book, including (but not limited to) errors, omissions, or inaccuracies.

Any company information, products, website addresses, phone numbers, or links printed in this book are offered as a resource and for illustration purposes. They are not intended in any way to be or to imply endorsements.

Details and names in some anecdotes and stories have been changed to protect the privacy or identities of the persons involved.

Note: Laws and regulations provided in this book are offered to provide you with additional insight into different jurisdictions. However, these laws, regulations, and frameworks are subject to amendments, name changes, revisions, and sometimes invalidation. We recommend you research and stay up to date with changes to the specific jurisdiction that's of interest to your church. Be aware that websites offered as sources or citations at the time this book was written may have changed or vanished by the time you read this book.

To my uncle, Nathaniel Kingsley, whose belief in the vision of a fifteen-year-old me changed many lives, especially mine.

But everyone who hears these words of mine and does not put them into practice is like a foolish man who built his house on sand.
(Matthew 7:26)

SUMMARY OF CONTENTS

Acknowledgements	1
Preface	3
Introduction	6
Part One: Privacy Basics	**17**
Personal Information and Data Inventory	18
Privacy Principles	40
The Law	56
Church Privacy Notices	70
Part Two: Church Operations	**103**
Church Freelancers, Vendors, Contractors, Gig Workers, and Employees	104
Church Bookstores, Gift Shops, Cafeterias, Gyms, and Clinics	145
Church Leadership, Counseling, and Mental Health	171
Small Church Privacy Challenges	196
Children	211
Part Three: Church Communication and Technology	**217**
Cybersecurity, Website, and Applications	218
Church Email, Social Media, and Cameras	239
Church Bulletins, Directories, and Announcements	261
Prayer Requests, Hospitalizations, and Funerals	272
Part Four: Privacy Violations	**287**
Data Breach Costs	288
Data Breach and Cyber Liability Insurance	293
Conclusion	309
Appendices	313
More Recent Privacy-Related Book Releases	346
Connect with Grace beyond the Page	347
About Grace	350
Ways You Can Engage with Grace throughout the Year	352
Available Anywhere Books and E-books Are Sold	354
Special FREE Bonus Gift for You	356
Additional Training Resources	357
Notes	359
Index	367

Contents

Acknowledgements ... 1

Preface ... 3

INTRODUCTION ... 6

    Protect Your Privacy ... 6

    Should Your Church Take Privacy Seriously? ... 7

    Who Is Responsible for Church Privacy? ... 11

    What Can You Do about Church Privacy? ... 13

    How to Use This Book ... 15

PART ONE: PRIVACY BASICS ... 17

    1. Personal Information and Data Inventory ... 18

        Personal Information ... 18

        Sensitive Personal Information ... 20

        Personal Information in Your Church ... 24

        Hoarding Information ... 33

    2. Privacy Principles ... 40

        Privacy Principles ... 41

        Privacy Roles ... 43

        Who Knows What? ... 47

    Onions in Church Leadership … 48

3. The Law … 56

    Privacy Laws That Apply to Your Church … 57

    Privacy Framework … 60

    Get Consent and Avoid Privacy Invasion and Intrusion Lawsuits … 62

    Avoid False Light and Defamation Lawsuits … 64

    Avoid Negligence and Data Breach Lawsuits … 66

4. Church Privacy Notices … 70

    Privacy Notice … 70

    Privacy Policy … 70

    Privacy Statement … 71

    Tailoring Privacy Notices … 71

    Creating Your Own Privacy Notice … 72

    Usability, Design, and the Structure of Your Privacy Notice … 75

    Privacy Notices and Layered Notices Templates … 77

    Let's Create Your Own Privacy Notice … 78

    Sample Layered Privacy Notice … 85

    Privacy Statement … 87

    Internal Privacy Notices … 88

    Event Privacy Notices … 89

Internal Rules for Collection and Storage ... 96

Basis for Granting Access or Approving Access to Personal Information ... 98

Authority and the Process of Approval of Access to Personal Information ... 100

PART TWO: CHURCH OPERATIONS ... 103

Church Freelancers, Vendors, Contractors, Gig Workers, and Employees ... 104

Costly Vendor Problems ... 106

Working with Contractors, Freelancers, and Vendors Directly ... 106

Freelancers and Gig Workers on Online Platforms ... 107

Freelance Platforms ... 111

What Type of Access Permission Does the Freelancer Need? ... 117

What You Should Know about the Freelance Platforms You're Using ... 121

Rules to Protect Your Church on Freelance Platforms ... 122

Communication with Your Freelancer ... 123

Paying Your Freelancers ... 123

Church Employees ... 124

How Do You Get Contractors, Freelancers, Vendors, or Volunteers to Comply with Your Privacy Policy/Standards? ... 128

Training for Church Employees ... 131

Granting and Approving Access to Personal Information ... 135

Incidents ... 135

Perform a Risk Assessment of Your Church ... 140

Salaries, Raise Negotiations, and Privacy ... 142

6. Church Bookstores, Gift Shops, Cafeterias, Gyms, and Clinics ... 145

The Importance of a Church Bookstore ... 145

Personal Information Collection ... 145

Risks to Personal Financial Information ... 146

Vendor Management and Card Payment ... 146

Payment Card Industry Data Security Standard (PCI DSS) ... 147

Four Areas Most Privacy Laws and Regulations Spotlight ... 154

Secure Sockets Layer (SSL) ... 155

The Value of Applying Secure Sockets Layer (SSL) ... 157

Other Considerations for Your Church Bookstore's E-commerce Site ... 158

Privacy by Default and Privacy by Design ... 159

Church Gym ... 162

Church Clinic ... 163

Health Fairs ... 164

Protecting Health Information ... 165

Gym Services ... 165

On-Site Clinic ... 167

Health Fair ... 168

7. Church Leadership, Counseling, and Mental Health — 171

    Authority Abuse — 171

    Misusing the Mic — 174

    Accountability — 175

    Let's Talk about Sex — 179

    Why People Need Counseling and Privacy — 184

    Mental Health: What People Are Saying Versus How They Are Doing — 188

8. Small Church Privacy Challenges — 196

    Benefits and Challenges of Being a Small Church — 196

    Don't Compare Yourself to Others — 197

    Being Small Is Not a Defect — 198

    No Substitute for You — 198

    Small Churches Perish Too for Lack of Knowledge — 200

    Data Traders and Criminals Love Small Churches — 202

    Trusting the Wrong People and Things — 203

    A Plan Will Save Money — 203

    Privacy Consciousness — 204

    You're Too Busy for This! — 205

    Privacy Regulator — 205

    Over-Accommodating — 206

    Give Away Multiple Hats 206

    Privacy Assembly 207

    The Value in Being Small 207

9. Children 211

    Collecting Children's Personal Information 212

    Child Caregivers 213

    Importance of Collection 213

    Church Websites and Children 213

PART THREE: CHURCH COMMUNICATION AND TECHNOLOGY 217

10. Cybersecurity, Website, and Applications 218

    Cybersecurity and Data Privacy 218

    Cybersecurity Versus Information Security 219

    Effectiveness of Apps for Team Collaborations 222

    Personal Identifiable Information (PII) 224

    You're Only as Strong as Your Weakest Link 224

    Seven Simple Steps to Stay Secure on Online Apps 225

    Manage Apps, Collaborative Software, and Services 226

    Collaborative Apps and Services for Managing Church Worship Services 227

    Bible Apps 233

11. Church Email, Social Media, and Cameras 239
    Church Email 239
    Social Media 243
    Cameras 252

12. Church Bulletins, Directories, and Announcements 261
    Church Bulletins 261
    Prayer Announcements 264
    Directories 264

13. Prayer Requests, Hospitalizations, and Funerals 272
    Prayer Requests 272
    Hospitalization: Privacy Even during Sickness 276
    Privacy and Funerals 280

PART FOUR: PRIVACY VIOLATIONS 287

14. Data Breach Costs 288
    Preparedness 288
    Financial Risks and Assessment 289

15. Data Breach and Cyber Liability Insurance 293
    Coverage 294
    General Liability 299

    Insurance Terms 300

    Cyber Liability Insurance 301

    Calculate Coverage 302

    Data Breach Insurance 303

    Shop Around 303

    Don't Purchase More than You Need 305

CONCLUSION 309

APPENDICES 313

    Appendix A: Sample Privacy Job Descriptions 314

        Position: Privacy Advisor 315

        Position: Privacy Coordinator 318

    Appendix B: US Federal and State Privacy Laws 322

        US Federal Laws 322

    Appendix C: International Privacy Laws and Regulations 326

    Appendix D: Other International Privacy Guidelines 334

    Appendix E: Major Retailers' Data Breaches 336

    Appendix F: Mrs. Lindqvist's Story 339

    Appendix G: Additional Church Data Breaches and Invasion of Privacy Lawsuits ... 340

    Appendix H: Onion Rings Template 343

Appendix I: Great Privacy and Cybersecurity Books 344

More Recent Privacy-Related Book Releases 346

Connect with Grace beyond the Page 347

About Grace 350

Ways You Can Engage with Grace throughout the Year 352

Available Anywhere Books and E-books Are Sold 354

Special FREE Bonus Gift for You 356

Additional Training Resources 357

    Privacy Success for Church Volunteers and Employees 357

    NEW Church Privacy Team Course 357

    NEW Expert Resources 358

    Connect with Grace Online 358

    Notes 359

    Index 367

Acknowledgements

Readers, readers, readers! Accept my bearlike hugs. I thank God for giving me the foresight and direction and I thank Him for you! You caught the vision for this book from the start. After tasting the goodness of *Church Privacy 101*, you demanded more, and you kept me pondering even at 3 A.M. Thanks for sharing your personal stories of church leadership and doing so for the good of the greater church. To all the church and synagogue leaders who have impacted my life and this book, God knows you're a gem and are too numerous to name. You've fed, influenced, and shaped me into a heaven-bound Grace. I'm grateful and want church privacy practices to improve for you and for those you care so much about!

To my relentless editorial team, Callie, Joyce, Lady Rhoda, Josh, Sam, Gabrielle, Olson, Juliet, Brette, and NAD Publishing, you've seasoned, spliced, chopped, and fine-tuned this manuscript into a beautiful book. Thanks for staying committed through the thick and thin. Thanks for making this series a success and a resource for churches all over the globe.

I thank the many lovely endorsers, churchgoers, and leaders I've met along the way, some of whom have already contacted me about how *Church Privacy 101* and *Church Privacy: Who Cares? You!* impacted their lives. Your encouraging words are like a million sweet smelling flowers and herbal tea. They keep me writing.

To my extraordinary mentors and friendtors: Marcia and Frederick, Tanya and Carl, Car and Kevin, and Georgia, you should be thanked more often. Thank you. You deserve a hug right now.

To my amazing family, friends, professional circles, leadership circles, privacy students, and awesome church and Sunday school family, I love you! Let me say that again. I love you! Your prayers and encouragement mean so much to me. To the University of Toronto, Edinburgh Napier University, and the University Bookstore. Thanks for your resources.

To some of the authors who have done much more than inspire me, Karl Vaters, Kay Arthur, David Arthur, Pete De Lacy, Jo Saxton, Kimberla Lawson Roby, Dr. Henry Cloud, Dr. John Townsend, Valorie Burton, Lysa TerKeurst, Wayne Barber, Eddie Rasnake, Richard Shepherd, and Dr. Willie Jolley. Many thanks.

Grace

If there's a book that you want to read, but it hasn't been written yet, then you must write it.

(Toni Morrison)

Preface

As a church planter's daughter, I was born on the mission field. Although I cherished the thrills of adventure and exploration, and meeting some of the most amazing people, the frequent relocations, open doors, and foreign places, languages, and dialects often left me longing for privacy and stability. I felt awkward in churches where everyone seemed to know the personal details about everyone else, and I questioned whether God actually intended it to be so. As a child, in my imagination I sent anonymous notes to church leaders about issues I felt needed improvement. My concerns ranged from poor selection of children's refreshments to the lack of a recess between Sunday school and the worship service. In college I published a periodical to increase visibility for the youth in the church. After graduation I felt a calling to create more awareness and to address neglected issues within churches. One of those burning issues I hadn't read of or heard anyone speaking about was privacy. I was haunted by my observations of many mentally distressed churchgoers leaving the church wounded and enraged by privacy violations. I knew I needed to step up and help. I have.

I love helping churches. I help churches and members handle privacy issues. I desire for churches to be compliant with privacy laws and regulations. But most importantly, I want churches to foster trust and to create lasting relationships within their communities. I am an entrepreneur, a global privacy expert, and the founder of The Privacy Advocate, a privacy consulting firm in Washington, DC. I confess, I wasn't always a privacy purist or a good privacy steward. I've betrayed confidences, hurt others, and made careless privacy mistakes. If you haven't, great. Pray for those of us who have learned the hard way. I relish this opportunity to openly share my knowledge.

Privacy is a human need. It's about respecting human dignity. Privacy is important for churches because a church is a place where humans interact on many levels and personal information is shared. There are many situations where privacy needs should be respected:

- when someone is going through a difficult time and requires counseling

- when churches collect personal information for event registration

- when taking care of children

- when taking prayer requests

- during financial transactions

- during sermons, in published works, and in prayer meetings

Privacy needs are sometimes met in churches, but in my experience, they are often neglected. Members of the clergy often take a wait-and-see approach (that is, they wait for someone to complain about privacy before considering it an issue). And if anyone does have an issue with privacy, too often they just tell other members, and that's as far as it gets. Unfortunately, privacy is one of those needs that church leaders do not truly appreciate until they have been gutted and embarrassed.

I thought it was time to address the gaps and ensure that more churches are equipped and empowered to understand and respect privacy needs. So in 2011 I took a leap of faith and spoke about privacy at a church conference. The conference attendees loved their first-ever church privacy session, but an important element was missing. While my PowerPoint presentation and worksheets were a start, they were not enough. Individual churchgoers wanted a solid resource to help them make a case for privacy at their home churches. In the ensuing years, my passion for privacy led me to write *Church Privacy 101* to achieve just that.* The book addresses aspects of church privacy in relation to its impact on people and relationships within the church community, such as people who are new to the church, people who have been in the church for a long time, and even people who have left because of privacy violations. It covers how members living a healthier and more peaceful private life make their church a privacy influencer in their community and beyond. The book also addresses privacy decisions in parenting, marriage, courtship, friendships, and workplaces and general privacy advice for churchgoers. If you value privacy, you no longer need to have those awkward conversations with your church leadership, family, or friends because *Church Privacy 101* provides you with information to begin making a difference.

I began to work more extensively to help churches properly manage privacy in relationships, use privacy to strengthen ministries, and meet legal and regulatory obligations in their business and

---

* *Church Privacy 101* is available at Amazon, Barnes and Noble, Apple Books, and wherever books are sold.

operational activities. Of course, once church leaders learned about my first book, they wanted one dedicated to the issues they specifically faced. This book, *Church Privacy Team*, is for church/ministry leaders, operational managers, and church decision makers. While my companion book, *Church Privacy 101*, will help you better understand privacy from your members' perspective, this book will specifically help you understand the importance of privacy from a leadership perspective. It will expound the importance of protecting privacy in your personal life and in the lives of others as well as provide you with the tools needed to optimize privacy in your church processes, governance, and leadership. *Church Privacy Team* serves as a companion guide to my church privacy courses, coaching, privacy implementation, and governance consulting services, providing a comprehensive resource that will help your church be accountable and proactive before a breach or privacy violation occurs.**

Scott Berkun once wrote, "Advice is cheap, decisions are hard."[1] Every organization needs reliable information and advice so they can then roll up their sleeves and make hard decisions on complex privacy issues. You have hard decisions ahead. This book will make those decisions a lot easier to make. But most of all, this book is a ministry to serve you and others. Its purpose is to invite your participation on privacy concerns because, as a church, privacy is your business too.

It really doesn't matter how slow you are going as long as you do not stop.
(Unknown)

To one who has faith, no explanation is necessary.
To one without faith, no explanation is possible.
(Thomas Aquinas)

** Details about courses are available for you in the back of this book. You can also join my informal privacy conversation community for free and be part of our bimonthly Q&A.

Introduction

Protect Your Privacy

In 2019 St. Ambrose Catholic Parish Church in Ohio hired Marous Brothers Construction to do work at the parish. Every month the church paid the company an installment via wire transfer and received confirmation from the bank. Two months later St. Ambrose received a troubling call. According to Father Bob Stec, Marous Brothers wanted to know why the church had not paid the installment for the last two months, totaling approximately $1,750,000. Father Stec was confused. "This was shocking news to us, as we have been very prompt on our payments every month and have received all the appropriate confirmations from the bank that the wire transfers of money to Marous were executed/confirmed."[1]

The church called the FBI to help figure out why the contractor had not received the payments the church had wired to the contractor's account. After an investigation, the FBI found that there was nothing wrong at Marous Brothers Construction; the issue was with St. Ambrose. Two St. Ambrose email accounts had been hacked.[2] According to news sources, it appeared that St. Ambrose workers may have clicked on emails or attachments that looked legitimate but were in fact designed to give identity thieves access to the parish's network. Unnoticed, the hackers monitored private emails within St. Ambrose and stole enough personal information about Marous Brothers to open a bogus bank account in the company's name. By impersonating the owners of the two email addresses at St. Ambrose, they convinced other workers at St. Ambrose that Marous Brothers had changed their bank account. The thieves then made a phone call to St. Ambrose to inquire about a purported late payment. An unsuspecting worker who answered the call remitted the $1.75 million to the forged account without first verifying it with other contacts at Marous Brothers Construction. Father Stec painfully concluded the story of what happened: "The money was then swept out by the perpetrators before anyone knew what had happened."[3]

Situations such as these are common. Churches are frequent victims of cyberattacks, and church members are subject to theft and fraud. But if you think a cyber thief is only after your church's money, you're mistaken. Not only does money vanish from virtual collection plates, but criminals also monetize the personal information they steal. For example, church members' passwords, names, credit card numbers, and other financial and personal information are illegally collected and sold.[4] Identity thieves don't waste any information. They steal money but also violate privacy.

Long before cybercriminals steal money, they first violate the privacy of their victims. How? Hackers violate privacy by compromising passwords and accessing and reading personal emails of the email account owner/church worker to find out about the business affairs of the church, including employees, roles, vendors, and people with authority and access to money. Cybercriminals are not always about stealing identities, reading personal conversations, and stealing financial account passwords. Some hackers have different goals. For example, exposing churches by leaking confidential documents, clergy's emails, and other personal information that could embarrass the leadership and disrupt the streaming of church services. These are all privacy issues. Our personal information is now widely accessible electronically. These days, thieves can steal more personal information with a computer than showing up at your church with a weapon. Keyboards can do more damage to your church than bombs, physical vandalism, or arson. And what's scary is that your church could be next.

If you are working on something that you really care about, you don't have to be pushed. The vision pulls you.
(Steve Jobs)

Should Your Church Take Privacy Seriously?

Protecting and preserving the privacy of your church members and workers is imperative. But doing so goes beyond faith alone; it takes planning, strategy, information, and special tools and techniques. If you think your church has more important issues to worry about or that privacy protection isn't an issue your church needs to consider, you might think differently after what happened at St. Ambrose and after you read the rest of this book.

St. Ambrose was not an isolated incident. For hackers to gain access to a computer, all they have to do is persuade or deceive the account owner, or anyone else at the church, into allowing them a chance to segue into the computer network. They can then access an account or impersonate the user, stealing what church folks often shrug off as unimportant but is even more important than money—personal information. Uncontrolled access to personal information allows for a multitude of crimes to be committed, as the following examples illustrate:

1. Human error led the Southern Baptist International Mission Board to lose control over the personal information of thousands of its current and former employees in a massive privacy breach. Stolen information included names, contact information, and even some health information.[5]

2. At the First Presbyterian Church of Birmingham, malicious email attachments were opened by unsuspecting church workers, allowing hackers to take over the church computer system with CryptoLocker ransomware. The church was locked out of its records and was asked to pay ransom in order to regain access.[6]

3. At the St. Pius X Catholic Church in Greensboro, North Carolina, criminals impersonated the email address of the priest in order to solicit church members and the public to buy iTunes gift cards.[7]

4. The Michigan Catholic Conference was robbed of personal information from its human resources and employee wage reporting system. Sensitive personal information that could be quickly monetized by criminals included Social Security numbers, dates of birth, and addresses.[8]

5. At a cathedral in Des Moines, Iowa, $680,000 raised to support homeless and abused women vanished from the electronic collection plate.[9]

This list goes on and on, with CBS News reporting that the FBI has over four hundred active investigations into account takeover fraud and is opening new cases every week.

The information collected by churches is attractive to criminals because it's so lucrative. Personal information has more value than the actual equipment it's processed or stored in, such as church monitors, cameras, computers, phones, and other electronics. Thieves can use or sell the personal information they obtain as is, or they can create or clone multiple accounts from one person's personal financial information.

On the dark web (the Internet's black market), personal information sells just like illegal substances. The going rate in 2021 for personal information is eye-opening:

- cloned credit or debit card information: $25–$35

- credit card with account balance up to $5,000: $250+

- online payment gateways (i.e., Stripe, PayPal, and others): $50–$1,000, depending on the account balance

- US Driver's License/ID: $100–$185, depending on the state

- passport: $1,500–$6,500, depending on the country

- health/medical record: up to $1,000 per record, depending on the health record details[10]

You simply don't know when a hacker is waiting for just one vulnerable church worker or a weakness in your church computer system. Any church worker who accidentally sends an email (with personal information) to the wrong person could be the cause of your church's data breach. But there's good news: it's preventable, and churches can take concrete steps to protect the confidentiality of their business information and the privacy of their church members. Because most data breaches are the result of human error, the best way to prevent breaches is to train church employees, volunteers, and contract workers on information privacy.

Education, training, compliance, and best practices are not only the right things to do, they also help prevent lawsuits and regulatory penalties and fines. Church members in the US have sued churches over privacy breaches and won. And even when members don't have the courage or legal right to sue, regulators in the state where your church is located can still sue on behalf of their residents who are impacted by the breach your church caused. In *Duncan v. Peterson,* a minister, Richard Duncan, and Moody Church sued Erwin Lutzer, the senior pastor of the church, and Bervin Peterson, the chairman of the board of elders, for false light invasion of privacy. *Snyder v. Evangelical Orthodox Church* involved the public dissemination of private information to a congregation despite a church official's promise not to do so.

Beyond this, your church's insurance company can decline coverage or file a lawsuit against the church depending on the situation. This can happen if the insurance company investigates and discovers the church could have prevented the breach or reported it sooner. Failure to protect against privacy breaches can be enormously expensive to your church. You don't have to become a privacy expert, but every minute you delay managing privacy could cost you thousands or—like St. Ambrose—even millions of dollars.

Besides the growing number of technology-related data breaches, *people* violate other people the worst: violations of privacy happen in non-technological church settings more frequently than you might think. Ministers, pastors, bishops, deacons, priests, and other members of the clergy who disclose personal information gleaned during private counseling sessions, for example, can face legal repercussions. Lawsuits by church members against other members and church leadership are becoming more prevalent, with *The Wartburg Watch* noting that "people have brought an increasing number of lawsuits against pastors for invasion of privacy and other tort claims arising out of the disclosure of confidential information by a pastor or other church official. The result of these suits has brought recognition that the obligation to maintain confidentiality is not only a moral obligation, but also often a legal one."[11]

The increase in lawsuits is partly related to the fact that privacy laws are mushrooming now more than ever. Many states now treat privacy violation as grounds for a lawsuit. The concept of a privacy violation can involve one or more of the following:

- intruding into someone's solitude or peace and quiet

- publicly exposing private facts about another person

- using another person's image, name, or resemblance without permission

- publicly misrepresenting someone or putting the person in a false light

Knowing the many different ways that a church can accidentally cross the line is increasingly difficult to grasp without the proper information, insight, or training. But once a lawsuit is filed against your church, it becomes public record. It doesn't matter if the plaintiff wins or loses the case—the church bears the most losses in the long run. Negative publicity is not good for any church, especially if you can prevent it. In a famous case from the 1980s, a single mom sued the Church of Christ for invasion of privacy, intentional infliction of emotional distress, and more. The story gained national attention and made the *New York Times* and *The Phil Donahue Show*.[12]

> *Even if you are on the right track, you'll get run over if you just sit there.*
> (Will Rogers)

Who Is Responsible for Church Privacy?

Whether it's a hacker breaking into church systems due to weak security and inadequate privacy training or a preacher violating the privacy of members, a church should be more concerned about trust than almost any other organization. And as an organization, all of its members are responsible for privacy. But it should have one person who is solely accountable for privacy. Churches must take an organizational-wide approach to privacy. No matter who in the church obtains personal information, the church is ultimately responsible for the privacy protection of that information and anyone who works with it.

You should extend privacy requirements to church members, workers, vendors, contractors, and volunteers collecting personal information on behalf of the church to support its operation. To be clear, this is not just about entering data into a church computer or collecting it online via a website. Collection also happens when people working on behalf of the church interact with someone one-on-one, ask for personal information, and write it down. For example, an EU court ruled that the Jehovah's Witnesses were illegally collecting personal information obtained from the people they spoke to during their door-to-door preaching because they didn't obtain consent before doing so.[13]

You may not be the Jehovah's Witnesses, but does your church organize community outreach? Do you evangelize on the streets? Do you engage in door-knocking or in other forms of community engagement? Do you obtain consent or permission before you take people's names, addresses, phone numbers, emails, ages, or personal information about them or their family members?

Do you know the rules regarding privacy that apply in the outreach situation I just listed? How would it make you feel to discover your church is guilty of privacy transgressions similar to those that have plagued larger corporations? Odds are your church is making similar mistakes. More than two-thirds of all countries (137) currently have privacy laws, and states are rapidly following suit.[14]

California enacted one of the most stringent privacy laws in the world, the California Consumer Privacy Act (CCPA). These strict laws are motivated by people's increased use of the Internet and increased adoption of new technology products and services. Prevalent use of technology presents opportunities for organizations to over-collect, overuse, over-retain, and overexpose personal information with little limitation. This applies to churches as well.

The scary trend of some laws and regulations is that they now apply to organizations regardless of where they're located. Your church doesn't have to be in California or the European Union to be subject to their laws—if you have virtual members or people who are residents in those jurisdictions interacting with your church online, their laws could apply to you. Have you noticed that with the rise of virtual worship, several activities spanning membership, donations, tithes, baptisms, and confessions require personal information to be processed? With some churches inviting participants from all over the world, you should be concerned about how privacy laws and regulations in other jurisdictions apply to you. With churches now processing personal information of members in different states and countries, there may be more laws or regulations that apply to your church now than ever before.

Being aware of and fulfilling all these privacy concerns and requirements might sound like an expensive proposition. It's not. I will outline a bootstrap approach that shows how all churches can get started the right way regardless of budget constraints. Managing privacy is not all about big budgets or hyped projects aimed at making a handful of people title-rich. It's about instilling a compassionate culture and influence, communication, and good practices that are consistent with the beliefs and values within the church. How? Your church's privacy mission is helping others walk in physical, mental, emotional, and spiritual freedom—by respectfully and empathetically walking a mile in people's shoes when responding to their need for privacy.

Of course, church culture can make privacy challenging. Your church may never make the list of "100 Best Places to Work," but it's the best place to work. You work together, pray together, worship together, and make a difference in the world together. Team relationships are sturdier because people rarely quit those jobs. This is good! The downside is, churches don't want to hurt people's feelings, so they don't hold them accountable enough (even major corporations hold business partners, vendors, employees, and others accountable). Risks and growth require you to show responsible love. You can't achieve privacy in your church without accountability: it's ingrained in privacy principles.

Imagine a worker has turned in her resignation or no longer wants to volunteer at your church. What happens to the loads of personal information she has processed for months or even years? Do you have an exit interview conducted to see what data she has at work or at home or what she needs to delete, shred, or return? This is not just a consideration for commercial organizations. You need established processes for departing employees and volunteers. To comply with your privacy obligations, you need to make accountability your policy.

> *The Bible tells us to love our neighbors, and also to love our enemies;*
> *probably because generally they are the same people.*
> (G. K. Chesterton)

What Can You Do about Church Privacy?

Despite the profusion of stories about the serious threat info-thirsty hackers pose, many churchgoers remain oblivious and indifferent to the need for privacy protection. They are like the bystanders in the days of Noah who saw a man building an ark but, rather than preparing for the rain, continued eating and drinking (Matthew 24:38). Don't make the mistake of assuming that thieves are only targeting the big churches or companies like Equifax or Home Depot. Scammers on the hunt for personal information will not respect the size or innocence of your church. They are on the lookout for personal information and will glean it from any source that is careless enough to divulge it. And if anything goes awry, a church faces the same liabilities as a corporation—this includes lawsuits, hefty fines, regulatory penalties, imprisonment, a wrecked reputation, and loss of trust, members, and partners.

Your church is ripe for criminals to prey upon the personal information in your charge. Some criminals belong to international consortiums like Evil Corp., a Russian hacking group that locates and attacks weak Wi-Fi connection spots. But more likely than not, your data breach will occur closer to home. Data thieves are in your church neighborhood. Some have volunteered or worked at your church, visited your church, hugged you, or shaken your hand. And when church employees work from home, it requires even more care and diligence because human error is the cause of most data breaches. Technology is not the problem most of the time. The errors that insiders make can lead to legal battles that can drain your treasury or threaten projects and your overall mission. Awareness and training are crucial.

What can you do? Get to know your privacy obligations. Set goals, formulate a good strategy, and gather expert advice. Think of the technology and processes your members' personal information goes through like doors. Each piece of personal information your church collects, even if it's stored for later use, creates an opening for many threats. And just like a door, it won't lock itself. A door needs additional security for restricting access—bolts, locks, or alarms—so be sure to check your church's privacy doors. Are they locked? Do the people you assign to handle personal information know about best privacy practices? Are they trained? To restrict access to personal information and protect the members you serve, you must act. *Now.*

Church Privacy Team is designed to help you identify the types of privacy you must preserve, give you protective measures to implement, and teach you how to manage the personal information with which you've been entrusted. Every step you take and every set of activities you apply from this book will help you secure many vulnerabilities that threaten valuable personal information. This book will help your congregation or ministry, whether it is a small prayer circle or a large gathering. You'll be able to assess the ways in which you're vulnerable to privacy breaches or violations and learn how to prevent them.

It is time for all churches to recognize the importance of protecting privacy. Doing the right thing before it's required is the best policy and the best privacy practice. I realize that privacy can be a difficult conversation to have, especially in church circles and even among individuals. People can be disinterested, nonchalant, and dismissive. They may even accuse the prudent of being unreasonably paranoid or self-centered.

But beyond their legal obligations, churches have a theological imperative to respond to privacy concerns. As the parable of the lost sheep (Luke 15:4) suggests, if even one sheep out of a hundred complains that his privacy has been violated, a caring shepherd seeks to help resolve his concerns. The shepherd goes after the sheep. The individual privacy needs of every member of the flock are important; it doesn't matter if the other ninety-nine sheep do not feel that their privacy is violated. A good shepherd does not judge the one that exercises their right to speak up. (Indeed, 1 Corinthians 6:5–7 says you should appoint the right people to handle complaints and put processes in place so concerns don't end up in court.) Still, a shepherd is not able to control what the sheep does. What you can control is first understanding what privacy is about, then doing what laws and regulations say is best to do. In this way, you can ensure you're equipped to go after and rescue the sheep that has lost their privacy.

Who is wise and understanding among you? Let them show it by their good life, by deeds done in the humility that comes from wisdom.
(James 3:13)

How to Use This Book

Church Privacy Team is an actionable companion book to *Church Privacy 101* that will allow you to get relevant information needed to make the hard decisions about privacy. This book is a step-by-step guide designed to offer you practical solutions, let you enjoy significant privacy improvements, and help you understand diverse privacy matters so your church can retain the trust of its members and community. Each chapter explores and breaks down a privacy topic and includes actionable steps you and your church can take. Starting with a narrative of a particular privacy concern or topic, each chapter also contains activities that offer you opportunities to reflect on where you stand on action items, allow you to record questions as they come up in your assessment and implementation, and help you plan your next move. After reading about each topic, you'll have a checklist to help you assess what your church has already done about that specific topic and what you could be working on next to reduce or control privacy risks. You'll grow used to planning, execution, accountability, and documentation in order to implement these concepts.

Together, *Church Privacy 101*, *Church Privacy Team*, and the companion privacy course will give you and your church all the information, skills, and guidelines needed to better protect privacy. You can find information about the privacy course on my website: www.ChurchPrivacyBookSeries.com.

This book is for small, medium, large, mega, and gigachurches. It's for all churches regardless of how members meet, their location, or the extent of online activity. It's for churches and ministry managers/organizers, ministry leaders, chief ministry officers, chief financial officers, chief operations officers, and church staff, including other clergy, leadership, administrative staff, missionaries, and counselors. It's also ideal for employees, volunteers, freelancers, contractors, vendors, and other church workers. Regardless of their title, anyone in church who processes people's personal information digitally, physically, verbally, and otherwise needs this book.

As Matthew 6:34 suggests, responding to the need for privacy today is better and easier than solving a breach tomorrow. Don't put it off. This doesn't mean you have to do everything all at once—as the saying goes, "Don't try to boil the ocean." When applying that to good privacy practices, you're better off dividing up the seemingly overwhelming privacy ocean into one cupful at a time with the limited resources you've got than trying to deal with the entire ocean of requirements and problems at once. If you follow this book one step at a time, applying privacy in your church will become simpler and rewarding. It will help you see what's important and assess where you are currently, and it will show you how prepared or unprepared you are to face your members and regulators should they come knocking with privacy concerns. This book is also designed to help you prioritize and focus on a few critical tasks so you can start achieving them today. I'm right here for you! With that said, grab some coffee or whatever beverage you drink at this time of the day, and let's get started!

We are what we repeatedly do. Excellence, then, is not an act, but a habit.
(Will Durant, *The Story of Philosophy*)

Part One
Privacy Basics

1

Personal Information and Data Inventory

Whoever is careless with the truth in small matters cannot be trusted with the truth in important matters.
(Einstein)

You can't protect what you don't know—or what you don't know you have. The first step in any privacy plan is to figure out what personal information your church has about congregants and workers. If you skip this chapter, you'll be on a path to wasting a ton of money and time. Waiting even a minute longer puts you and your church at risk.

But before you dive into performing an inventory to discover what you have, let's first understand what personal information is.

Personal Information

Personal information is any information that in a particular context and/or when combined with other personal data can identify a person directly or indirectly. It can be used to contact or locate the individual. For example, the personal data on your driver's license and passport identify you. Personal data can show where you can be located (your work or home address) or how you can be contacted (phone number or email address). Personal information is also any data that is related to or can be associated with or traced back to the person who's identified. Personal information is what privacy laws and regulations deem that it is. This means the context and source of the data play a huge role in defining what type of data is or isn't personal.

A first name can help identify a person you've casually come in contact with or someone you occasionally see. For example, I know Eden. I volunteer in a community program with Eden. In our group of thirty volunteers, there's only one person by the name of Eden. If you or someone who doesn't know her calls out that name, on a good day, if she is not feeling somewhat suspicious, Eden will step up. But identifying a person in other contexts is not always that easy. In many situations, a piece of important information by itself (such as a first name) might not sufficiently identify a person, but when collected in combination with other sets of data, it becomes personal *and* identifiable information.

Examples of personal data include:

- your first and last name

- home address (and apartment number if not a family home)

- email address (even the one that's not made up of your first and last name)

- ID card numbers (from driver's license, Social Security/national ID, and employment badge)

- medical records

- financial records

- birthdate

- photos

- mobile phone details (number, location data, and other traceable data)

- Internet protocol (IP) or Internet address of your computer and other connected devices

- physiological attributes and biometrics such as voice, fingerprints, palm print, etc.

Let's say you don't know who Eden is, but I told you she found the designer umbrella you misplaced. I described Eden as a very friendly, five-foot-tall, slender, fair-skinned, dark-wavy-haired lady with a huge dinosaur tattoo on her neck and arms, and that her standard greeting is "Hey, Boo!" Based on the physiological attributes I described and the context, you could easily distinguish Eden in our group of thirty volunteers and snag your umbrella back. That description was personal and identifiable. But try searching for Eden online with just her first name and those attributes. You won't find her. But a first name combined with a last name can help identify a person, link to other information about the individual, and allow you to trace the person online where you could gather more information about them. If I said, "Eden McGraw," you could go online, find Eden's profile, and confirm that's the Eden you're searching for when you see her profile picture. You may also find several pieces of information associated with Eden: where she lives, what school she attends, where she works, and people she knows. Unfortunately, busybodies, malicious individuals, and criminals rummage deeper. Having access to Eden's Social Security number or national ID number combined with her first and last name would reveal more about her. Armed with that information, you could trace and distinguish Eden from, let's say, two hundred other Eden McGraws in her region or country. Having access to Eden's phone (or password), computer, online accounts, people close to her, and her private communications could reveal even more personal information. For instance, it could reveal Eden's emotional or psychological state, her financial and health records, her personal decisions, her private photos, where she shops, what websites she frequents, what she eats, her entertainment preferences, her private struggles, her political affiliation, her beliefs, and her opinions—all the information Eden doesn't want certain (arguably most) people to know about her.

Sensitive Personal Information

Let's take one step back and look at Eden's health. Eden's medical history—treatments, prescriptions, diagnoses (whether in the past, present, or future)—is considered sensitive personal information. While it's critical to protect personal information, sensitive personal information is a special class or category of personal information that requires stricter protection. It needs additional protection against misuse by unauthorized individuals, including church members and employees. This is because, if Eden's sensitive personal information is revealed to the wrong person, it could have a significantly damaging, negative impact on Eden (i.e., financially, psychologically, and/or emotionally). Eden could be denied health insurance coverage due to discrimination over certain health conditions being exposed. Eden's bank account information—for instance, her ATM PIN, credit card data, account passwords, and the answers to her bank account security questions—is also sensitive personal data. Eden could become a victim of identity theft—she could lose all the funds in her accounts or be denied the use of her credit or bank cards. This could result in late bill payments, which would negatively affect her credit score. Depending on the context and the jurisdiction where Eden resides, her religious beliefs, views, political opinions, ethnicity, sexual orientation, genetic data (including her DNA), and biometric data (including her retina, fingerprint, facial characteristics, palm print, and voice) would also be considered sensitive personal data. The privacy laws and regulations in your region determine what type of personal information is sensitive.

What Personal Information Isn't

Any information or data that does not identify or link to a specific person directly or indirectly is not personal information. This means any information that isn't traceable to or associated with a particular person. In the context of a data breach, and depending on the applicable privacy laws or regulations, information that isn't personal can be defined as information that's encrypted, anonymized, redacted, obfuscated, or has other forms of manual or technical privacy protections that cannot be easily compromised. This definition is based on the assumption that if a criminal made away with such data, some regulators would calculate this as a low to no-risk situation to the people the information is about. Here is an example of a low to no-risk situation: although a laptop was stolen from your church, the criminals are unable to access the personal information or data inside due to the protections you proactively applied to that data and the device itself before it was stolen.

At the same time, information can be linkable to a person but, depending on the source of the personal information, may not be considered personal information by some privacy laws or regulations. That includes certain data collected by the government. For instance, if Eden buys a house, the government would make her real estate records or property deeds available as *public record*. And let's say Eden rents a room in her home to a student. If Eden later brings a lawsuit against her tenant, the government would treat the related court proceedings or court data as public record. With the exception of personal information of children or minors, court records are available to the public.

Other identifiable information that is not protected by the government (laws and regulations) as personal information because of the source, contexts, and jurisdictions of the information is called *publicly available information*. This is information such as your full name, home address, phone number, and email address that are part of a public directory or phone book. Publicly available information can also be found in a post published by the person the information is about. For instance, Eden owns a blog site and posts information there about her personal life, particularly her travels. Each blog post includes her contact information. Another type of information that's considered publicly available is a person's public profile. In this case, that would include Eden's profiles on LinkedIn, Twitter, Facebook, YouTube, Instagram, and other public media platforms. Lastly, information that isn't protected as personal information can be information that's shared and published as part of a person's interview with the news media. For example, Eden regularly helps create awareness of how therapy dogs help improve the quality of life for individuals with mobility impairments and hearing loss and also veterans with post-traumatic stress disorder. Eden interviews with local news organizations and speaks fondly about her well-trained therapy dog, Autumn, and the health benefits she enjoys because of having a therapy dog. That personal information is now in the public realm and is no longer protected as personal information because of the context and the source. In a different context, if a nurse in Eden's doctor's office takes in personal information about Eden's health or her disability from her medical file and shares it with another patient or a visitor, the nurse is in violation of Eden's privacy. Eden can take legal action.

Why is protecting personal information important to your congregants and the government? Wrongful disclosure or misuse of personal or sensitive information can cause congregants harm, such as physical safety issues, embarrassment, emotional distress, financial hardship, or discrimination based on ethnicity, political affiliation, philosophical views, and medical history. The government has a duty to protect its citizens. It relies on your church to do its part to protect people.

Your church has a moral, legal, and regulatory obligation to identify and manage the personal information it handles. Your church should understand the types of personal information and related risks so it can properly protect the information. Protecting personal data of congregants and church employees builds trust. That's an enormous benefit to the church. Besides, in doing so, you won't need to worry about hefty regulatory penalties, fines, lawsuits, and related liabilities. The government imposes harsh consequences on organizations that violate people's privacy or apply inadequate protection to the personal information they hold.

You're doing great.

Now that you understand what personal information and sensitive personal information are, you'll need to locate, identify, and categorize the different types of personal information about your congregants and workers. Carrying out a personal information inventory makes personal information much easier to manage, protect, and report. Have you conducted this type of inventory? It's not as difficult as you think. Let's talk about how this inventory is done.

Begin by making an inventory of the scale, location, and type of personal information you are dealing with. Sounds dreadful, I know. Look at it as a scavenger hunt. What you need to discover are answers to these eight questions about your church:

1. What personal information does your church collect or use? If you don't know, you won't know what to protect and which privacy laws and regulations apply.

2. How sensitive is the personal information your church collects? The severity of a data breach can depend on the type of personal information involved, and knowing this will help you determine your risk level and how much money you'll spend to investigate and recover from a potential breach.

3. Who does the personal information belong to? This is relevant because laws and regulations may be different for someone residing locally versus individuals who are from out of state or residents of other countries.

4. When and how do you collect it? How this information is coming into the church—online, over the phone, or in person—is relevant.

5. Who is doing the actual collection? If the information is being collected by someone else on the church's behalf, you need to understand the legal responsibilities of the third party you

contracted to gather the information or the church volunteer who is collecting personal information during outreach on the streets.

6. Where is the data stored? Knowing where the personal information is stored is crucial for understanding whether your existing protections (if any) are enough.

7. Who has access to it? Understanding which departments, ministries, leaders, or employees access this personal information to accomplish their work is also necessary for determining protection.

8. Who would be affected if your church or ministry experienced a data breach? The number of people impacted matters to regulators (it influences the penalties or fines if the breach is your fault), and who is impacted matters when notifying those affected so they can take the necessary steps to protect themselves.

I know it's a lot, but below you'll find a step-by-step process you can follow to help you answer these critically important questions.

Personal Information in Your Church

Begin by creating an inventory of *what* personal information or data your church collects. Be honest and don't limit yourself to the items I've listed below. The purpose of this exercise is to help you reflect on your church's data processing activities and the personal information that comes in as a result. Information could be collected through programs, initiatives, projects, events, missions, physical/online stores, members' giving/gifting—the possibilities are many. You'll need to document those processing activities and the related personal information you collect.

Personal Data You Collect from Church Members and Employees

☐ full name

☐ gender

Personal Information and Data Inventory

- ☐ home address
- ☐ email address
- ☐ home phone
- ☐ mobile phone
- ☐ age and birthdate
- ☐ marital status
- ☐ race/ethnicity
- ☐ sexual orientation

- ☐ driver's license number
- ☐ Social Security number (SSN)
- ☐ other government-issued ID
- ☐ background check information
- ☐ criminal records, arrests, or imprisonment
- ☐ fingerprints (for those who work with children)

- ☐ employer name and contact information
- ☐ employee files
- ☐ health/mental health/medical records
- ☐ vaccination card/records

- ☐ prescriptions
- ☐ family/individual counseling notes and records

- ☐ financial account/credit card/debit card
- ☐ passwords (employees and events portals)
- ☐ communications (digital or non-digital)
- ☐ social media accounts
- ☐ photos and videos
- ☐ IP computer address
- ☐ religious beliefs/faith
- ☐ political affiliation/opinions
- ☐ union membership
- ☐ insurance beneficiaries

Other Unique Personal Data Your Church Collects

- ☐ _____
- ☐ _____

Depending on the country, laws and regulations may be stricter about certain types of sensitive personal information. The definition of *sensitive* and what data is classified as such is not consistent across all state, national, and international jurisdictions. For individuals who engage in your church activities but are residents of other countries, pay special attention to how the laws and regulations in their jurisdiction define sensitive personal information. Indicate the definition in your internal policies for all workers, contractors, and volunteers, and prioritize the security of that information first.

Next, identify how you collect data. Think about the forms people fill out and what information you require on those forms. Which ministries/departments have forms? If you don't have forms, you should. How else do you collect personal information? Do you write it down on paper when talking on the phone, request it by email, or enter it in your phone or laptop during a conversation? Even small churches often use event invitation apps (for example, Eventbrite, Zoom, or Perfect Potluck) to collect personal information. Check personal information sources in your church, and add more sources to the list if necessary.

Sources of Personal Information in Your Church

☐ counseling records

☐ marriage records

☐ birth records

☐ christening and baptism records

☐ confession records

☐ death records/funeral programs

☐ directory (email, physical address, phone)

☐ health records (clinic visits)

☐ mental health records

☐ employees (hiring, payroll, fingerprint)

☐ disability records

☐ nursery/childcare records

Church Privacy Team

- ☐ financial records of donors/partners
- ☐ tithing or offering envelopes/records
- ☐ giving/donations (apps, website, checks)
- ☐ online/physical bookstore records

- ☐ church bulletin (visitation addresses, hospital room numbers)
- ☐ prayer requests
- ☐ communication (all types)
- ☐ education/training courses
- ☐ small groups
- ☐ senior and youth records
- ☐ new member registration
- ☐ membership/general ministry forms
- ☐ volunteer application forms
- ☐ leadership position forms
- ☐ church leadership voting forms
- ☐ conference registrations
- ☐ church videos, photos, social media postings
- ☐ outreach/evangelism

The next step is to look at *who* is doing the collecting—which ministry or activity collects personal information. Document who handles the process—is it an individual, certain ministry roles, or entire departments? Consider making a checklist of who is collecting the information.

☐ individual ministries and department leaders

☐ event planners or organizers

☐ ministry volunteers

☐ technology manufacturers

☐ computing devices

☐ membership registration coordinator

☐ secretary

☐ clergy

☐ service providers or apps

☐ treasurer

☐ members

☐ other _____

Then investigate *where* the data is being stored. Knowing where personal information resides is crucial for understanding your data security needs. Is the information centrally stored or dispersed? If stored online, is it encrypted? If stored offline, is it secure or not?

Storage of Personal Information in Your Church

- ☐ desks
- ☐ file cabinets
- ☐ ministry offices
- ☐ email accounts
- ☐ cloud storage
- ☐ employee laptops/phones
- ☐ stored by a third party (e.g., vendor, contractor)
- ☐ someone's home or office
- ☐ personal storage devices (e.g., thumb drive)
- ☐ church-owned storage devices
- ☐ other _____

The final step is to assess who has access to this information and what policies are in place to guide that access. Are there currently any church rules that address the importance of protecting the types of personal information you checked? Are they addressed in any internal church policies even if those policies are not a privacy policy? Who is responsible for protecting each of the sources you've checked and enforcing the policy?

Who has access to these sources (physically and electronically)?

_____

_____

_____

What policies are in place for the protection of and access to these sources?

_____

_____

_____

_____

_____

Has anyone been designated to take charge of the protection of and access to these sources?

_____

_____

_____

_____

_____

Do you have a way of knowing if someone has accessed, copied, misused, or stolen personal information from these sources?

☐ Yes ☐ No

At this juncture you will want to begin building a spreadsheet (or get one from the Church Privacy Team course) to begin recording all forms of personal data you collect. That way, you don't need to start from scratch to build a structure. You should record what kind of data, how it's collected, who is collecting it, where it's stored, and who has access to it.

Tip: For best results, perform this inventory regularly. Once you complete the first inventory, decide how often you'll perform the inventory, and create a schedule (for example, every six months or quarterly). Make periodic personal data inventory a standard business process for your church.

Church Privacy Team

Value: Once your church has this down, your privacy efforts will be more habitual and effective, lending your church greater credibility and even serving as a model of best practices in this area. Earning the trust of your members is a great value.

Action Steps: You've assessed the types of personal information or data your church collects. Now it is time to take the inventory. Have you designated someone within your church to handle this responsibility? Jot down your answers.

_____

_____

_____

When can you start working on this goal?

Day _____ Month _____ Year _____

What's your target date to complete this goal?

Day _____ Month _____ Year _____

What questions would you ask me?

_____

_____

_____

_____

_____

Hoarding Information

Churches hold on to papers and files with personal information for a long time. It's okay and lawful to destroy personal information on forms and other materials after you're done using them. Once upon a time, when I used to watch TV, I remember the A&E reality series *Hoarders*. One good result was that the show forced me to give possessions away and become a minimalist. I survive with only three pairs of jeans to my name. If I narrow it down to the ones that aren't ripped (in the wrong places), that brings my tally down to one and a half. In the few episodes I watched of *Hoarders*, the hoarder featured was warned that if they didn't let go of their vast collection of stuff, they would risk being evicted. Police officers eventually showed up. The authorities' interest was public safety, such as reducing fire hazards and other harms to the person.

Hoarding personal information is no different. In the eyes of privacy authorities, I don't want your church looking like the woman with seventeen dogs and five cats or the family with 22,000 pounds of trash. The risk of hoarding personal data in a church is that the information is likely to get disclosed to the wrong person, be misused, or get lost. Hoarding unnecessary personal information is a huge hazard. It's a risk. Remember that, and never, ever forget it. Examples of risks are people getting hurt, negative publicity, lawsuits, and regulatory penalties. You don't want that for your church. Whatever you do or spend to avoid this, it's cheaper than going to court.

What happens when you hoard?

1. Hoarding eats up your budget—your project or building funds could go into paying regulatory fines.

2. You increase your accountability or responsibility for that personal information. More personal information means dealing with more requirements to protect it.

3. You spend more to protect what you hoard.

4. You have more potential liabilities.

5. You're required to comply with rules of privacy and data protection laws. And the law will ding you for not deleting personal information you don't need. You don't have a retention policy.

There are privacy issues with donating and trading in old computers and devices too. There's no telling where they will end up. A gentleman followed me on Twitter recently. When I read his Twitter profile, I realized he was in the business or hobby of finding what people leave behind in old phones and other devices they pass on to others or throw away. There's a market for leftover personal information. It trades and sells the information to interested buyers. Encountering this guy reminded me of Ms. Watson. Who is she? Read on.

Ms. Watson's Story

I want to share Ms. Watson's story with you. But I'd like to tell the story in the form of a letter to you or the leader of your ministry or church. Since you're reading this book, plug your name into the blank and read on.

> Dear [your name],
>
> I hope you're good and coping well. I'm reaching out to you now to make you aware of an important issue. I believe you will be interested in this news for two main reasons: (1) I know you love donating items you no longer use to secondhand stores, and (2) I am very much aware that you might no longer have interest in the news whether it's coming from the TV, newspapers, or your electronic devices. It is based on these two reasons that I feel the need to update you on happenings concerning donating items to secondhand stores.
>
> WTHR News made a shocking discovery concerning the Goodwill Industries of central Indiana. This discovery was brought about by the observations of Emily Watson, who shops at Goodwill outlet stores at least once a month. She noticed that in addition to the typical merchandise expected to be found at Goodwill stores (e.g., furniture, books, and clothes), sensitive documents (e.g., bank statements, pay stubs, divorce papers, tax returns, medical and dental records, insurance documents, checking and savings account information, Social Security numbers, and credit and debit cards) were also being sold. To Ms. Watson's utter amazement, when her discovery was brought to the attention of the manager, the response she got was that none of what the manager had found appeared harmful. Can you let that sink in for a moment?

The manager didn't cringe at the sight of people's bank statements, Social Security numbers, or insurance documents. And believe me, I've been in Ms. Watson's shoes in many of the secondhand stores in my locale. This is the norm in most of the secondhand stores scattered all around. The shops simply don't care or maybe don't realize they should care about what is being sold to customers as long as money is coming in. Do you realize how easy this has made the jobs of criminals who engage in identity theft? Someone can just walk into a secondhand shop and leave with loads of highly sensitive personal documents. When some of the people whose sensitive documents were contacted, most of them had different stories as to how the documents had gotten to the store, while others simply couldn't say how. In all, they were so happy to have the documents retrieved.

In 2019, identity theft accounted for about 20.33 percent of the fraud cases reported to the Federal Trade Commission (FTC).[1] It equally ranked as the highest fraud committed that year, posting a staggering 46.4 percent increase from what it was the previous year. Identity theft reports received by the FTC in 2020, ranked by state, also showed no sign of any form of decrease on the crime.[2]

Given the figures on identity theft over the years, you would think these shops would have strategies in place to check and resolve issues such as these. However, evidence and facts on the ground are pointing to the contrary.

My dear [your name], I do know how much you're fond of donating items to charity. So, believe me when I say this information isn't aimed at making you stop. I just want to alert you to the reality so you don't fall victim to this careless and shameful act. That being said, my advice is that you always make sure you take your time to go through items you are donating to charity. Every last one of them! I kid you not! Read for yourself this article about a privacy breach at Goodwill.[3]

Spread love, protect privacy.

Cheers and Peace!

Grace

Now you know about *Hoarders*, the guy I met on Twitter, and Ms. Watson. Boy, were those interesting! They make you stop and think. Let's look at action items that'll keep regulators happy and hopefully keep them from penalizing your church. Regulators like to see you doing what's right. There are ways you can prove that you manage your data retention and disposal.

Assess What Your Church Is Doing about Retention and Disposal of Personal Information

- ☐ Our church has reviewed retention requirements for relevant laws and regulations that apply to us.
- ☐ We have a retention policy.
- ☐ We have a personal information retention plan.
- ☐ We have a retention schedule for paper and digital records.
- ☐ We have a vendor who provides disposal of personal information per our state law.
- ☐ We have an arrangement with a local store such as Staples to securely shred papers.
- ☐ We have invested in a shredder for every department and ministry.
- ☐ We encourage workers to shred church materials they take home when no longer in use.
- ☐ We understand that computer storage of personal information at our church is regulated. Whether it's located in the church or with a vendor, our storage is our responsibility. If anything goes wrong, our church, not the vendor, could bear most of the responsibility.
- ☐ We have applied appropriate security according to requirements to protect our personal data storage.

- ☐ We train workers to use strong passwords on their computers so personal information is protected.

Assess What Your Church Is Doing about Old Devices

Sometimes we upgrade certain devices and must dispose of the old ones.

- ☐ We donate old devices—such as computers (laptops and desktops), printers, tablets, or phones—to schools.
- ☐ We donate old devices—such as computers (laptops and desktops), printers, tablets, or phones—to other churches.
- ☐ We donate old devices—such as computers (laptops and desktops), printers, tablets, or phones—to our workers.
- ☐ We donate old devices—such as computers (laptops and desktops), printers, tablets, or phones—to members.
- ☐ We donate old devices—such as computers (laptops and desktops), printers, tablets, or phones—to seniors.
- ☐ We donate old devices—such as computers (laptops and desktops), printers, tablets, or phones—to anyone.
- ☐ We trade in old devices—such as computers (laptops and desktops), printers, tablets, or phones—to manufacturers.
- ☐ We delete the data, but we also use outside professional services to wipe the devices.
- ☐ We wipe data from cameras and video recorders and related HD cards.
- ☐ We back up the data in devices and check drives, ports, and openings on the side, top, back, and bottom of the devices.

☐ We remove and destroy DVDs, CDs, USB drives, SD cards, memory cards, card readers, SIM cards, floppy disks, cassettes, and VHS tapes from all devices before donating them.

Do you know how many of these external drives people find at thrift stores? Do you know how much personal information people find in them?

Tip: Create a checklist of what to do and what to check when donating different items. Create a document titled "Donated Items Checklist" or a title that makes the most sense to your church. Use the checkboxes I've provided you with. You can do this in thirty minutes max. Any church, regardless of resources, can do this. Share the document with everyone so they know what's expected. Address data disposal in your privacy policy to drive the point home.

Value: Having a checklist minimizes the liability that could result from disclosing or losing personal information that can negatively impact members, donors, employees, visitors, and others who serve and support your church.

Action Steps: You've assessed what your church is doing about proper disposal of personal information and reuse of devices. The items you did not check are your action items to work on: list them. Have you designated someone within your church to handle this responsibility? Jot down your answers.

_____

_____

_____

What's your target date to assign someone to take this responsibility/when will you begin the tasks? Day_____ Month_____ Year_____

What's your target date to complete these tasks?
Day_____ Month_____ Year_____

What questions would you ask me?

_____

_____

_____

_____

_____

Earthly goods are given to be used, not to be collected. . . . Hoarding is idolatry.
(Dietrich Bonhoeffer)

2

Privacy Principles

There's some truth about all of us we don't want repeated!
(John K. Jenkins Sr.)

Privacy is about people, not inanimate objects or organizations. Privacy refers to the personal matters you want to exert control over so that you can have peace of mind, preserve your dignity, and live securely, confidently, and freely. Everyone has personal information they control or want to control, whether it's positive or negative. For example, your bank account, finances, and passport are positive information. But that doesn't mean you want to share that information with everyone. Right? You may have made a poor personal choice in your past that you deeply regret (who hasn't messed up). But even though some people know about it, you don't need everyone to know.

Privacy rules, privacy principles, laws, regulations, and fair information practices require that every person, government, and steward of personal information comply. This means you and anyone who handles other people's personal information—your church included. Your church must incorporate privacy principles to protect personal information—ethically, morally, fairly, biblically, and according to specific requirements of relevant privacy laws and regulations.

Privacy has become essential for all businesses. People care about why and how their personal information is collected, used, and shared. Of course, these days, technology, innovation, and frequent exchange of information raise risks for both the people the personal information is about and the organizations that process personal information.

Now that you've identified the types of personal information your church may have access to (Chapter 1), it's time to consider *how* to handle personal information based on privacy principles.

Let's get started by identifying privacy principles that influence the laws and regulations your church needs to comply with. Your church workers and volunteers will make fewer mistakes when using these principles to guide them in every aspect of personal information handling. Your church will lower its risks because you're now well-informed about how privacy and data protection work and why they are important.

Privacy Principles

These are the golden rules of privacy that your church should follow immediately:

1. **Notice/Openness/Transparency:** give people a notice explaining your privacy practices, what information you collect, what it is for, and how you handle, protect, and share the information (some refer to this as a *privacy policy*, but it's a notice, a legal one).

2. **Choice/Consent:** give people choices. Ask for their permission regarding the collection of their personal information. Simply ask them to check a box to decline the collection, withdraw consent previously given, or unsubscribe from your emails.

3. **Collection Limitation:** don't take more personal information than you need to use (think about the commands on how to gather manna in Exodus 16:16).

4. **Purpose Limitation:** stick to one purpose for collecting the personal information; don't recycle the information for other purposes without the person's permission (even with all your good intentions), and don't hoard personal information—if you no longer need the personal information, let it go by deleting it.

5. **Participation/Access:** give people a way to contact you to correct, view, or delete their personal information.

6. **Quality/Accuracy:** make sure you verify that the personal information you hold is correct and current.

7. **Security:** protect personal information in all forms by maintaining physical and technical safeguards. Having adequate security protections helps prevent criminals and unauthorized people in your church from stealing or exposing private information.

8. **Accountability:** start a privacy program by assigning someone to take charge of managing, assessing, monitoring, and keeping your church compliant with these principles and relevant laws and regulations.

Assess If Your Church Is Already Incorporating These Principles
Our church has already incorporated these golden rules into our internal church policies:

☐ notice/openness/transparency

☐ choice/consent

☐ collection limitation

☐ purpose limitation

☐ participation/access

☐ quality/accuracy

☐ security

☐ accountability

It's best to get your employees thinking about these privacy principles right away. Here's one exercise you can do to get started: Start good privacy practices with any of the paper or digital forms you give members and visitors to fill out, such as forms for joining the church and registration forms. See how your forms line up or comply with the principles I've explained, and modify them accordingly.

More broadly, does your church have ongoing privacy awareness discussions, workshops, or webinars so that church workers, members, and leaders understand that privacy is a human need? A privacy expert can help facilitate or moderate privacy awareness discussions, workshops, or webinars that your staff and ministry leaders can engage in. It's one of the best ways you can communicate these privacy principles to get everyone on board with your legal and regulatory obligations and responsibilities, which I'll explain in the next chapter.

Privacy Roles

You still recall the principles we just went over? Having privacy principles down pat is well and good, but they need someone to put them into action in order to reap the benefits. Shall I zoom in on the accountability principles to show you how? The privacy roles I'm about to discuss for putting privacy principles into action are different from the roles you would find in most church environments. Similar to "Take Your Child to Work Day," let's pretend it's "Take Your Church to Work Day"—and I'm taking your church with me so you get to learn about the many different privacy roles that exist. Each role performs its own significant function. Each role covers a particular area of expertise and accountability to make sure people's privacy needs and the legal obligations of the organization are met.

By adding privacy roles, you add accountability to your privacy practices, and regulators praise accountability. But don't let the number of potential roles intimidate you. I'm not suggesting that you need all the roles listed below. You might need only one or two of them depending on the scope of your church's personal information collection or processing activities. Even if you end up just having one privacy person in your church who wears multiple hats, knowing the details of all these roles will give insight on future needs or privacy solutions you may consider, even as a small church.

Privacy Roles and Responsibilities

A privacy coordinator keeps every church department leader on their toes about their privacy responsibilities. They know tasks that need to be completed by certain deadlines to meet compliance requirements. In other words, they harmonize the church's administrative activities related to privacy laws and regulations, which I'll discuss in the next chapter. They do this with different groups within the organization by serving as their point of contact for privacy-related concerns and to provide a progress report to the leadership. A coordinator may review internal and external requests about personal information and also review privacy complaints and escalate privacy concerns to those in other privacy roles to track and resolve the issues. They also directly support the privacy expert. I view this role as the privacy office manager.

A **privacy analyst** works with different departments/roles to identify privacy risks, assesses risks, monitors risks, researches privacy controls, ensures privacy policies are implemented, and communicates updates to regulatory requirements.

A **privacy manager** manages the privacy program, processes, policies, procedures, and privacy staff and other privacy roles. They report to the privacy director or data protection officer.

A **privacy project manager** manages essential privacy program projects and compliance activities and compliance road maps by collaborating with other departments to assure deadlines are met.

A **privacy officer/chief privacy officer (CPO)** is a senior-level executive whose responsibility is to make and manage personal information decisions and risks across the organization in compliance with laws and regulations.

A **data protection officer (DPO)** manages compliance risks by advising the organization about its obligation to customers, employees, and members and to laws and regulations. They serve as the face of the organization to the public. They help assess privacy complaints and concerns and interact with privacy regulators or authorities. (Note: this is a legally required position in certain organizations that collect and process personal information on a certain scale.)

A **privacy engineer** focuses on technology products (apps, software, platforms) to ensure they're designed by default to protect, preserve the privacy of the users, and comply with laws and regulations. They help the organization properly communicate to users how their products work and how people can control their privacy preferences.

A **privacy expert/consultant** is an independent expert or consultant who helps an organization in whatever capacity it needs to apply best practices and achieve compliance. For instance, they can carve out a neat privacy roadmap, assess the activities your church engages in on a daily basis, give advice on high-priority steps to take, and may also make recommendations on setting up a privacy program as well as hiring, program goals, strategy, implementation, operations, communication, training, and technology solutions. An expert knows how privacy works to the finest details—they operationalize the theory and deliver the results.

Can you picture these roles? Privacy roles are pretty cool.

Depending on what you can afford, I recommend a part-time or full-time privacy coordinator, either hired internally or outsourced to a consultant. If your church wants to put together a job description to help hire a privacy coordinator, you can see a sample job description in Appendix A. It's for informational purposes only because every church or business environment is different. Many factors that are exclusive to your church will control what your job description will look like. If you don't tailor a job description to your unique environment, specific privacy needs, and the tasks you want done, the person who responds will likely not be the right person for the job. But we can change that.

In the absence of a privacy coordinator, designate someone within the church to take on that role. You need someone who takes initiative, likes to learn, and collaborates well. You can consult a privacy expert to coach this person so they can start getting the job done.

Teams That Work Closely with and Support Privacy Roles and Decisions

A personal chef, dog walker, flea market flipper, or truck driver can work alone. Privacy roles? No. They don't work in isolation. They need other teams or expertise to be able to succeed and achieve their goals. Here are a few of the business functions that collaborate with privacy roles and privacy teams.

The legal team/attorney researches and analyzes privacy, security, and technology laws and regulations. They conduct legal reviews of privacy policies and contracts. They negotiate contracts and privacy compliance clauses with third parties, vendors, and contractors who handle personal information.

Human resources manages privacy pertaining to personal employment information—employees' payroll, health information, benefits, and evaluations.

Information technology (IT) manages and maintains computer systems and software and ensures they are current, operating as intended, and properly connected to form a secure network that protects personal information.

Information security and cybersecurity ensure that any information (not only personal information) is securely exchanged, distributed, processed, and stored by humans, computer systems, the Internet, and in physical or non-digital forms.

Product development develops concepts and strategies for products and services that can better serve the needs of customers, members, employees, or users and align with privacy principles.

Policy management develops corporate policies to ensure alignment (i.e., review privacy policies and all the organizational policies and standards to make them align with the overarching goal of the organization).

Customer care and service intakes privacy complaints, feedback, and requests for access to personal information. They provide support to meet people's privacy needs and foster trust as a result.

The finance team contributes resources to cross-functional risk management in the organization. As the costs of resolving a data breach and related fraud incidents are quite high, reducing privacy risks is important to the finance department. Also, data breaches and noncompliance can result in business disruptions, reputational damage, and loss of revenue due to penalties or lawsuits, it makes sense for a finance department or team to be fiducial and monitor whether the organization is reducing all risks and staying compliant.

The internal audit team evaluates and manages risk throughout the organization. An in-depth audit can help the privacy team measure where they are in meeting their legal compliance goals. Audit teams identify problems or gaps and allow management to fix them within a defined time frame (ahead of external auditors discovering those gaps or flaws).

The training department develops or procures training content and affirms that every employee, volunteer, vendor, and contractor understands their roles, responsibilities, rules of behavior, and acceptable behavior while at work and ensures they use work equipment and personal information in accordance with policies.

That concludes my pretend "Take Your Church to Work Day." What an adventure that was! That's a lot of departments and roles, and not every business or church will have all of them. But churches grow in different ways, and the more ministries or departments that support and collaborate with your privacy team, the faster your church can discover and address gaps regularly. You can see how the different departments bring their unique perspective and insights to privacy practices. Privacy is everyone's responsibility in church, so everyone must have some level of knowledge through awareness and/or participation. I'm here to encourage you to do what you can afford to do now but also help you envision what you'll need in the future as you grow. Today you only need committed people from each ministry to rally around and support the person you designate to fill the privacy role.

Identify the folks responsible for specific privacy practices, and make their roles official by announcing them to your congregation.

If you're operating on a shoestring budget, I recommend getting committed members to form a team to coordinate privacy education. Educating people is the best way to spot risks, reduce liabilities, prevent privacy violations (keep members from getting hurt), and stay compliant with privacy laws and regulations, which you'll soon learn about in the next chapter. If you've already worked privacy into your policies, your team can double-check that everyone complies by participating in mandatory training and awareness. A privacy coordinator can act as an internal auditor for all your departments. But start now, then create a budget for privacy, and grow with it.

Who Knows What?

How does your church manage who has personal information? Who knows the private matters and private experiences of members who entrust the church with such information? How does your church protect private discussions and personal information about people? I created the Onion Model to explain how personal and sensitive information should be better managed by churches. This model might sound silly, but it really works.

I'm always in the kitchen cooking, and I love purple onions—so much so that when I was drafting *Church Privacy 101*, I meant to type "1 Thessalonians 4:11" (to make a point about how the church and churchgoers should mind their own business) but mistakenly cited the Scripture as "1 Thessal*onions* 4:11." Of course, that red squiggly spell-check line in Microsoft Word called me out. I wondered, *What's Microsoft's beef?* I stared at the last six letters for a while and then eventually exclaimed, "Oh, my Lord!"

Do you see the *onions* in "Thessalonians"? I was inspired, and now onions have become my privacy model.

The onion provides a perfect analogy for understanding how you can manage personal information at your church, but to understand how it works, let's test-drive the Onion Model in your personal life. Let's imagine a couple from your church has found out they're pregnant. They disclose information about their pregnancy to others depending on the relationship they have with them. First, they pray and talk to God. Next, they see a gynecologist during the first few weeks of being aware of the pregnancy, then they talk to their best friends, parents, and siblings. After that, they tell their church buddies and coworkers according to the layers of their onion. If they were to cut an onion horizontally in the center, what they would see would be a number of rings. My onion model takes that compartmental, aerial view of the rings. God is at the core of the onion. The next ring is the person or group closest to the couple (in the context of a new pregnancy). In this example, the gynecologist would be on this ring—they're the expert. And then the information would move out from there, one ring at a time. The last ring of the onion might be the government. Huh? Yes, I can explain. When the baby arrives, they will need to register the baby's name for hospital records, file for a birth certificate, and obtain a Social Security number before they leave the hospital.

The couple has a Pregnancy Onion that applies specifically to the personal information about their pregnancy, but they likely have other onions too, such as a House-Hunting Onion or an I-Got-a-Raise-at-Work Onion. This goes to show that a person can have many onions as they choose to address different private matters in their lives.

The Onion Model is in each of our own heads and is expressed through our behaviors and decisions, but oftentimes the problem with privacy is that people—and churches—forget who they trust or don't trust and why. It's said, "Loose lips sink ships." Oversharing will encourage a breach. It's important for you and your church to get the Onion Model out of your head and document it. Let's try that.

Onions in Church Leadership

Churchgoers always start with God at the center of their onion, and the same is true for churches. As I mentioned earlier, each ring after that is a particular individual or group that you trust with certain personal information about you or others. As the rings get farther and farther away from God, they represent the groups or individuals you trust a little less. The farther the ring is from the God ring, the fewer details or information the people in that ring will have.

Without an onion, a lot can go wrong. As I discuss in *Church Privacy 101*, people leave churches they once loved enraged that leaders and members violate privacy or allow others to meddle in onion

Privacy Principles

rings they don't belong in. The church needs to apply the Onion Model to personal information about its members—especially people who seek the counsel from members of the clergy about different aspects of their lives. Some church leaders can be very careless and casual when discussing personal information with others who do not need to know that information. Use of the Onion Model is pragmatic for effective church leadership and sound privacy practices. Let's say you're a minister, and a member discloses personal information to you about someone else. If your spouse is not one of the other people the member disclosed the information to, then don't tell your spouse. They are not in that particular ring of the onion with you. If your spouse does not need to know, you shouldn't pass on that information to them. You cannot earn trust for your spouse. Trust is nontransferable.

Similarly, there are ministries within the church that require deep sharing so that the members of those groups can get the support and healing they need. Privacy makes these types of groups effective because participants have a safe place to be vulnerable and transparent. These groups exist so participants are comfortable disclosing very personal experiences to others who are either directly or indirectly facing similar issues or challenges, such as substance abuse, sexual abuse or rape, mental health concerns, and marital issues. This type of group would need its own onion. For privacy reasons, members of the church shouldn't show up at these meetings just because they want to see what goes on there. That onion is *closed*.

How do we get better at managing who knows what? By making onion rings explicit. Let's say a ministry leader, Frederick, is considering taking on a role at a congregation in another state. He interviews and receives an attractive job offer and decides to take it and start work in six months. This could be Frederick's onion with respect to this personal decision:

Onion title: "Job Offer Onion"

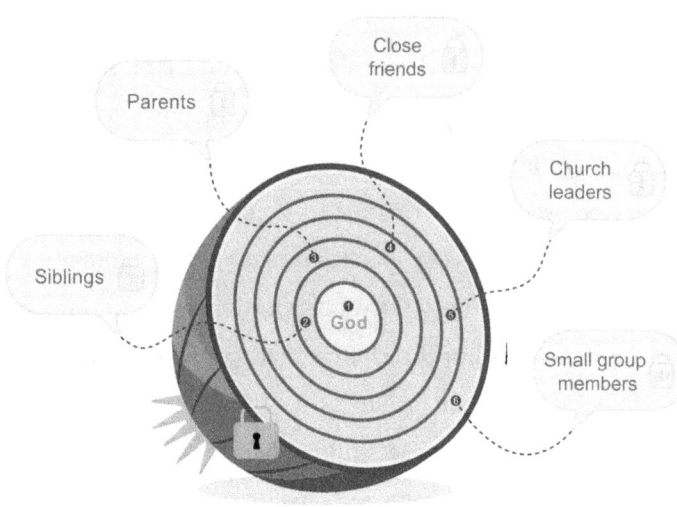

Figure 1. Frederick's onion (trust assigned according to individual groups)

While everyone in this onion will eventually know about the new job and the move to another state, they are on different onion rings based on their need to know and Frederick's level of trust for each group. As a result, the time when they receive the news is different. How much information they receive will also be different. Why doesn't Frederick tell everyone in the onion at the same time, including church leaders and the church groups to which he belongs? Because that's what privacy is all about. Privacy is not only about carefully selecting who you share personal information with, but it's also about the level of information and the timing that would give you, or someone such as Frederick, the most peace, focus, and control.

Churches that don't create intentional onion rings risk information leaks, losing their credibility, losing members, fostering resentment, and attracting lawsuits. The next onion is an illustration of a ministry within a church. This juicy onion belongs to Rosa, a devoted ministry director. It shows that the director shares certain information with Annah that she doesn't share with Steph, Ellie,

Queenette, or Harriet at the same time or with the same level of detail. This doesn't mean that Annah is holier than everyone else or that she attended the same high school as the director's niece. It might be due to the type of situation Rosa is handling at the moment, or because Annah has earned the level of trust required, and there's more value in giving her information before the rest of the ministry members are informed.

Onion title: "Ministry Onion"

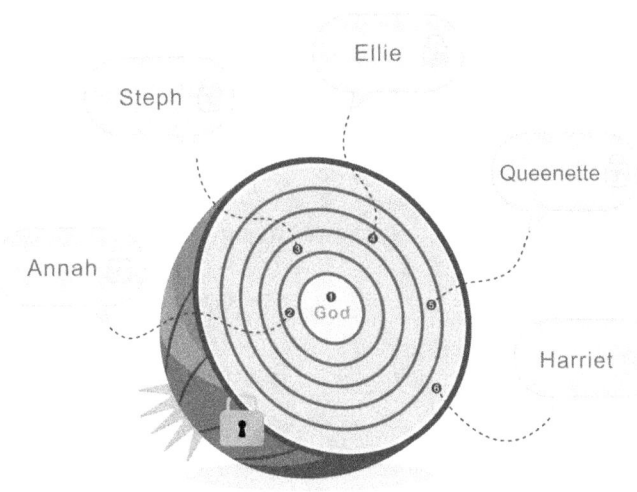

Figure 2. Rosa's onion (trust assigned according to individuals)

Assess How Your Church Determines If a Person Should Be Included and Where in the Onion
Before including anyone in an onion or picking which ring of the onion a person or group in your church belongs on, your church should first answer who, what, why, when, and where in order to properly place the person. How should you do that? It's easy. When deciding where in the onion a person belongs, assess them against the following criteria:

Do the tasks that need to be done with personal information require this person?

☐ Yes ☐ No

Why/Justification:_____

Do the decisions that need to be made using personal information require this person?

☐ Yes ☐ No

Why/Justification:_____

Does the type of personal information involved require this person's professional expertise?

☐ Yes ☐ No

Does the ministry that the task/decision involves require this person's involvement?

☐ Yes ☐ No

Does the person understand our privacy rules on handling this type of personal information?

☐ Yes ☐ No

Has the person read, understood, and acknowledged our privacy policy?

☐ Yes ☐ No

Has the person participated in privacy training/awareness that the church has offered?

☐ Yes ☐ No

Has the person proven they're trustworthy and reliable in similar matters?

☐ Yes ☐ No

Other questions: _____

☐ Yes ☐ No

Assess If Your Church Analyzes the Amount of Information and the Timeframe for Sharing

After assessing the person against the criteria and verifying they are a great candidate for an onion, our church does the following:

☐ We determine when they should have the personal information.

☐ We document the justification for the timeframe or date.

☐ We determine if the person has a need to know all of the personal information involved.

☐ We document the justification (if they do).

☐ If they should only know limited details, we define which elements of the personal information they need to know.

☐ We document the justification.

Consider this list as you populate an onion. It helps you determine if there's any value or risk in sharing personal information with a particular person. All types of personal information are not equal. Some are more sensitive than others, and you need to track what you share, how much you share, and with whom you share. That's why analyzing and prioritizing people and information in the onion is crucial. For example, in our illustration, Annah is the first to know and has the most information. What should the director do about Steph? How soon should Steph have the personal information? This can be as simple as saying, "Inform Steph three weeks after Annah has been informed," or whenever that date is on your calendar (it should make sense to you). The interesting thing about onion rings is that, depending on the situation, Steph may be given the exact same information as Annah but later in the process.

Be sure to brainstorm and document your onion candidates until they stick in your mind. And when you don't know whom to trust with personal information, make onion rings. Avoid relying on emotions when it comes to deciding whom to trust with other people's personal information in church. Trust should be on merit and necessity. Small churches give members and volunteers all kinds of personal information because they don't have many people to help out. Big churches do the same out of a prolonged and uncorrected bad habit of sharing personal information with people whether they have a need to know or not. For the most part, it's based on unrelated loyalty to the recipient of the information, not trustworthiness. Members' privacy gets violated this way. But the good news is, we now know better. A small church has an easier onion, as it has fewer people and departments, but even if you have zero formal departments, create an onion made up of trusted members and volunteers. And if you're a bigger church, most definitely create onions for the various ministries in your organization.

I've included a printable template (in Appendix H) so you have a bigger onion and can manually brainstorm and add/remove people in your onion. On my website, www.ChurchPrivacyBookSeries.com, you can also download a free editable digital copy if you prefer an electronic version.

Tip: The more creative you are, the easier it is to get people to listen and buy into your initiative. One way to do that is to assign privacy roles and then get students within your congregation to support people in these roles. Further, don't make privacy practices and compliance efforts a task people approach with fear and trembling.

Value: A great privacy culture is an opportunity for the church all-around. You'll deliver value to your city's law school, business school, or technology institutions by offering students internship opportunities they can adorn their résumé with while they give you valuable support free of charge. Present these efforts as a positive experience everyone desires, needs, and can be creative about achieving. It gives you another excuse to celebrate your workers by acknowledging people who come up with bright privacy ideas that help you improve church privacy processes.

Action Steps: You've assessed the model your church uses to determine how it is sharing personal information about its members and visitors. The items you did not check are your action items to work on: list them. Have you designated someone within your church to handle this responsibility? Jot down your answers.

_____

_____

_____

When can you start working on this goal?

Day _____ Month _____ Year _____

What's your target date to complete this goal?

Day _____ Month _____ Year _____

What questions would you ask me?

_____

_____

_____

_____

_____

*A clear vision, backed by definite plans, gives you
a tremendous feeling of confidence and personal power.*
(Brian Tracy)

3

The Law

Your most unhappy customers are your greatest source of learning.
(Bill Gates, *Business @ the Speed of Thought*)

Laws and regulations tend to be clunky, intimidating, bookish, and unfriendly. But privacy laws ought to hold your interest because privacy is a human concern you can relate to. People have the right to expect privacy and to be left alone. Privacy is a civil issue similar to equality, freedom, and liberty—everyone has the right to enjoy privacy. Privacy rights help protect people and their personal information, body, thoughts, space, and speech from being violated, harmed, abused, or suppressed by other individuals, organizations, or the government. Privacy rights prevent invasions of one's privacy that may result in financial, emotional, and physical harm or even death. Depending on where you live, individuals and/or governments can take legal action against privacy offenders.

Here are five instances that may lead to privacy violation lawsuits:

1. **Intrusion of Solitude or Intrusion upon Seclusion:** observing or recording a person in a situation or place the person would believe to be private, such as a restroom, bedroom/house, giving birth, in a private conversation, or carrying out any activity in a secluded space where the person would reasonably expect to have privacy.

2. **Appropriation of Identity, Name, Image, or Likeness:** using a person's likeness, name, image, or voice to advertise or promote ideas, beliefs, or products without the person's permission.

3. **Public Disclosure of Private Facts:** publishing private facts about a person that the public doesn't need to know, where the information being shared is offensive and can harm the person's reputation.

4. **Portrayal in a False Light and Defamation:** telling part of a story that can give the wrong impression about a person (or flat-out lying about the person), causing them emotional distress and/or harm to their reputation.

5. **Data Breach and Negligence:** losing or exposing personal information due to error or failure to properly secure personal information.

Privacy Laws That Apply to Your Church

Now that you've become familiar with privacy principles, it's a lot easier to understand the different grounds for lawsuits. Knowing the principles will also make it easy to understand the purpose and focus of privacy laws and regulations. That's because all modern privacy laws and regulations were written based on those privacy principles. This is the reason why one of the initial steps here is to understand the principles, then the laws and regulations. Next, know how, when, and to whom a particular law or regulation applies and what specific types of personal information and activities are covered. Some privacy laws do not apply to nonprofit organizations, but many do—in the same manner that they apply to corporations. Charitable and faith-based organizations have responsibilities and are accountable under some of the same privacy laws that apply to government entities.

It's also important to examine privacy laws that do not apply to nonprofit organizations. Why? Because when examined closely, you might find that the commercial activities of your church make these laws applicable. For example, the EU's General Data Protection Regulation (GDPR) applies to nonprofits, including the activities of individuals in churches. Canada's Personal Information Protection and Electronic Data Act (PIPEDA) applies to for-profit or private-sector organizations, not to nonprofit organizations, but commercial activities can change its applicability.

There are many comprehensive state and industry-specific laws that apply to commercial and nonprofit organizations that handle health information and employment information and process financial transactions using credit cards and bank information. Churches collect personal information through tithes, offerings, bake sales, book sales, and other events that involve credit card processing and registration. In some cases, health information is collected, as some churches have clinics and schools. As a result, some laws also apply to churches.

In a nutshell, you shouldn't treat privacy laws and regulations at face value. Some interpretive elements are hidden below the surface. You're not a privacy expert or a privacy lawyer. Besides, you have other things to do and shouldn't try to tackle legal analysis. If your church doesn't have a privacy expert or lawyer to help with analysis and research, the companion course to this book shows detailed steps for getting certain aspects started in the meantime, and it connects your church with privacy experts, privacy attorneys, and other essential resources. Designate someone to perform good legal research and analysis on laws applicable to your church. This way you won't waste time spinning your wheels, and you'll save money by reducing your risks. Also see Appendices B and C for lists of additional laws, regulations, and industry codes to make brainstorming easier for you or your church attorney if they're not specialized in privacy. They'll get familiar with the universe of privacy and data protection laws and regulations that apply in your particular context.

Once you have help, identify at least two to three specific laws or regulations that apply to your church, then organize them, and focus on those.

Local Laws:

_____
_____
_____
_____
_____

The Law

State/Provincial Laws:

_____
_____
_____
_____
_____

National/Federal Laws:

_____
_____
_____
_____
_____

Industry Codes/Regulations (i.e., if your church is producing or publishing media, music, film, or art, engaging in marketing and advertising, or offering health-care services or services to children or schools, specific codes or laws in these industries may apply):

_____
_____
_____
_____
_____

International Laws (i.e., if your church has international members and handles their personal information, international privacy laws may apply):

_____

_____

_____

_____

_____

Privacy Framework

There are different paths available that you can chart to stay on top of all the laws, regulations, or requirements that apply to your church. Frameworks (sometimes called standards, recommendations, or guidelines) are made for this. Some frameworks incorporate requirements from multiple laws and regulations to give organizations a more streamlined guide. Others focus on one regulation or law. Certain frameworks focus on a specific industry. Depending on the framework, you could map required privacy safeguards, processes, and management documentation back to the specific law or regulation that applies to your church.

Frameworks are not mandatory tools, but you'll love the helpful recommendations and guidelines. They are a blanket to-do list: you pick and choose which measures pertain to your unique activities (e.g., the types of documentation to develop, vendor management, security, and training). Overall, they improve how you manage risk associated with collecting personal information but leave the decision-making up to you. Some frameworks may not be suitable for your church—but may work well for the church next door. Your unique activities and handling of personal information may not be like another church. You can also use multiple frameworks if your needs are not completely covered by just one framework.

The Law

The National Institute of Science and Technology

Among many service and publications, the National Institute of Science and Technology (NIST) offers standards, frameworks, and guidelines. These are generally known as NIST 800 series. Before you say that these are for the federal government, let me invoke the clever Secret deodorant tagline coined in 1972: "Strong enough for a man but made for a woman." The same applies to the NIST 800: strong enough for churches but made for the federal government. This framework will guide you through how to approach compliance, but at over 450 pages, it can feel overwhelming. Its implementation guide comes with recommendations downloadable from the NIST website.[1]

International Privacy and Information Security Principles and Frameworks

On the international side, here are a few examples of frameworks or general privacy principles to consider:

- Organisation for Economic Co-operation and Development (OECD) (https://www.oecd.org)

- Asia-Pacific Economic Cooperation (APEC) (https://www.apec.org/press/features/2013/0903_cbpr)

- International Conference of Data Protection and Privacy Commissioners (https://privacyconference2019.info)

- ISO/IEC 27000 family (https://www.iso.org/isoiec-27001-information-security.html)

However, just like a tax person knows how to navigate tax paths that benefit your church, you still need to consult with a privacy expert who can guide you in following privacy laws based on your unique situation. Churches should be aware that in some cases, laws and regulations that are incorporated into certain frameworks can drastically change with only a two-year notice. One major problem is that your church may not even know a particular law or regulation has changed (or if there's a new one), especially if you don't have anyone managing privacy for your church. If you have a lot of work to do in the privacy area, and your privacy situation is complex, even a two-year grace period can fly by quickly, and your church could struggle to achieve compliance. In essence, throwing tons of money into privacy compliance at the last minute doesn't guarantee success. A privacy expert who understands what you need can actually help you save money while helping you comply.

Get Consent and Avoid Privacy Invasion and Intrusion Lawsuits

A church could face a lawsuit if it's not transparent about the personal information it collects, handles, or uses. The Lord hates a lying tongue (Proverbs 6:16–17) and so does the privacy authority in your state. "The Lord detests lying lips, but he delights in people who are trustworthy" (Proverbs 12:22), as do many privacy laws. And make no mistake: it's not just church members or visitors who can sue a church for privacy violations. Donors, partners, and employees can sue also. In addition to individuals, regulators can sue following data breaches and other privacy violations.

Even if you don't have a privacy expert yet, there are steps you can start taking now to avoid legal and regulatory lawsuits. First and foremost, to avoid violating a person's privacy, your church must get consent from the individual for the personal information it collects, uses, manages, and shares. Making sure you have consent allows your church to know you're not overlooking people's needs. Also, you can defend yourself if the person claims they did not know how you were going to use their personal information. Having proof could calm the person down, keep both of you out of a legal battle, and save your relationship. It's essentially a good privacy practice to remove or take down an element of personal information you posted about someone when they object to it. Even if they did initially give permission for you to use it. Be transparent about how you'll use the information so the person can make an educated choice. Make sure the person consenting is of legal age to consent (the actual age depends on your jurisdiction). You should also ensure the person is mentally capable of understanding their choice or decision.

There are two types of consent:

1. **Written/Verbal Consent:** The person signs a form or checks a digital checkbox indicating you have their permission to use their personal information in the way you've stated on the form. Legally, consent is a huge deal. If there are potential risks to sharing their personal information,

tell the person, just like when a medical doctor is about to prescribe medication and tells you about its side effects. Aren't you usually glad they did? Often those side effects sound worse than your symptoms, but the doctor is not trying to scare you—they're being transparent about the risks so you can decide if the benefits outweigh the likely side effects. Same with consent. If you need someone to consent to two different uses of their personal information, let the person know so they can choose. If you give them two checkboxes, they can check the box that suits their preference. That's a form of written or express consent. They may consent to the church using their email address to confirm a men's conference ticket they purchased, but they can object to receiving marketing email for other church events. Also, consent can be verbal. For example, banks use verbal consent to transfer funds when you initiate transfers over the phone. But your church is not a bank, and you need to use discretion with verbal consent. So I recommend getting written consent, whether digital or physical, so you can track and manage who you have permission from and what their choices are.

2. **Implied Consent:** This is when the person knows how you're going to use their personal information and doesn't object when you require that information. For example, a member purchases study materials from your church's bookstore and asks to have the materials shipped to them. At checkout, you ask for their full name, mailing address, and email address. They understand that the bookstore partners with third parties that deliver goods (e.g., FedEx, UPS, or USPS). Their name and address are needed to deliver the supplies they requested—even their email address to let them know the status of their order. By making the purchase, the member implies that they agree to the bookstore using and sharing their personal information to process and complete the order. In the eyes of the law, your bookstore has a legitimate business reason to collect this customer's personal information—even if there is no formal/physical consent signed.

Assess How Your Church Handles Consent Related to Personal Information Collection

When we collect personal information we obtain

☐ Written Consent   ☐ Verbal Consent/Permission

Before we publish personal information in written form we obtain

☐ Written Consent ☐ Verbal Consent/Permission

Before we post on the Internet, website, blog, or social media we obtain

☐ Written Consent ☐ Verbal Consent/Permission

Before/after taking photographs of people at events, in order to use their image(s) we obtain

☐ Written Consent ☐ Verbal Consent/Permission/Release

Before/after videotaping people at events, in order to use their image(s) we obtain

☐ Written Consent ☐ Verbal Consent/Permission/Release

Before/after recording or obtaining voice or audio, in order to use the recording(s) we obtain

☐ Written Consent ☐ Verbal Consent/Permission/Release

Before/after obtaining music and other art forms, in order to use those mediums we obtain

☐ Written Consent ☐ Verbal Consent/Permission/Release

Remember, whenever possible it's best to have express consent.

Avoid False Light and Defamation Lawsuits

As a church, you're in the business of telling the truth. The problem is that even when you tell the truth, depending on what that truth is, people may suffer mental distress and damaged reputation as a result of your church publishing facts about them via any writing, preaching, speaking, filming, or blogging or on websites.

False light is invading someone's privacy by making a false statement to the public about the person and as a result causing mental distress. For example, you may conclude that I'm not a trustworthy citizen because the police are always coming to my house. While this may be true, you've never seen me be arrested or charged for anything. In fact, it may be that my security alarm system signals the police when the alarm trips, and that is why they come to my house. You see the police officers check my windows and doors and exchange handshakes when we part. But when you make a public statement about the frequent visits of the police to my home, you leave out the context about my alarm system and my handshakes with police officers so that I appear as a troublemaker. You show or post photos of police officers at my property. In another example, you may say publicly that I'm a computer hacker but omit the fact that I'm paid by the government to break into government computer systems and that I do it ethically to protect and defend my country. You give the public a false impression of me. (Keep in mind that the definition of *false light* varies by state or jurisdiction.)

If you don't know how you should check if your statement or message puts someone in a false light to the public, or is defamatory or slanderous, here are questions you could use to weigh your message:

- Is the information true, half of the story, or false?

- Is identifying this person necessary?

- Will my description of the person make the person easy to identify?

- Will what I'm sharing be highly offensive to a reasonable person?

- Will this have a negative impact on the person?

- If so, what negative impact will it have?_____

Don't make your spoken or written statement if you know the information is offensive, a half-truth, or will invade the privacy of the person if the way you present it is misleading or creates a false impression. Don't imply that it's truth without portraying all angles of the story from a balanced perspective. Don't share the information if you won't bother to verify whether the information you have about the person is true. Don't identify the person if identifying the person is unnecessary and harmful. If your description, accusation, or association of the person with a specific thing makes them easily identifiable and linked with something negative, don't share the information. And definitely don't say anything if making the statement and identifying the person will have a negative impact on the person's life and you are aware of the type or level of negative impact this would have on the person (for example, emotional distress, embarrassment, loss of trust, or financial loss).

Defamation is the act of communicating false statements that are harmful or would hurt a person's reputation. The statement doesn't need to be made to a large number of people. A person can sue you under libel laws if you write or print the statement or under slander laws if you speak it. For instance, it would be slander for you to tell people verbally at my place of work that I steal credit card information and defraud people. You know this is a false statement. You know your statement will harm my reputation, but you make the false statement anyway. (The definition of *defamation* varies by state or jurisdiction as well.)

Don't make your spoken or written point if you know it's false or know that identifying the person is unnecessary to making your point. Similarly, don't describe a related event or person to make them easily identifiable.

All churches, including small churches, should be aware of this before any church employee or volunteer speaks or publishes information about people on the church website or blog, especially concerning people they disagree with. By taking these precautions, you avoid hurting people. Having information from different sources doesn't always mean you have knowledge of a person, and you shouldn't repeat what you hear or read as fact or truth. Assessing what you're doing allows you to apply fairness. (Check out my discussions on abusing pastoral/clergy privileges in Chapter 7.)

Avoid Negligence and Data Breach Lawsuits

With so much information being exchanged on the Internet, it's easier for people to make mistakes and it's much easier for hackers to access and capitalize on personal information. New privacy laws and regulations are also making it easier for people to sue. As a church, you don't want to have a reputation for being untrustworthy or careless. So you should step up your game, as trust is on the line and your credibility is at stake. You need your members, employees, community, and regulators to have confidence in you. Besides, noncompliance can quickly empty out your church treasury.

So how can you avoid lawsuits? By doing as much as you can as quickly as you can. You can start with education. Education is important because it helps with prevention (remember that prevention is better than a cure!). Understand that in any industry and organization, training is a highly effective management tool. A data breach can happen to any organization. The more informed your church is, the more prepared you will be. Moreover, regulators pay attention to training to determine your level of due diligence in keeping people well-informed and aware. So what can you do? The most feasible option for both large and small churches is to bring in an expert to speak and answer questions. Give the expert a list of concerns. All churches need a quarterly or biannual checkup (i.e., a review of concerns and practices), especially if you don't have a privacy expert in-house. When you've done all you can, put on your armor and stand your ground (Ephesians 6:13).

To comply with laws and regulations on personal information your church collects, you should do the following:

- Make your own privacy rules. Base your church policies on the laws or regulations that apply to your church.

- Appoint a knowledgeable person to take charge of your privacy rules/policies and principles.

- Check or track if people are following or breaking your privacy rules/policies.

- Get privacy education. Take privacy courses.

- Take mandatory annual privacy training and biannual or quarterly refresher courses.

- Attend reasonably priced privacy seminars/workshops/Q&As with a privacy expert.

- Since noncompliance poses legal and regulatory risks, discuss privacy in business meetings.

Don't expect to apply good privacy practices or be compliant with privacy laws and regulations if you don't consider and incorporate the above items. Compliance won't happen by itself.

Tip: Extend privacy training to all members and former members, not only workers. There are ways to train unique audiences according to their level of responsibility. Know what interests them, how you can attract and retain their attention, and how they prefer to learn. Remember, some of your members are also volunteers who work on the same tasks as your employees. The earlier they are privacy-aware or trained, the better. If you have an education department, contract a privacy expert to teach courses they could help you develop based on risks in your unique church environment.

 Value: When you make members aware, it will change their behavior, even in their private lives. If they're applying healthy privacy practices at home, they'll do the same in church. You won't have to worry about lawsuits if you have done your due diligence. Learning about different grounds for lawsuits is a win-win for the church and for its members.

Action Steps: You've assessed what your church needs to consider and work on. The items you did not check are your action items to work on: list them. Have you designated someone to oversee these responsibilities? Jot down your answers.

_____

_____

_____

When can you start working on these tasks?

Day _____ Month _____ Year _____

What's your target date to complete these tasks?

Day _____ Month _____ Year _____

How have you been negligent with how you portray others? Write down ways to correct this.

_____

_____

_____

What questions would you ask me?

_____
_____
_____
_____
_____

When it comes to privacy and accountability, people always demand the former
for themselves and the latter for everyone else.
(David Brin)

4

Church Privacy Notices

*Do the right thing, do the best you can,
and always show people you care.*
(Lou Holtz)

Privacy Notice

Continuing our conversation on statements that could have legal effects, a privacy notice is a public notice or a legal statement that your church makes. That statement is made to the public about your lawful practices as they relate to personal information. Consider your audience to be regulators, the general public, the media, customers, partners, church members, and website visitors. Most websites have notices. If you scroll down to the very bottom of a web page, you'll find it. Website privacy *notices* are often labeled *privacy policy*, but in reality, they're legal notices. Privacy notices are not limited to websites. Depending on the context, notices can be in a paper form such as the one your doctor's office puts on a clipboard on top of the forms you fill out. A notice should be clear and truthful about how personal information is handled because there are legal consequences for incomplete, deceptive, unfair, or false statements in your privacy notice.

Privacy Policy

A privacy *policy*, contrary to the naming confusion, is essentially an internal document that communicates to employees, vendors, contractors, and volunteers what is expected of them. There are multiple policies within any given organization that address employee behavior in different aspects of the organization. Privacy policies in churches are no different. You need them to communicate expectations for protecting privacy in your church.

Privacy Statement

A privacy statement describes your church's stance on privacy. It can be used as a short opening paragraph for your website privacy notice. Making a strong privacy statement will establish credibility. It doesn't hurt to let website visitors know why your church cares about privacy and that it is committed to preserving privacy because it's the right thing to do. Emotionally connecting to people builds trust. It's also useful internally (as the introduction of your privacy policy document) when addressing church workers about privacy. I will give examples on this later.

Tailoring Privacy Notices

Tailor your notice to represent what your church is doing. That is, your current privacy practices. Avoid copying another church's privacy notice. If you copy, you'll likely inherit their legal headaches. I advise my clients that the people they're copying may be in a different business realm and using different business models. Even if they're in the same industry, no two organizations are the same regarding what personal information they process or how they process it. The truth is, this applies to the church as well. Same God. Same Bible. Same mission. But different personal information handling practices in every church.

Be Sure You Can Defend It
When you're tempted to copy and paste another organization's privacy policy or notice, think about this: remember that you've got to be able to defend what's in your privacy notice. Every word. Every sentence. Every processing practice you include. And every element of personal information you list and what you say you do with the information. The content of your notice is unique to you. You're

the only one who can explain why you made this legal and public notice and what you use personal information for. Your notice is like a toothbrush. You know what you use your toothbrush for. Right? But you can't say what another person uses theirs for. It depends on who you ask. Toothbrushes have amassed many uses from applying hair dye to cleaning tile grout, keyboards, carpet stains, tires, toasters, shoes, and stove tops. Copying some other organization's privacy notice is like coming across a stray toothbrush and using it to brush your teeth. Awful! Don't do it. Never copy a notice you don't know much about. It might cause your church legal headaches down the line.

Creating Your Own Privacy Notice

It's not that difficult to start drafting your own notice. When creating a privacy notice, you should first practice not referring to a notice as a "privacy policy" just because everybody else does. It's a notice. A notice explains how you justify the collection and use of people's personal information and shows that your practices are legit or justified. What do I mean by legit? Collection of personal information has to be for a legitimate business need. Hint: your business need is to serve people. Right? What are the ways you serve people? The different ways you serve people's needs create the need for processing personal information. See, you're getting it already.

To address the personal information you will collect, you must break the notice down into sections. Keep it brief and make it as clear as water. Your privacy notice should address how you collect personal information, why you collect information, when you collect the information, and how it's secured. I'll walk you through each.

Below, I have laid out the different sections you'll need to start populating with information that's unique to your church's environment and privacy practices. We're focusing on a website notice here. No worries if you get stuck creating your own. I filled out one for you to use as a template. You can take a peek at it just a few more paragraphs down.

Privacy Notice Content
A privacy notice should include all of the following sections. Brainstorm and gather information before you write. Take one section at a time. Check off each section as you complete it. Your notice

doesn't have to be perfect. It needs to be an accurate representation of what your church is doing with personal data. You're going to polish it several times before you let your church attorney peek at it.

In our church's website privacy notice, we've included the following:

- [ ] general information about our church and our commitment to a positive privacy experience
- [ ] what personal information we collect
- [ ] how we gather/collect personal information
- [ ] what we do with the personal information we collect (i.e., the purpose and use)
- [ ] our privacy team's contact details
- [ ] third parties we disclose or share personal information with
- [ ] people's privacy rights (i.e., their right to access, delete, correct information, or withdraw consent)
- [ ] what people should do to exercise these privacy rights (e.g., make requests via email, phone, or postal mail)
- [ ] the security of any links from our website to other websites
- [ ] how we secure personal information
- [ ] how we handle or update changes to this privacy notice
- [ ] children's personal information (age appropriateness and how we handle children's information)
- [ ] different ways people can contact our church
- [ ] how to make a complaint or send feedback
- [ ] list of governing privacy laws and regulations that apply to our church
- [ ] our official headquarters' or location's address, phone, and email address

Church Privacy Team

 Tip: You can have additional information in your notice as long as the information is important for the audience or website visitors. Regulators recommend keeping it short, easy to understand, and very organized to help the readers. Write policies and notices for people. Write policies and notices that don't leave readers feeling confused or stupid. Make them feel empowered and smart.

 Value: Your transparency shows your users, members, partners, and visitors that you value privacy. They'll trust you. Transparency doesn't mean you have to give every detail of what you do.

 Action Steps: You've assessed what content needs to be included in your church's privacy notices/policies. The items you did not check are your action items to work on: list them. Have you designated someone within your church to handle this responsibility? Jot down your answers.

_____
_____
_____

What's your target date to assign someone to take this responsibility/when will you begin the tasks?
Day_____ Month_____ Year_____

What's your target date to complete these tasks?
Day_____ Month_____ Year_____

Do you read privacy notices on websites? How can you make yours easier to understand and exciting to read?

_____
_____
_____

What questions would you ask me?

_____
_____
_____
_____
_____

By failing to prepare, you are preparing to fail.
(Benjamin Franklin)

Usability, Design, and the Structure of Your Privacy Notice

Regulators prefer you keep your privacy notice short, practical, and easy to read; users will appreciate this as well. There are different ways to achieve that. Regulators will grade and ding you publicly on the reading difficulty of your notice. If your audience needs a dictionary to understand your notice, that's not a good sign. Pay attention to these items, which will make your notice easier to read.

Layering

Create a layered notice to give it several levels of information. Make sure the first page of your notice has clickable or linked content. For instance, the following two items should have links that direct the readers to the topics they want to read:

- a summary or privacy statement page with all the topics covered in the notice

- an outline page

Combine these two items if you prefer. The main purpose of layered notices is so that your audience can click specific topics they're interested in instead of scrolling through numerous pages searching for the topics they want to read.

Structure

Give your notice a structure so it's easy on the eyes to skim through. Include the following:

- bullets, boldface, wide margins, lists, and short sentences and paragraphs
- icons

Plain Language

Writing the notice in regular language will make it easier to understand. Remove the following from your notice:

- technical language or "tech-speak"
- legalese
- "church-speak" or church jargon

Reading Level

The reading level of the notice should be relatively low so that most adults, youth, and children will be able to understand it. A sixth-grade to eighth-grade reading level is recommended.

Visibility

It's important that the link to the notice be big enough for people to find and read it. Follow these guidelines:

- Use 12-point font. (Some laws specify font size and typeface that's easy to read. Fine print is prohibited.)
- Place the link to your privacy notice where it's easy to find on your website.

Tip: Consider your audience and remember that some readers may find your privacy notice too complex, especially the elderly and those who learned English as a second language. Any content you write for the general public should be at an eighth-grade reading level or three levels below the level of education of your specific audience.

 Value: A privacy notice is doable by a church of any size. Designate someone to start the first draft. Circulate the draft to others assigned to be part of creating this document. Share feedback. It will save you money in the long run. By the time you get a privacy expert and/or a lawyer to review and finalize it, you should have already done the bulk of the work instead of paying the lawyer to ask you for the information, come up with a template, and do all the writing. Your notice should be usable. Usability means transparency, accountability, and good customer care. Members and regulators will discern if you're pulling the wool over their eyes. They'll also notice if you're committed to privacy.

Privacy Notices and Layered Notices Templates

To recap, a privacy notice is a public notice. Basically, it's a legal statement to the public, customers, users, and regulators informing them that you collect particular types of personal information. It also discloses your privacy practices on activities related to collecting and handling personal information. Your privacy notice may not be the most prominent link on your website, but it's still a public notice and a legal statement. It could be used against you.

Where Do You Get a Template?

I'm glad you asked. Some churches just copy another congregation's privacy notice and, in doing so, inherit their legal headaches. I know you wouldn't do anything like that. You know better. What your organization does on a daily basis with information determines what your church privacy notice says. Why should your notice say you make technology products when you don't? That's embarrassing and tacky. Cutting corners can hurt you legally. Write your own. Save your Tylenol for another occasion.

Tell me, if you were caught wearing somebody else's underwear, what would be your defense? Could you persuasively defend why you were wearing it? Could you defend why it exists, its history, or its future? Could you defend why it was important for you to put on someone else's underwear when you could have looked for and bought your own drawers? You may absurdly say, "It was convenient." When you're tempted to copy and paste, think about this underwear analogy. Every word in the notice has a purpose. That purpose should align with what you, not some other church, are doing with people's personal information. Every sentence and paragraph has meaning to the regulators and other readers who stumble upon it. If it scares you to read it, it's not yours. You copied.

Let's Create Your Own Privacy Notice

Your privacy notice should show how you justify collecting, handling, and using people's personal information. It should demonstrate that your privacy practices are legit. You're aiming to help people, not impress them.

That's why you have a notice visible for people who visit your church website. They're your audience. Your message in the notice is technically saying to the public, regulators, and the media, "Here's what info we collect, our purpose for collecting it, and how, why, and when we collect it. Here's how we share and secure the information, the choices or rights people have, and how we handle personal information legally." Don't get it wrong.

Your church may have a privacy notice specifically for employees that resides on your employee-only web page. It can be on paper, not just digital. The rule of thumb is the same: address how and why you collect and break the information down into bite-size sections. Keep it short. Don't copy what I have. Understand the sample first, then use it as your guide. The key is to make it your own. If you have a privacy notice already, revise it. Use everyday language and scrap the gobbledygook or jargon. Once you get the important information in your notice, you can get creative with it as long as it enhances readability.

What you see below is simply an example. Let's call the church in this example Sarah Laughed Twice Church. Notice how easy it will be for readers to glide through this notice.

Sample Privacy Notice Sections or Outline

1. General information (in a nutshell)
2. Our contact details
3. Our privacy team's contact details
4. How we get your personal information
5. Your privacy rights
6. Sharing your personal information
7. Links to other websites
8. Your right to complain
9. Changes to this privacy notice
10. Children's information
11. Managing customer contact
12. Visitors to our website
13. Make a complaint
14. Laws—CCPA, GDPR, your state law

Privacy Notice Sample

Welcome to Sarah Laughed Twice Church website's privacy notice.

As a member of our church family, or as a visitor, this page exists to inform you and to give you control over your personal information that we collect in the course of your activities on our website. For example, our website and services provide web forms. Through our online forms, depending on the services that you're requesting, we may ask you to provide your personal information, including your full name, home address, email address, telephone number, date of birth, prayer requests, credit card number, other financial account information, and your country or state of residence.

This privacy notice also informs you about what you should expect us to do with your personal information when you contact us through this website or use our services.

We cover several topics on this notice, but we have created topic headings to make it easier for you to select the information you wish to read with regard to how we handle personal information.

We believe you should know the following:

- why we are collecting your information

- how we collect your personal information

- the purpose of processing your information

- how long we store your information

- whether we share the information with third parties

- whether we intend to transfer your information to another country

- whether we do automated decision-making or profiling

Our Contact Details

The Sarah Laughed Twice Church is the primary collector of the personal information we process, unless otherwise stated in this notice. There are two ways you can contact us: by email or postal mail.

Our postal address:
Sarah Laughed Twice Church
4400 Data Inventory Way
New York, NY 20703

Our email address: info@sarahlaughedtwicechurch.org

Privacy officer contact details: reach our privacy officer at info@sarahlaughedtwicechurch.org or via our postal address.

How We Get Your Personal Information

Most of the personal information we process is provided to us directly by you for one of the following reasons:

- You have requested information about our services.

- You have registered to download materials from our website.

- You have met us at an event and given us your business card.

- You have established a relationship with us as a partner or client.

- You have filed a complaint or made an inquiry.

- You have made an information request.

Your Privacy Rights

Under privacy laws, you have rights we need to make you aware of. Keep in mind that different laws provide similar but sometimes different rights. The rights available to you depend on our reason for processing your information. But if at any point you have questions about exercising any of these rights, please let us know right away. You are not required to pay to exercise your rights. We have one month, or 45 days in some cases, to respond to you.

Here are common privacy rights:

- Right to refuse sale of your personal information: You can ask us to not sell your personal information to third parties. We don't sell your personal information.

- Right of access: You can ask us for copies of your personal information. This right always applies. There are some exemptions, which means you may not always receive copies of all the information we process.

- Right to rectification: You can ask us to rectify information you think is inaccurate. You also have the right to ask us to complete information you think is incomplete. This right always applies.

- Right to erasure: You can ask us to erase your personal information in certain circumstances.

- Right to restriction of processing: You can ask us to restrict or suppress the processing of your information in certain circumstances.

- Right to object to processing: You have the absolute right to object to the processing of all or some of your personal data for direct marketing purposes.

- Right to data portability: When you request information that we hold about you, we will provide you a copy in a readable format such as an Adobe PDF, a Microsoft Word document, or another document format.

Exactly how long do we keep your personal information?
For information about this, please see our retention schedule.

Do we share your information?

- We will not share your information with any third parties for the purposes of direct marketing.

- We use third-party data processors who provide different services, such as data storage. They will not share your personal information with any organization apart from us.

- In some circumstances, we are legally obliged to cooperate and share information with law enforcement in response to court orders.

- We may also share your information in the event of a nonpayment for services or debt.

We use the following third-party services:

- Mailchimp: This allows you to download free content and receive follow-up emails.
  - Privacy Notice: https://mailchimp.com/legal/privacy/.
- Stripe: This processes your payments on our web page.
  - Privacy Notice: https://stripe.com/privacy.
- BigScoots: This provides hosting for our website.
  - Privacy Notice: https://www.bigscoots.com/privacy-policy.
- WordPress: Our site is built on WordPress.
  - Privacy Notice: https://wordpress.org/about/privacy/.

Links to Other Websites

Where we provide links to websites of other organizations, this privacy notice does not cover how that organization processes personal information. We encourage you to read the privacy notices on the other websites you visit before giving your personal information.

Your Right to Complain

We hold ourselves to high standards when it comes to processing your personal information. If you have queries or concerns, please contact us at info@sarahlaughedtwicechurch.org.

If, after helping address your concerns, you remain dissatisfied, you can make a complaint to your state's privacy regulatory authority about the way we process your personal information.

Changes to This Privacy Notice

We keep our privacy notice under regular review to make sure it is up to date and accurate: this notice was last updated on June 7, 2024.

Children's Information

We do not provide services to children or collect their personal information online. The information in the relevant parts of this notice applies to children as well as adults. Although children may read and understand this notice, we do not provide services to children or anyone under 18 years of age.

Managing Customer Contact

Our customer contact information is restricted only to communications relevant to the customers' needs or inquiries. You have the right to object to our processing of your personal data. There are legitimate reasons why we may decline your objection, which depend on our purpose for processing your information. For more information on your rights, please see "Your Privacy Rights."

How You Can Contact Us

Email or write us by postal mail.

Social Media

We use Twitter for social media interactions. If you send us a private or direct message via Twitter, we delete that information within 30 days and continue communication with you via our secure email account provided we have your email address. It will not be shared with any other organizations.

Emailing Us

We use Transport Layer Security (TLS) to encrypt and protect email traffic in line with government guidance on email security. Most webmail, such as Gmail and Hotmail, use TLS by default. We also monitor any emails sent to us, including file attachments, for viruses or malicious software.

Visitors to Our Website and Analytics

When you visit www.sarahlaughedtwicechurch.org, we do not use a third-party service to collect Internet log information and details of our visitors' behavior patterns.

Cookies

We do not use cookies. But pressing play on a YouTube video on our website would set a third-party cookie. Cookies are tiny files that latch on to your computer when you visit certain websites. They remember what you do on the site, such as your password and preferences, for your convenience. You can accept or decline cookies.

Search Engine

Our website does not search queries or log the results. That means you can't enter keywords to conduct searches.

Security and Performance

We use a third-party web application firewall from Oracle Dyn to help maintain the security and performance of our website. The service checks network traffic for unusual activities directed at the website. *Traffic* means the volume of website visitors and users' activities, requests, or demands. A firewall is a computer device that helps filter out unauthorized or suspicious traffic that may affect the website negatively.

Now let's see about making this notice easy to navigate for your members and visitors.

Sample Layered Privacy Notice

If you really want to score good privacy points with regulators, don't just have a good privacy notice. Make it a layered privacy notice. Here is an example of a layered notice from the National Institution of Health (NIH). Health sector regulators are some of the strictest (in a good way), as privacy of personal health information is critical and is loaded with privacy implications. Layered notices roll up information into links, which offer smaller chunks of information so the reader isn't overwhelmed and website visitors don't give up before getting to the section of the notice they're looking for. Showing the headings allows for skimming, which makes it easier for users to glide through. Visitors only see the text if they click on the link or the plus sign to expand the topic. Be friendly to users.

In this example, additional privacy policy content is rolled into the last three expandable bullets on the bottom of the page. This way the privacy policy is not too lengthy and doesn't require the users to scroll. Some organizations may put these expandable sections on the left side of the web page (i.e., where you see the items under "About NIH"). There are different styles, but the goal is the same.

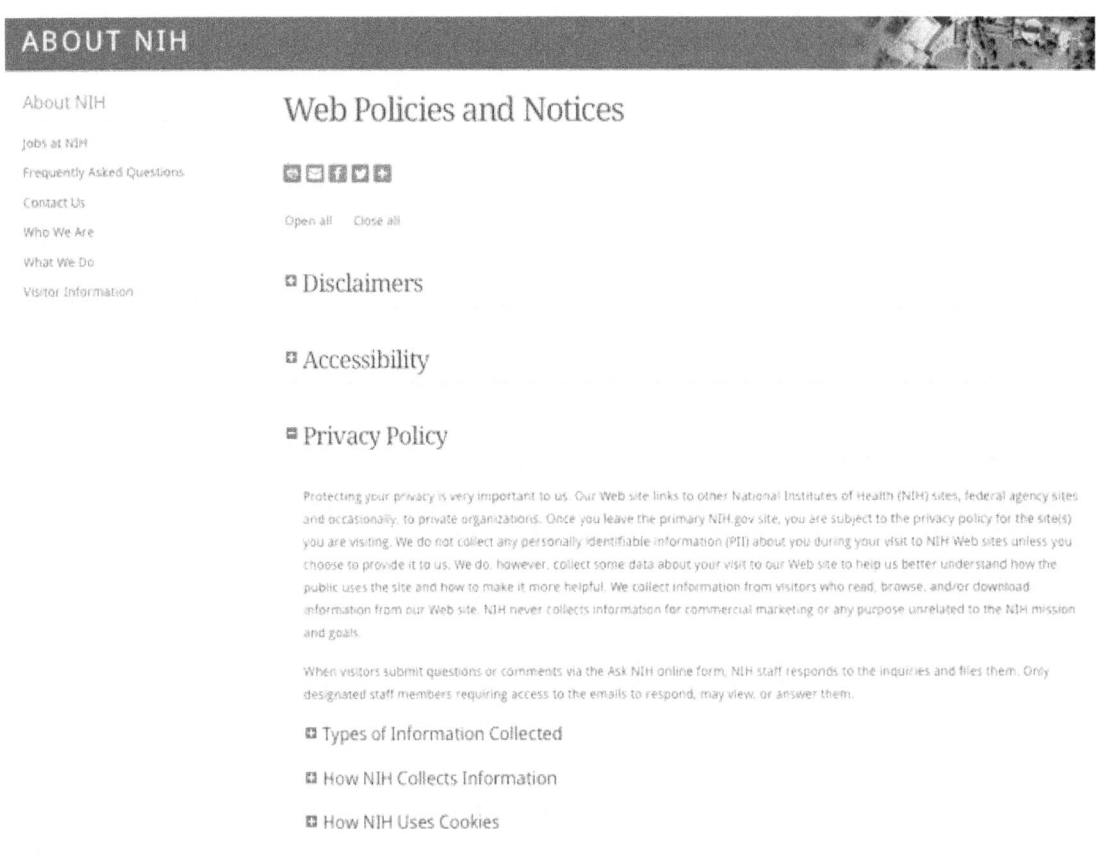

Figure 3. NIH web policies and notices

Speaking of being friendly to users, the font size, structure, language, and tone of your notice matter. The rest of your web pages or messages can't sound welcoming and friendly, but then when people get to your privacy notice, it sounds detached or like the readers are in a courtroom. Don't the ushers in your church smile and say, "Welcome"? In the same way, you should introduce your privacy notice in a way that is welcoming and lets people know you care and are committed to protecting their privacy. That's called a *privacy statement*. I mentioned this earlier. There is one in the NIH example above. And in the next paragraph, I snagged another example from a university's website to show you how it's done.

Privacy Statement

A bookstore is one of the places where a church takes payment cards. Sometimes the bookstore has an online presence, especially in recent years, as more churches have moved their bookstores online. I want you to focus on the statement under the privacy and security heading. Here's how a university's bookstore implements a privacy statement before it delves into its privacy notice. A statement helps members, customers, visitors, and even employees know what stance the store takes regarding information privacy. This excerpt was used with special permission from University Book Store's website.[1] More about bookstore privacy in Chapter 6.

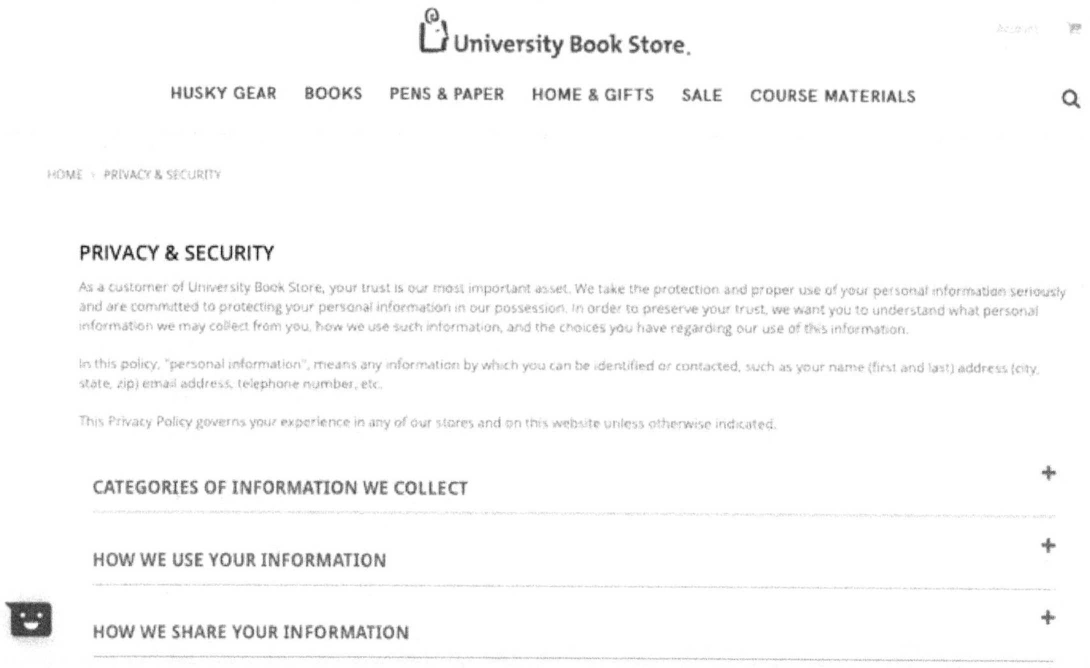

Figure 4. University Book Store privacy and security page

Internal Privacy Notices

We've already discussed the external privacy notice, but there are other types of notices. You'll need to create an internally facing notice that is designed for your employees because the usage and collection of their personal information is different from the public's. Don't fret. Take the same external notice and tailor it to personal information you collect from employees and other workers. That is, don't forget to name specific types of personal information you collect or hold about your employees, such as health insurance benefits, bank account information, credit report/background check, and beneficiary information for retirement accounts and life insurance. That notice is what they will read when supplying you with personal information for employment purposes. Rinse and repeat. If you have a web page that only members visit, tailor a notice for members based on the types of personal information you collect.

Event Privacy Notices

Church conferences and events need privacy notices, no matter their size. Many churches hold both online and in-person events—both require the same level of diligence to protect personal information. Inform and remind people why you collect personal information and how you use it. Even if you think they should already know, it's your responsibility. Your legal obligation is to provide a privacy notice before people give you their personal information. For instance, provide one during registration (in-person or online). Put a sign in the hallway about cameras or event photography and privacy. Include the privacy-related notice in any correspondence you send out to registrants before, during, and after the event. Get their permission or consent ahead of time. Give registrants who didn't consent before the event a chance to do so when they arrive at your event.

Registration

Events (whether physical or digital) require attendance and registration. Whether the event is a church cookout, anniversary, potluck, fish fry, picnic (you name it), registration helps the organizers plan to avoid running out of food, seats, or event materials. I don't like to hear that there is not enough fish left after I've stood in line for a while watching other people eat fish, especially when both my Dixie paper plate and my stomach are empty. That's just one reason for collecting personal information for church events. Registering with their personal information also keeps attendees updated in case the event is canceled or postponed. A third reason is that it gives organizers a chance to communicate what to expect, such as the agenda, event prizes, and notices about photography and social media. A notice is a critical privacy principle.

Church Privacy Team

Event Banner Privacy Notice (To Use on Location and in Hallways)

Here I have an example of the content displayed on an event sign at a university. This would be displayed in the hallway at an event your members and visitors are attending. Of course, your church event and situation could be different depending on if you do any photography, but the point is, it is good to inform attendees of what your church is doing about photography and the privacy of the attendees. First, you need to let people know what their choices are about their photo being taken. Next, you need to plan ahead to make sure you have a process for receiving requests and questions from attendees who desire to withdraw consent of their images or photos being used for marketing or other purposes. Then there are people who did not consent but want to know if you have any photos of theirs stored. The goal is making information and choices available to attendees. Let's look at this example of a sign posted at the entranceway of an event in Edinburgh Napier University:

> The use of photographs and data protection: Photographs taken will be used solely to promote the activities of Edinburgh Napier University and may appear in any of our promotional material in printed or electronic form including website, social media, in multiple publications, course leaflets or prospectuses. Please note that websites can be seen worldwide and not just in the UK where UK law applies. We store photographs securely on the University's network in a password-protected folder for no longer than five years, however, some of the photographs could be selected for inclusion in our historical archive and be retained indefinitely. For further information about today's event please contact . . .[2]

Event Planner and Photographer

Get your event planner and photographer on board with the attendees' permissions. Consenting to the use of their photos requires a release form attendees can sign. Small churches have fewer people and thus fewer people to ask permission for group photographs. If someone ever emails their photos to be posted on the church website or social media, have the person expressly state in the email that they want those photos to be used for that purpose. It's not a bad idea to say to event attendees, "Hey, if you don't want other attendees of the event to post your photo on social media and tag you, let people know before you smile for a photo with anyone, including our event photographer." You're not passing the privacy burden to your attendees. Rather, you're reminding them to restate their privacy preferences as often as necessary. (In Chapter 1 of *Church Privacy 101*, I share a true story about a Mrs. Lindqvist who was sued by fellow church members over a group photo she'd posted online. You can also read this story in Appendix F.) Being candid and reminding attendees to respect privacy is not only empowering for all but also helpful in preventing legal battles among members. Even if those battles are not yours, they can indirectly cause harm. Going out of your way to show diligence is a sign that you're aware of privacy needs. It shows you care.

Not everyone will be excited that their photo is on the church's Facebook page, website, or other church publication. This is yet another opportunity for your church to show its community that it cares about privacy and its members' well-being and peace. Okay, let's assess how your church is doing.

Purpose

Remember those privacy principles I touched on in previous chapters? Remember the one that specifies you should stick to one purpose or use? That's the principle! Don't spam people with emails promoting other church events; unless they specifically ask to be notified about other events, use information for this one event. Be in the moment. Give registrants a choice to subscribe to your emails and to be alerted about future events. Give them a choice to opt out when they're no longer interested. They'll appreciate your church the more for this important gesture.

Assess What Your Church Is Doing about Registration and the Type of Data Collected

☐ We establish the purpose for each type of personal information we collect for an event.

☐ We limit personal information to what's necessary for the event.

☐ We do not collect health information, date of birth, age, marital status, or personal contact information.

☐ When acknowledging people's birthdays at events, we only share month and day, not year.

☐ We consider the risk of every personal information element we collect.

- ☐ We give registrants a choice to participate in or decline from receiving emails unrelated to the event.

- ☐ We limit the use of personal information to what we indicate in our notice to registrants.

- ☐ Workers who handle registration for online and physical events receive privacy training on handling personal information.

- ☐ We brief our workers about information handling prior to the event kickoff and every day of the event.

- ☐ Registration forms in paper copy are protected when in use and shredded when no longer needed.

Assess Whether What Your Church Is Doing Aligns with Privacy Notices for Events

- ☐ Each event that attendees register for has a privacy notice they can read before completing the form.

- ☐ We have a link to the privacy notice on each email we send afterward.

- ☐ Workers or volunteers who handle registration for in-person events have taken personal information handling training.

- ☐ Printed registration forms are protected and shredded at the registration desk when no longer needed.

Assess What Your Church Is Doing about Event Privacy Notices for Photography and Images

- ☐ We inform attendees in the event's notice that there will be event photography and videography.

- ☐ We use banner stands at the entrance of events and near registration booths to inform attendees about photography and videography privacy and how they can express their choices.

- ☐ We inform people that they can contact us. We provide an email and a phone number if they do not wish to have their photo used for marketing, publicity, social media, or our website.

- ☐ We have signed releases from attendees who are identifiable in the images we use for publicity and on other materials.

Assess What Your Church Is Doing about Photo Permissions for Social Media

- ☐ We use our event privacy notice to inform attendees about the steps we take to protect the privacy of their photos and how we use those photos on social media.

- ☐ We also include in our event privacy notice that attendees of our events should let friends, family, church members, workers, and others they meet at our event know their privacy preferences if any of the following applies to them:

  - They do not wish for their images to be posted on social media.

  - They do not wish to be tagged in a photo or image posted on social media.

  - They do not wish to be described or have anything related to their personal lives mentioned.

  - They do not wish for their images to be texted or emailed in any form.

  - They do not wish for their images to be published on a commercial or personal website.

Assess What Your Church Is Doing about Marketing Privacy

- ☐ We review marketing requirements and laws in our jurisdiction and in other jurisdictions.

- ☐ We give people a choice to opt in to receive our email or newsletter about future events.

- ☐ We do not market future events to people just because we have their email addresses.

- ☐ After they opt in, we confirm that they wish to receive our emails in the future.

Church Privacy Team

- ☐ After they opt in, we give people an opportunity to change their minds anytime by including an unsubscribe link in the email.

- ☐ We let people know the timeframe it would take to process their request according to the law.

- ☐ We do not market to children. We get parental consent to communicate online with children or anyone under thirteen years of age.

Assess What Your Church Is Doing about Permissions for and Publicity of Photos or Images

- ☐ We use a release form when a person's photo is prominent or identifiable.

- ☐ We allow the person in the photo to withdraw consent at any time in writing (via email and other means).

- ☐ We keep permission or consent as a separate section from the website privacy notice on the registration site. (Note: A woman sued Chipotle for the use of her image. The photographer did not obtain a release.[3])

 Tip: Your church's event registration web page is the perfect spot to start. Before people start filling out the online registration form, they need to see a privacy notice on that page. Not in microscopic fine print. Make the notice easy to spot. Explain the photography and the use of photos at your event. Make it your policy that when people take group photos or videos, everyone in the photo is informed on how the photo will be used, where it will be posted, and what information will be given related to the photo (for example, tagging and other descriptors). The notice should also inform event attendees of the opportunity to give consent or decline consent for the church's use of their photos. Allow people to make these choices as they check in. The event planner, privacy expert (if any), church attorney, and photographer should be in the loop when it comes to executing event privacy. For large churches, your professional photographers should comply with your policy on photography. For small churches, this is even easier to apply because there are fewer people. Don't focus on the church's obligation alone. Again, attendees take photos of other attendees and post them online. Include in your notice that attendees should also remind other people (those they pose for photos with) what their privacy preferences are. This may sound minor. But it isn't. Earlier, I mentioned Mrs. Lindqvist, who was sued by fellow church members over photos she posted of them online. Such cases can tear apart long-standing relationships in the church community. Save your members' relationships and save them from liabilities at the same time.

Value: A privacy notice is a monumental boost to your events. People will now look forward to your events. They can relax and enjoy themselves instead of spending their energy dodging cameras because they don't want their photos showing up on Facebook, Instagram, or the church's slideshow. Those who attend your event will have the confidence that their photos will not be used without their express consent.

Action Steps: You've assessed what your church is doing about event privacy. The items you did not check are your action items to work on: list them. Have you designated someone within your church to handle this responsibility? Jot down your answers.

_____

_____

_____

What's your target date to assign someone to take this responsibility/when will you begin the tasks?
Day_____ Month_____ Year_____

What's your target date to complete these tasks?
Day_____ Month_____ Year_____

What questions would you ask me?

_____

_____

Church Privacy Team

_____

_____

_____

Internal Rules for Collection and Storage

It's a best practice to limit the personal information you collect to what's necessary to provide the person with the services they need or request. Your internal privacy policy or rules for protecting personal information should specify where personal information is to be stored and also where storage of that information is forbidden; for instance, you don't want personal information stored in employees', members', or volunteers' cars, left openly on someone's dining table at home, or on an unencrypted device that, if stolen, can be compromised. Personal information should not be left on desks or in someone's house unattended or unguarded. Your policy or rules should specify that it is to be locked up or protected when not in use. When information is on a device, the device should be encrypted. This includes encryption for laptops, desktop computers, and thumb/flash drives. Your policy and/or training should also be specific to places you know people are likely to leave personal information. Let's use cars as an example. Don't just say, "In a car." Get specific, such as on seats, under the seats, in the trunk, and in the glove compartment. Personal information should not be shared via social media—WhatsApp, Facebook, Instagram, and other social media platforms. Look at the following list and check whether any of the following are being shared via your church's social media platforms. (Note: they shouldn't be shared via this medium.)

- prayer requests

- medication, health information (condition or treatments), or hospitalization information

- account information (password, username, credit card, or bank account)

- location (vacation, travel plans, or errands or the precise conference, event, or church you're in and what room)

- personal information of other people you don't have consent from (Many apps tag photos and videos you take of others with location information.)

- criticisms and opinions (These could be seen as slander and/or libel. Slander is what you say, and libel is what you write about someone that could be damaging to the person's reputation. These types of statements can also be emotionally harmful.)

People don't typically admit they leave personal information in their cars. It's embarrassing, and they don't want to get in trouble. Don't ask them; they'll lie. So what should you do instead? Rather than sending out a survey, during privacy and risks discussions, call out the storage locations or places that are forbidden, like the car example we just went over. I'm sure someone will race to their car after the discussion and remove church documents that contain personal information. That's what good awareness and training does. It helps highlight good behaviors and corrects irresponsible conduct. Some people don't realize that thieves break into cars for personal information. Car radios, shopping bags, and cash are no longer as lucrative as they once were. Personal information can make more money over time than other items left in a car that you believe are valuable. Periodically, you should send out a memo to workers and volunteers highlighting places where you don't want personal information of church members to be kept. It will cause people to rethink the privacy risks associated with their habits.

Tip: You can't protect what you don't know. That's why I recommended earlier that you pinpoint where the information should be stored. Sometimes the location may not be as obvious as you'd think. If you're a large church, talk to ministry leaders, and you'll find out where everything is actually located. Assess all the processes and procedures for handling personal information in departments where personal information is used.

Value: Knowledge is power. It sounds cliché, but when you use your rules to share with your members, workers, and volunteers why you're concerned about privacy, people will begin to dialogue. Be sure to listen. After a privacy discussion, use insights you gleaned there to talk about your expectations, and then update your policy with the new ideas that'll change people's behavior to make them more privacy conscious. Incorporating feedback from those conversations will strengthen your policy. Did I say *policy*? Yes, your internal policy that your workers and members read, not a website notice.

Action Steps: Have you identified the leaders in your ministries who will be responsible for protecting these personal information sources? Have you designated someone to assure that all these sources are protected? Jot down your answers.

_____

_____

_____

What's your target date to assign someone to take this responsibility/when will you begin the tasks?
Day_____ Month_____ Year_____

What's your target date to complete these tasks?
Day_____ Month_____ Year_____

What questions would you ask me?

_____

_____

_____

_____

_____

Basis for Granting Access or Approving Access to Personal Information

Not everyone in the church is entitled to see or handle personal information the church holds, only those who need the information to carry out their duties or jobs. If there's no need to know, they should not have access or know the information. Before your church allows anyone to access personal information, you should evaluate whether the person should have the access. Consider the following criteria:

- Is the type of work they'll perform using this information specified and needed?
- What is their role (specify if volunteer, contractor, clergyperson, ministry leader, employee, or other role)?
- Have they read, understood, and signed the privacy policy?
- Have they received privacy training?
- Are they trusted/reliable?

Create a document with your rules based on the above criteria. Here's an example of a privacy rule that I just made up: "Sharing a person's identity or financial or health information is forbidden unless consent has been explicitly obtained and verified and the reason for sharing is justified according to the privacy policy of the church." Pass this rule around with the other rules you've created. Have a meeting to explain it, and check if everyone has read it and signed off. Take questions because the key to making this effective is engaging your people. Privacy practices thrive when there's an abundance of conversation and participation. Turn individual rules into an internal policy for privacy. Make your expectations known every opportunity you get. A policy can be as long as you want to make it. But don't get carried away. Keep it short so people will actually read it and easily remember to do what you expect of them.

Tip: No matter how long you have known someone, it doesn't mean you can trust the person with personal and sensitive information. Verify that they understand your rules, policies, and the risks. Don't base your selection on age, gender, race/ethnicity, profession, social status, how long the person has been with the church, or how much they've given (time or money) to the church. Small churches should not hand responsibilities to people simply because they take the load off the leadership. Not a good idea.

Value: When you use this method, there will be no surprises. Everyone will be on the same mission to protect personal information.

Authority and the Process of Approval of Access to Personal Information

You should create a policy that has clear rules and procedures for how workers are approved to access personal information. I mentioned that the granting of access should be based on the criteria I discussed in the previous section and that it should be approved. I recommend designating a handful of people to approve access. For starters, the following approval authority will help:

- A ministry leader makes the decisions to grant/approve access in their individual ministry.

- A privacy coordinator or manager reviews the decision (this could also be someone in a position above the ministry leader).

- At least two other people or leaders weigh in on the decision to grant/approve access.

Depending on how your church is structured and how many people you've hired into privacy roles, you can decide who should be an approval body. That's why the bullet points offer you examples, not a prescription. Every situation and church is different.

Create a document titled "Access and Need-to-Know: Approval Authorities," or name it what suits your church. Include the roles and specific names of people who will approve access. Once you have your list, you can copy and paste it into your privacy policy for all church workers. Drop it in any communication where you need to remind ministries about your procedure.

How you'll implement privacy depends on the structure of your church. For example, some churches have a main corporate authority and then regional and local congregations. Decisions can be made from top to bottom. In this case, there's a privacy role and program management at the top dictating what the regional and local congregations should do. That's fine. Let's focus on your church at the local level. You can decentralize decision-making to make approvals easier to manage. Let the local congregations handle their approvals. Another option is to have a hybrid model, a combination of a central role who approves access and a lower-level leader who does the same. That lower-level leader could be a ministry leader who initiates an access request for a worker or volunteer. For churches without branches or several congregations, ministry leaders, preachers, and other clergy can report to the designated person in charge of privacy such as the privacy manager or privacy coordinator. The crux of the matter is, having more than one person approve access to personal information is best. Small churches should assign someone to be accountable for privacy. Their title doesn't matter. You need an objective person who will be the final approving authority for requests.

Tip: You should make sure leaders have a person or two at different levels in the church leadership hierarchy to assess the integrity of their decisions about accesses they grant. This way there are checks and balances. The tip here is, accountability will work well so long as the people checking on the decisions remain objective.

Value: Using this method will help you keep personal information handling in check. You have two types of volunteers in your church: one is in your church's neighborhood or visits, and one is a member. Either way, make your volunteers privacy savvy. Depending on their tasks, they may need training. Unless they're helping rake leaves outdoors, they need to read and understand your privacy policy about handling personal information. This will keep you mindful of who you give personal information handling tasks to and how much it may expose the church to privacy risks and liabilities.

Action Steps: You've learned how approvals should be handled. Assess how your church handles approvals and write down how it differs from my example. Then write down what needs to be changed so you are handling approvals appropriately. Those are your action steps. Have you designated someone within the church to take this responsibility? Jot down your answers.

_____

_____

_____

Church Privacy Team

What's your target date to assign someone to take this responsibility/when will you begin the tasks?
Day_____ Month_____ Year_____

What's your target date to complete these tasks?
Day_____ Month_____ Year_____

What questions would you ask me?

_____
_____
_____
_____
_____

Tell me and I forget.
Teach me and I remember.
Involve me and I learn.
(Benjamin Franklin)

Part Two
Church Operations

5

Church Freelancers, Vendors, Contractors, Gig Workers, and Employees

Every morning in Africa a gazelle wakes up and knows that it must run faster than the fastest lion or it will be killed and eaten. Every morning in Africa a lion wakes up and knows it must outrun the slowest gazelle or it will starve to death. It doesn't matter whether you are a lion or a gazelle, when the sun comes up you'd better be running!
(Dr. Willie Jolley, It Only Takes a Minute to Change Your Life)

Best privacy practices are like good running shoes that'll make you and your team run like the fastest gazelle. Information criminals will need to work very hard to catch up with you. To make this happen, you'll need everyone on your team to be on the same page about privacy expectations. Contrary to popular belief, policies are not just a bunch of rules. A privacy policy is the way your church communicates its expectations with the following people:

- employees of the church (all levels of workers and leadership)

- contractors, freelancers, and suppliers of services (such as cleaning services, maintenance, technicians, equipment, caterers, decorators)

- partners (including the local area food banks, health workers, media, and law enforcement)
- volunteers (for events and ministries)

Privacy policies are central to safe behavior around personal information. They inform people of what's expected of everyone, or a specific group of people, and why. A privacy policy should have different sections or topics to address various concerns, such as the scope of personal information the church is concerned about and related consequences of losing personal information. Other items a policy should include are the negative impacts of a privacy violation or breach to whom the policy applies, who has been designated to enforce the policy, and the church's legal responsibilities and obligations. When you have a privacy mission and vision statement, workers will realize your church is a privacy rockstar. They'll commit to your stance. Better yet, incorporate this in job descriptions and when you interview candidates. Do the same for freelancers, contractors, vendors, and volunteers. I'll jump on the topic of freelancers next.

Before a privacy policy is written, your church should do an inventory of what privacy laws and regulations require. Tally up what people's needs are with regard to privacy. Know what your obligations are, both to people and in order to comply with privacy laws and regulations.

If you have a policy for vendor management, then the church can tweak the same policy to hold all workers who are not church employees to a high standard of privacy protection similar to your church's employee privacy policy. Sometimes external workers (vendors, contractors, or freelancers) are hired but are not thoroughly checked because the church may not know the right questions to ask or what measures must be in place to protect privacy. Many churches simply assume their vendors will do what is right.

Depending on the level of access the person has been given to church information or computer systems, a privacy policy can require that the worker regularly scan and safeguard their laptop, computer systems, or networks that are connected to the church's network to assure they do not pose a risk to your church. The policy can state that there are disciplinary or legal actions that will be taken for noncompliance. Similar to an internal privacy policy for your employees, the policy for contract workers can specify that if they don't comply, they could face termination. The following are examples of major data breaches related to contract workers, vendors, and employees who were noncompliant with policies. Although these breaches did not occur in a church, churches are not immune to similar breaches. I want you to notice the impact on customers and how much money was spent to recover from the error.

Costly Vendor Problems

- Target spent nearly $148 million after a data breach caused by gaps in its security was overlooked.[1]

- Home Depot spent an estimated $179 million due to an attack caused by credentials stolen from one of its vendors.[2]

- Saudi Aramco faced an extortion of $50 million because one of its contractors leaked customer data.[3]

- Eli Lilly publicized the email addresses of over seven hundred patients taking the drug Prozac by sending a mass reminder email to all who had subscribed, exposing subscribers' email addresses.[4]

Next, let's look at people you hire directly and the ones you hire through third parties online.

Working with Contractors, Freelancers, and Vendors Directly

Many churches work with independent contractors, freelancers, and vendors directly. These freelancers work for themselves, which means you hire them directly by visiting their website or calling them with no third party in the middle. Some examples of freelancers you might hire are photographers, event planners, and web designers. If you're going to give these types of workers documents that have personal information, communicate your standards for handling and protecting personal information. Ask the freelancers what they do to protect information. Some freelancers already have this in the contract document they will send you to sign. If it's not included, ask them to include a clause that says the freelancer is forbidden from duplicating or sharing the personal and confidential information that will be part of the project and that they're also not allowed to use it for unauthorized purposes. If you already have privacy and security expectations for contractors/vendors written, just email those to them. They'll cut and paste the expectations into the contract document you'll both sign. The church and the freelancer should reach an understanding before signing. Just because someone was referred to you doesn't mean you should let your guard down. Next, let's talk about freelancers and gig workers who sell their services through online platforms, meaning you pay a fee to the platform/third party to hire these workers.

Freelancers and Gig Workers on Online Platforms

Gig workers are also freelancers or independent contractors who are hired for short-term work by multiple clients. You'd find them on online platforms such as Guru, Upwork, Truelancer, Fiverr, FreeUp, Giggrabbers, AnyTask, Freelancer, and PeoplePerHour, among others. These platforms are like eBay or Amazon but focus on selling services instead of products. After creating an account, you can access millions of freelancers or gig workers offering multiple services. In 2019 there were 57 million gig workers in the US alone, and their noteworthy contributions to the US economy were close to $1 trillion.[5]

In today's gig economy, it is important to learn how to protect your church. If you're the service or gig buyer on behalf of your church, read this section carefully. As I've always said, treat all contractors, gig workers, freelancers, and independent workers as your employees. Hold them accountable as you would employees. They pose the same risks depending on what they have access to.

Does My Church Need to Worry about Freelancing or the Gig Economy?
Yes. Independent workers have been around for a long while, and they are becoming more and more common. Lately, their numbers have increased exponentially because of the COVID-19 pandemic. The following are statistics recently compiled by WhatToBecome:

- Fifty-two percent of worldwide global gig economy workers lost their non-freelance jobs due to the coronavirus pandemic.

- In 2019, 57 million freelancers worked in the US.

- One out of every four workers in 40 percent of companies are freelancers or gig workers.

- Forty-four percent of millennials are freelancing.

- Ninety-eight percent of remote workers would prefer to continue to work remotely for the rest of their careers.[6]

The gig economy is flexible, allowing your church to hire people from all over the world to do all kinds of work. I have used freelancers from online gig economy platforms for ten years. As a technical communication major, I was bred to be a freelancer, so I relate to freelancers more than most people do. People with my background provide technical art, information architecture, scientific design, technical editing, technical writing, usability expertise, and numerous other skills after four years of an intense college program.

But there are always bad apples making claims of certain expertise and not delivering, which spoils the reputations of good freelancers. In today's gig economy, more people are online claiming to be experts in services I can't do for myself. Some are real experts. Others are unreal in every sense of the word. It's a jungle out there. But I have worked with and built great business relationships with wonderful freelancers in different parts of the world, including Nigeria, Russia, Kenya, Canada, the US, China, and more. To find a good freelancer, you just need to be very careful and do your homework. A good freelancer is the one who delivers what you need, enjoys your type of project, is easy to work with, and is not put off if you express privacy or confidentiality needs. If you're using a platform to find freelancers, read their profiles. Know what type of work they say they enjoy. Read what people say about the type of work you want done and how the freelancer handled similar work in the past. Tell them about your project; see if they're interested. Engaging a freelancer early is good so you get to know them. Maintain a list of freelancers you've reached out to that you liked and can trust with personal information so that when you need them in the future, you won't rush your decision and possibly end up getting scammed.

What Types of Services or Gigs Do People Buy from Online Platforms These Days?

Prayers. Yes, you can order prayers. For twenty dollars a shot, you can state your issues and have a pastor or clergyperson and their team of prayer warriors fast and pray their socks off—about your job, healing, good grades, you name it. There are other services. The guy who cuts my grass also writes and reads poems. The lady who hung my art frames is a banker but also cleans homes and hotels. The guy who did my yard work is a law student and does party/event setup and decorations. The lady who helped me with moving also sells photography services for twenty-five dollars and sings at parties. Another mover also does laundry and makes beds for under thirty dollars. All these can be ordered from online platforms. Now let's talk about what your church might order.

You can hire a temporary or part-time worker for bookkeeping, accounting, or data entry work. You can hire a VA (virtual assistant), a writer/editor (for documents or video or audio recordings), a graphic designer to design flyers, a researcher, a marketing specialist, a business process manager, a social media manager, and so many more. From platforms such as TaskRabbit, which connects you with someone locally who would come to your church facility, you can hire someone to wash your church automobile or church windows, organize a storage room, cook/grill for your ministry picnic, cut the church grass, handle event photography, or move heavy stuff in your building. Since we're talking about privacy here, every type of platform you order from has its own set of privacy concerns, but the benefit to your church is that you save a lot of money by hiring people in this way. Brick-and-mortar landscaping businesses may charge you $250 per month to mow the church's lawn when a gig worker will rejoice over cutting the same grass for $75. Another benefit is the great relationships you develop with the gig workers. You get to support individual skilled workers by helping them realize their entrepreneurial dreams. Plus, gig workers with office skills can help close the skills gap in skills your church volunteers do not possess. You don't need to hire someone part-time or full-time. You only pay for projects when you need help the most. All this sounds great, but regardless, you'll still do your due diligence to protect personal information.

As a ministry, small church, or large church, you need other people's skills and expertise to move your tedious church operational tasks forward so you don't get stuck, but you can't always hire a full-time person for everything. Whether hiring full-time or for one task, you must understand the risks involved. You can't rush through this. Know that the platform you find freelancers on may have rules to prevent bad behavior, but they won't go to the ends of the earth to fight for you, reimburse 100 percent of your money, or recover your intellectual property if a freelancer turns out to be a rogue. Some will give you credit toward another project. The credit may be less than the exact amount of the damage done. It's like expecting Facebook to fight for you because one of their users tricked you on its platform. It's not happening. Even if it happens, it's not their priority. If you think about it, pursuing your dispute does not make business sense for a freelance platform. In the end, you could lose more than you gain.

Are Online Freelancers Real People?
Some online workers are not real in the sense that they're not looking to help you as much as they're trying to deceive you and get your money. Go to the forums of the online platforms you're interested in and read the stories there. Some comments will shock you.

For example, one review was posted by a customer on Fiverr titled "Sellers Pretending to be from the US!" I laughed because it has happened to me before. A seller's profile said "US," but after I started engaging the seller and had a chance to vet them, I grew suspicious. I traced the freelancer to Bangladesh. I asked to see a particular website they'd listed as their work. It took the freelancer several days, and they still couldn't find it. I decided not to move forward with the freelancer. Since some platforms allow you to filter freelancers by location, some freelancers lie to increase their chances of being hired. Also, people can connect with friends in other countries to create profiles that deceive customers. The freelance platform may also believe they're based in the US, Canada, or Europe. It's not bad at all to hire freelancers in other countries—it's the misinformation and deception that are the problem.

Some platforms require freelancers and buyers to use the real names on their government-issued IDs. There's a little more accountability there. But even with that, there are scams and questionable behaviors. Check this out. I found this on a freelance platform forum. One seller said regarding the verification of sellers on that platform, "I have been here for four years and never have been asked for my ID, and my profile is not a photo of me." Would I give church members' personal information to this person to work with? Absolutely not!

Watch out for deceptive freelancers.

- Some are there to do what criminals do: extort money and intellectual property.

- Sometimes their cheap price is to reel you in. Then they will ask you to pay more before they start. If you don't agree, they lead you on but then strike in a way that forces you to cancel the order. But you've already given them so much information already—even passwords.

- They could even deface what they've already created for you just to spite you.

- Cancelling the order means you don't get to rate the freelancer for using this bullying tactic. So they keep doing this to more innocent buyers.

Of course, this is not to deter you from hiring freelancers. Great freelancers do exist. There are many who truly enjoy their work, will go above and beyond for you, and will deliver stellar service. It just takes prayer and diligence to find those types of talents in a world full of frauds. When you do find them, treat those freelancers with kindness and respect, and support them with more business to help them grow as they're helping you grow. It's a win-win.

Freelance Platforms

No matter the freelance platform you use, understand that they are in the business for profit, whether the money comes from the seller or the buyer. I have used Fiverr, Upwork, and TaskRabbit for church projects. Most of the experiences I've shared here are based on these three platforms. Definitely research platforms such as Guru, Truelancer, FreeUp, Giggrabbers, AnyTask, Dribbble, Freelancer, or PeoplePerHour to see how they work out for your needs. Most platforms cannot afford to use their time and resources to figure out who is right or wrong when there is a dispute or if personal information is at stake. It's your responsibility.

The Don'ts of Working with Freelancers on Online Platforms:

- Don't be in a rush, so start early. It's better to find freelancers far ahead of when you need them. This buys you time to do some research before you need to hire them. Don't focus on just pricing, skills, and reviews. Depending on the nature of your project, chat with the freelancer and ask questions about privacy and security.

- Do not give anyone your username and password. The freelancer could pass around your credentials to others. Sometimes the online seller is a network of folks, not just one person. You don't know who'll end up with your credentials. Applications such as WordPress, Squarespace, email campaign platforms, and others allow you to invite contributors to design content for you without them seeing your credentials. Ask the freelancer for their email so you can invite the freelancer into your platform. The email address they give you may be fake, then the freelancer may say, "Your invite is not working; just give me your main login information." If you do so, they can view your billing info, including your credit card, address, and more. Worse, they can change your password and hijack the ministry or church's website if you don't pay them more. That's a lot of control to give up to a stranger.

- Do not give "Administrator" permission for website work unless it's justified for the type of work. Make sure you remove the permission as soon as the work is completed. Realize that the person can lock you out of your own website. Indefinitely. They can also deface your website, blog, or whatever you're working on. This will cost you more to restore.

- Do not approve and pay for the service in full with the promise that they'll keep working on it afterward. Many freelancers will keep that promise, but others won't. Don't pay until you're satisfied with the work and have taken back access to your account or information.

- Don't share information that should be protected. That includes your personal information and that of other people in your church. Don't share confidential information.

- Don't give your home address, phone number, passport, or Social Security number to a freelancer.

What Freelance Platforms Will and Won't Do

- Yes, these platforms have a dispute resolution service, but there's no guarantee you'll get the result you desire. After a lot of going back and forth, some will encourage you to accept the quickest solution: cancellation.

- I mentioned earlier that some are not interested in pursuing a freelancer on your behalf in other parts of the world. Even if they're in your home state, it takes a lot of effort, time, and money.

- If there's a dispute, the platform will push for cancellation regardless of what it costs the buyer in terms of privacy or intellectual property. If this is going to waste their money or time, they prefer you pull the plug yourself (initiate cancellation), take the coupon they give you, and count your losses.

- They won't pursue a freelancer who suddenly drops out of the platform without warning. Some will vanish with your church's art concepts, ideas, business documents, and personal information in their possession.

What if the Freelancer Has Five-Star Ratings and Has Completed 200+ Jobs?

Five stars don't mean much when it's a scam. As I mentioned earlier, cancellation means you don't get to give a review or rate the freelancer even if they deceived you. They can keep doing this to more innocent buyers. You don't get to give them the one-star rating that they deserve once you cancel. They play the system well. If they can't upsell you, they create a problem so you're forced to cancel. If you gave away personal information of church members, cancellation won't help you. Cancellation doesn't hurt rogue freelancers. They'll just look for another victim.

If you look at what the freelancer delivered to you and realize the person you hired doesn't have the skills they advertised or didn't do the job, of course, the next step is to let them know what you didn't like and request a revision. Some will drop you for requesting a revision. Why? If they keep you, that means you may likely give them less than five stars in the end. In the meantime, you just wasted all the time you put in and lost important information.

But there are people who have really earned their five stars, and it's sad that the bad apples also have five stars. Don't just focus on the five-star reviews a freelancer gets, read the one-star and three-star comments in their profile to see what issues people have had with them. For example, did they overstate their qualifications or claim Harvard, Yale, or Oxford education yet delivered less than stellar work? They may have merely copied and pasted competencies and skills from another freelancer's profile page.

Freelancers Can Vanish Anytime

Freelancers can vanish in good ways and bad ways. A platform can unintentionally drop a freelancer from the platform because they didn't complete some requirement, or the freelancer can just drop out on their own without explanation. In some cases, they don't mean to abandon you. They don't have a way of reaching you if you didn't have another way to contact each other than through the platform. One way to prepare against that is to have alternate contact information so the freelancer can reach you if they get dropped from the platform or other emergencies happen. Agree on reaching out to the freelancer if the platform drops either of you or if the freelancer decides to leave the platform for other reasons. Some freelancers have a website or social media accounts they'll share. I remember one sharing their website information with me before I hired them. That's a good sign.

If you're still on the fence about online freelancers or you are unsure due to privacy implications, below are some ways to alleviate those concerns:

- How many years have they been developing/using their skills? Look at their training, education, integrity, or related achievements, which show their passion and commitment more than reviews ever could. Is there anywhere else you can read about the person's work? If not, trust your instincts and try the next freelancer. Keep in mind you want someone you'll enjoy working with. Don't settle for disrespect. No level of expertise is an excuse for unprofessionalism.

- Research freelancers' integrity and work ethic, and engage them in a chat to prove how they can protect personal information. It takes a lot of prep work. Pray and chat with the church's lawyer before you hand over your precious intellectual property. Don't give away any personal information that will negatively impact you or members of your church.

- Most platforms have a dispute resolution service. They will reach out to the freelancer and ask them to address your concern. But if the situation is too complicated, they can offer you a coupon and ask you to find another freelancer to work with. Again, they're a business and want to make a profit, not play detective. If you get compensation out of dispute resolution, great. So choose wisely.

Redact Personal Information

This takes time to do, but it is worth the investment. When you provide church documents to a freelancer, it makes sense to mask, cross out, or remove people's full names, addresses, phone numbers, and email addresses. Replace names with substitute names on the copy that you provide your freelancer. Delete email addresses, phone numbers, and photos from documents.

What Do You Need to Know about the Freelancer?

Again, it depends on what they're going to do for you. If the task you're giving the freelancer does not present the privacy risks I noted earlier, you don't need to worry. Don't stress the person. Their contact information and a well-understood contract will suffice. If it's a high-risk project where they'll view and/or use personal information about you or your members, you should know more about them. That could include the following:

- full name

- their website/blog site

- social media handles or profiles

- profile picture

- phone number

- email address

- country of origin/where they're based

- time zone differences

- qualifications/résumé

- proof/verification of skills (ask for samples if applicable)

- scope of work included in their offer (read and understand what's included and what's not included)

- price (confirm whether the fee amount is a fixed rate or an hourly rate)

Be upfront that the project is for a church. Some freelancers may have biases about churches while others love church-related work. That's why it's important to ask if this is the type of work they enjoy doing. Trust me, I know that even the government considers biases before allowing some workers to handle certain critical information.

Have a phone conversation to make sure this is the type of work they enjoy doing and to simply get to know them better. I do this often.

Remember that whatever personal information you collect from a freelancer, you're responsible for protecting it! It cuts both ways. Never forget that.

Consider the Type of Project You're Putting Out There and the Level of Access Required
What kind of work are you hiring a freelancer to do (web design, IT, content)? If the job requires design or content update of a website, this doesn't require you to grant administrative or owner-level access to a freelancer or contractor—you can grant access that doesn't expose personal or financial information. But if the job requires access to a database where members' or visitors' personal information can be accessed, or if the job requires access to the e-commerce section of the website where financial transactions are processed, these projects could have a negative impact on people if the access you give to a freelancer, vendor, or contractor is compromised. For these types of jobs, you need to check the person's background, credit history, job history, references, expertise, and application of privacy and

security standards, among other things. Write down what you're trying to get done and evaluate the risks. You might want to hire locally, not online. Consider the risk.

The Personal Information You Should Protect before Granting Access to Files and Accounts
Before you give access to church files or information, you need to decide what type of personal information you are giving the freelancer access to. You may need to block access to certain areas that contain personal information, or you may need to redact or remove personal information from the files. These are the types of personal information that will have a negative privacy impact if compromised:

- photos of church members
- full names and home addresses of members
- email addresses of members/visitors
- financial information or credit/debit card information of the church/members
- passwords and other account credentials
- employees' personal, health, and benefits information
- personal information of children

What Type of Access Permission Does the Freelancer Need?

Permissions depend on the tool or application you're building your website, blog, social media, or anything on. There are no universal labels or nomenclatures for access levels. I wish there were. But the idea is the same. Here are examples of permission categories and what they all mean:

- content editor: the person who creates the design, layout, and text that goes on the website, blog, or social media

- administrator: the person who can grant or cancel access to everyone who signs into the account (They can change the password of the main account.)

- reviewer: the person whose job may be to review the design and give feedback to the designer to make changes

I recommend that you visit the website of the application you want to build with/on and search the definition of the different permission levels or permission options.

More Permission Options

WordPress, Squarespace, Wix, Mailchimp, Canva, Adobe Express, and social media platforms (Facebook, Instagram, Twitter) all offer different types of permission options you can grant your freelancers. It is important to record the types of access you have granted so that you can maintain a log and track what each freelancer has access to. If you were to go online now and search "Squarespace permissions," you'd see a list of all the types of permissions you could grant a freelancer based on the work you want them to do. There are permissions for "Owner," "Administrator," "Content Editor," "Billing," and "Store Manager." Do this for other platforms/tools too. It will help you decide which permission is appropriate for the freelancer. If you're giving one person two different permissions, document those two permissions. Check on those permissions regularly so they're not misused. Ready? Here's an example of a simple table you could create now:

Table 1. Permissions given for website-builder platforms

Freelancer's Name	Platform Name	Tasks to be Performed	Type of Access Approved & Granted	Access Granted by Account Owner and Administrator, Main Street Fellowship Church	Start Date	End Date	Cancel Date

| Liz Habib | Squarespace | Add/Replace images Add/Replace link Update text on website | Website Editor (No access to personal information) | Rev./Bishop Carlos Gray | 1/20/23 | 2/22/23 | 2/22/25 |

Beginning and End Date of Access

The first lesson I learned in project management school was, every project has a beginning and an end; there's no such thing as an everlasting project. So document the beginning and end date of your project as well as any changes in the level of access you grant workers before and during the project. Don't be shy about sharing with a freelancer what your privacy expectations are for the access you'll give them. For instance, the permission you've granted them must not be shared or transferred to another freelancer or unauthorized person. Put that in writing. Make it clear. This means, supplement your contract/agreement document with a nondisclosure agreement (NDA) or a confidentiality agreement. You can have a different version for your independent contractors, vendors, employees, leaders, volunteers, and interns. An NDA does not protect information that is publicly available. It will protect your church against unauthorized disclosure of personal, confidential, and proprietary information. For example, a member list, a customer list, an event attendee list, health information, invention/product development, intellectual property, film concepts, or a personal financial information/donor list . . . I'm out of breath, but you get the picture. Our focus is on personal information, but I included confidential information in this example for you. It doesn't matter who you have an NDA with, incorporate these key elements. Add more elements if you'd like. Consult your legal counsel. It can be along these lines:

Church Privacy Team

Nondisclosure Agreement

This nondisclosure agreement (NDA) is entered into by/between Brookside Lutheran Bible Church [the Disclosing Party] located at 5 Loaves Ave., Capernaum, Illinois, and Eky Emma [the Receiving Party], Senior Web Designer at Bethany Web Design Inc., located at 29 Fig Tree Blvd., Capernaum, Illinois, for the purposes of updating the Disclosing Party's website, blbc.org. This agreement prevents unauthorized disclosure of personal information and confidential information as defined below. The parties agree that this NDA shall govern the rights and obligations of the parties involved in relation to disclosures made by the Disclosing Party.

Definition of Personal Information: For the purposes of this agreement, personal information shall include any information that relates to a person. Personal information includes membership information, passwords and access credentials, financial information, health information, contact information (email address, physical address, and/or phone number), biometrics, IP address, driver's license, photos, videos, and Social Security number.

Definition of Confidential Information: For the purposes of this agreement, confidential information shall include any information disclosed to the Receiving Party in written, electronic, and/or oral form including ideas/concepts, processes, designs, and strategies.

Exclusions: For the purposes of this agreement, the Receiving Party shall not be held accountable for (1) information that's publicly available, (2) a government authority's request for information, (3) information already known or made available to the Receiving Party prior to the agreement, and (4) authorized disclosures approved by the Disclosing Party.

Obligations & Accepted Disclosures: The Receiving Party shall protect the privacy and confidentiality of information in the interest of the Disclosing Party. The Receiving Party shall not disclose information to third parties or use the Disclosing Party's personal information or confidential information to pursue their own interests. The Receiving Party shall disclose information only to the Disclosing Party's representative specified and approved by the Disclosing Party, (i.e., Minister Ron Matthews). The Receiving Party shall return to the Disclosing Party any notes, files, and records at the end of their engagement with the project.

Terms: This agreement shall remain in effect until the Disclosing Party notifies the Receiving Party in writing releasing the Receiving Party from this agreement.

Severability: In the event of a legal dispute between the parties involved in this NDA where the court deems any term or part of the agreement unenforceable, the remaining provisions of this NDA shall still apply.

Signatures

This NDA shall be binding on the parties involved. It shall not be amended except by written agreement of the parties.

Disclosing Party
Name: Minister Ron Matthews, Media Ministry
Organization: Brookside Lutheran Bible Church
Address: 5 Loaves Ave., Capernaum, Illinois
Signature: _____
Date_____

Receiving Party
Name: Eky Emma, Senior Web Designer
Organization: Bethany Web Design Inc.
Address: 29 Fig Tree Blvd., Capernaum, Illinois
Signature: _____
Date_____

What You Should Know about the Freelance Platforms You're Using

You should know the following about each platform you are using:

- where they're based (Get their address.)

- who owns the platform or company

- what customers have written in their reviews

- what freelancers write on their online forum (Read what freelancers are saying about their customers and the platform.)

- their privacy policy and terms of use (Download and save these documents in a folder. Read them.)

- their phone number, including phone numbers for customer service, complaints, and dispute resolution departments

- their email, including email addresses for customer service, complaints, privacy concerns, and dispute resolution departments

Rules to Protect Your Church on Freelance Platforms

Realize that even with rules, some freelancers will twist your arm to give them more control of your personal and confidential information even if it's against the rules. So find the following documents on the freelance platform and read them:

- the privacy notice (a.k.a. "privacy policy" on the platform's website)

- rules of behavior for sellers/freelancers

- rules of behavior for buyers (that's you)

- consequences for noncompliance

- conflict resolution process

- service agreement/terms of use and indemnification (what the platform says is not its responsibility)

Communication with Your Freelancer

Deciding where and how you will communicate with the freelancer will help you control the flow of information. You could choose to communicate in any of these ways:

- Communicate on the platform where you found and hired the freelancer. (This is highly recommended!) You really don't need these other options below if you use the platform's inbox and call or video features. I typically use the inbox on the platform. No calls or video.

- Communicate via phone. (Don't give away your real phone number. Consider virtual or disposable phone numbers.)

- Communicate via social media. (Don't exchange or disclose password info or other personal information through social media.)

- Communicate via Skype/Zoom or similar tools. (If you communicate outside the platform and, for instance, you're using Zoom or other conference platforms, be careful about sharing your screen. Close files that have personal information if you find it's necessary to share your screen.)

Paying Your Freelancers

Remember that the freelance platform exists to protect you from faceless, online criminals who can steal your credit card information and/or your money. Pay your freelancers on the platform whenever possible. You have other options such as PayPal, Stripe, or Square, but I recommend paying through the platform. Stay there. It's safer.

 Tip: Remember that when you give anyone administrative access or permission, you're giving away the keys to the kingdom, so to speak—your personal information or church members' personal information. Depending on your role in your church, giving away too much access might mean jeopardizing other protected information in the church, not just personal information. When you grant administrative access, if you're dealing with a person who is evil or criminally possessed, they can take over your account and boot you out for any reason at any time. The major tip here is, don't hesitate to inform a freelancer what your data privacy expectations are for the access you've given them. For example, they shouldn't transfer or share the permissions you grant them. Put that in writing. See the NDA language I provided in the "Beginning and End Date of Access" section. If you suspect the freelancer is abusing their privileges, remove their access. Do that first before complaining or trying to resolve any issues with them. No matter how smart or talented a person is, don't let that intimidate you. They need to *earn* your trust. The greater risk will be on you if personal information is compromised.

 Value: You will be in control of the personal information assets in your care once you've considered all the possible risks. You can start managing those risks by applying the steps in this chapter.

Church Employees

There are roles or duties you should reserve for church employees, especially those tasks that have potential privacy risks. That is, save those roles for people you've gotten to know or will know for a while. These include workers whose background and references you've checked. They live in the local area. You have better assurance about the quality of their work and work ethic. Besides, their work relationship with the church is more dedicated whether you're hiring the person part-time or full-time. You need a privacy policy to influence, change, and control their behavior. The content of such a policy is very important. You don't want to just have impressive church-speak, legalese, tech-speak, and big words; you need a *message* that matters and that employees will understand and apply. Remember, you're sending them a message. Your employee privacy policy should have all of the elements below. Check the boxes so you know you have incorporated the elements.

Assess What Your Employee Privacy Policy Includes

- ☐ our purpose, principles, and objectives for protecting personal information
- ☐ scope: who the policy applies to (all employees)
- ☐ policy: the details of the policy address unauthorized/unlawful collection, handing, use, disclosure, alteration, storage, and retention
- ☐ responsibilities: expected behavior and password and access management
- ☐ definition of *personal information* for the purpose of the policy
- ☐ explanation of individuals' privacy rights
- ☐ violations: intentional and involuntary violation of policies, and the consequences
- ☐ explanation of authorized and unauthorized disclosure
- ☐ disciplinary action if not compliant (termination and legal action)
- ☐ incident reporting (the person, phone number, and email to report incidents to)
- ☐ proper handling of personal information
- ☐ remote work
- ☐ the person in charge or point of contact for the policy (title, email, phone)
- ☐ exceptions to the policy
- ☐ terms and definitions
- ☐ acknowledgment that employees have read and understood the policy

Tip: There's more to add depending on your environment. Remember, your privacy policy is a form of training, so include what's important to help change people's behavior. While you want employees to handle members' privacy properly, don't forget your employees also need a privacy notice to address how you handle their personal information. That goes for small churches too. You don't have employees? That's fine. Treat your volunteers like employees where privacy policies are concerned. Have a "Cell Phone Policy," "Social Media Policy," "Complaint-Resolution Policy," and "Work-from-Home Policy." You can download these and other templates at the course portal when you sign up for a course.

Value: When you create and use policies, everyone will be on the same page and will understand your mission, expectations, and privacy stance.

Action Steps: You've assessed what's included in your church's privacy policies for employees. Now you can customize your policy for vendors and other contract workers, including freelancers. You may choose to have a comprehensive privacy policy for both internal and external workers. It depends on your environment. Any items you didn't check are your action items to work on: list them. Have you designated someone within your church to handle this responsibility? Jot down your answers.

_____

_____

_____

What's your target date to assign someone to take this responsibility/when will you begin the tasks?
Day_____ Month_____ Year_____

What's your target date to complete these tasks?
Day_____ Month_____ Year_____

Church Freelancers, Vendors, Contractors, Gig Workers, and Employees

What questions would you ask me?

_____

_____

_____

_____

_____

Assess Your Privacy Policy for Freelancers, Vendors, Contractors, and Volunteers

Earlier, I mentioned a freelancer, vendor, and contractor privacy policy when I discussed the contract agreement. You need to get specific on what your expectations are, which largely depend on your church's environment or personal information processing activities. But generally, the content for your external workers' privacy policy should include these elements.

Our privacy policy for freelancers, vendors, contractors, and volunteers includes the following:

- ☐ our purpose, principles, and objectives for protecting personal information

- ☐ scope: who the policy applies to (vendors, contractors, volunteers), in this case external workers

- ☐ policy: addressing unauthorized/unlawful collection, handling, use, disclosure, alteration, storage, and retention

- ☐ responsibilities: expected behavior and password and access management

- ☐ definition of personal information

- ☐ explanation of individuals' privacy rights

- ☐ violations: intentional and involuntary violation of policies and the consequences

- ☐ authorized and unauthorized disclosure

- ☐ disciplinary action if not compliant (termination and legal action)

- ☐ incident reporting (the person, phone number, and email to report incidents to)

- ☐ proper handling of personal information

- ☐ remote work

- ☐ the person in charge or point of contact for the policy (title, email, phone)

- ☐ exceptions to the policy

- ☐ terms and definitions

- ☐ acknowledgment that they have read and understood the policy

How Do You Get Contractors, Freelancers, Vendors, or Volunteers to Comply with Your Privacy Policy/Standards?

If anything goes wrong with a vendor, the authorities might give you a break for your due diligence. But they get to determine if you did all you could: that you did your homework by researching the vendor's background, negotiating a clause into the contract, and monitoring your vendor for compliance. Small churches have vendors too. Any company that provides services for the handling of personal information or maintains any equipment that processes personal information is also a vendor. That includes anyone you hire to fix a computer, router, or network or anyone whose system connects to the church's network. How secure is their business? Have you ever thought about hired musicians? Singers? Some churches even hire people who handle fundraising. Are they hooking up their devices to your church's computer network? How secure are their devices? Who's holding these contractors accountable for personal information shared with them? I can't possibly name all types of vendors that work for your church. Remember, Target's multi-million-dollar data breach started through its vendor, an HVAC company. But Target footed the hefty bill and risked its reputation. Yes, a tiny air-conditioning business was the prime culprit for a world-class data breach. It goes to show that no company doing business with your church is above or below accountability.

Depending on the type of work and the risks, after you've assessed and proven their commitment to protect personal data, these are examples of how to get them to stay compliant: (1) give them a memorandum of understanding (MOU) or a memorandum of agreement (MOA) that spells out the mutually understood scope, purpose, expectations, and data protection obligations to ensure you're on the same page; (2) make sure your contract includes these expectations and a compliance clause (applicable laws, rules, standards, regulations, and your security and privacy policies); (3) ensure you define a timeframe for assessing the vendor's compliance during your relationship; (4) have a formal assessment process in place—it should require obtaining certain evidence to demonstrate compliance with data protection requirements; and (5) continuously monitor compliance and get updates.

Assess What Your Church Does to Get Contractors and Vendors to Comply with Your Privacy Policy/Standards

- ☐ We incorporate compliance responsibilities with applicable laws into the contract with our vendors.

- ☐ We specify our roles in the relationship (the church, not the vendor, owns the data).

- ☐ We specify what happens when the relationship ends, including what data they'll return or delete and the timeframe.

- ☐ We require full compliance with privacy and security policies of the church.

- ☐ We request to see the privacy policies for their employees and subcontractors.

- ☐ We monitor their compliance by exercising our right to audit the vendor for privacy compliance.

- ☐ We request to see their third-party audit report.

- ☐ We request their risk assessment and risk analysis report.

☐ We request a gap analysis report to compare their actual privacy and security performance against their expected performance with regulatory requirements or obligations.

☐ We review existing vendor contracts for what we agreed to and request an update if there are too many risks.

☐ We find out if there are any complaints or investigations on the contractor/vendor.

☐ We find out if there are any lawsuits against the contractor/vendor and why.

☐ We find out about their subcontractors' compliance track records and if they meet our church's standard.

Tip: The best time to get contract workers to apply the standards you want is at the beginning of the relationship. When you're volleying the contract document back and forth, it's harder to get them to step up their standards once you have a contract.

Value: Being sure that your vendors are in compliance with your privacy practices will protect your church from liabilities and your members' personal information from compromise.

Action Steps: You've assessed your church's privacy policies for vendors, freelancers, and other contract workers. Any items you didn't check are your action items to work on: list them. Have you designated someone within your church to handle this responsibility? Jot down your answers.

_____

_____

_____

What's your target date to assign someone to take this responsibility/when will you begin the tasks? Day_____ Month_____ Year_____

What's your target date to complete these tasks?
Day_____ Month_____ Year_____

Which roles will you absolutely *not* outsource in your church?

_____
_____
_____
_____
_____

What questions would you ask me?

_____
_____
_____
_____
_____

Training for Church Employees

When you appoint members of the clergy to take privacy roles, make sure they understand information privacy and data protection so they can communicate the risks to the church board or leadership. A privacy title is not enough. Plus, don't point them to the Internet to learn. You need to get quality and affordable training that's customized to your church environment. Training is more meaningful when tailored to your environment.

Tailoring the training is important because people only retain, own, and practice concepts that are directly connected to their role, tasks, experiences, or environment. If the training doesn't feel relevant, they'll lose interest. Many risks increase when people are not properly trained on or continuously reminded of how to protect information. Regulators levy hefty fines for employee errors or data breaches caused by the lack of or insufficient employee training. Having served as a subject matter expert for regulators, when I audit and find a great training program, that's good news. It shows that management understands its priorities. Remember, there is no substitute for training, so don't pinch pennies or time! Realize that training is your proof to authorities that your people know what's expected of them and do their jobs accordingly. A great policy by itself is not enough. You need training.

Different Types of Training and Education Approaches
There are several types available:

- **General training:** This gets everyone on the same page. Privacy is every worker's responsibility regardless of their role and whether they are employees or volunteers. To minimize threats to privacy, a general training on policies may include social media, email, password, computer use, rules of behavior, and physical security policies for personal information, incident plans, and procedures.

- **Role-based training:** This puts privacy training in the context of what workers actually do in their roles. This helps solve real work problems and can be applied based on real threats to the church's personal information assets as they occur. Role-based training fosters participation and feedback for improvements.

- **Privacy awareness:** This offers both informal and creative ways to remind people about their basic privacy responsibility. They can get a broad overview of privacy concerns and emerging issues. Brown bag lunches, dessert parties, contests, an external or internal privacy speaker/facilitator, or celebrating national privacy day are great ways to get people engaged in privacy awareness.

- **A privacy expert/speaker:** This involves inviting a speaker to deliver a keynote and/or a question-and-answer session. This will be best if the expert delivers a message that aligns with your privacy obligations and mission.

Training is an ongoing obligation, not a one-off-and-you're-done event. Your church should assess, monitor, and evaluate the training workers have received to ensure they are applying what they learned. You should then evaluate and update training to align with laws/regulations and new threats to personal information. Workers easily forget what they learn. You should have defined timeframes for offering refresher training and for updating training content. For example, you can offer a comprehensive annual training, quarterly refresher training/awareness, and quarterly updates to training content and policies. If you can afford to do these more frequently, go for it. It depends on your resources and the risks you're managing. Sometimes updates to training and refreshers can be flexible and situational even if you have timeframes set. That's fine. Some updates may become urgent because of an incident or privacy breach. I've been called upon by an organization's executives to revamp their training within a week because a significant incident occurred, and it was under investigation.

Assess What You're Currently Offering and the Different Avenues You Use to Deliver Awareness/Training

Privacy Training/Courses (online or in-person)

☐ Every 6 months ☐ Quarterly

Privacy Awareness (emails, memos, speakers)

☐ Every 3 months ☐ Weekly

Privacy Seminars/Workshops

☐ Every 6 months ☐ Annually

Church Business Meetings

☐ Every 6 months ☐ Annually

Privacy Policies/Processes, Procedures/Privacy Principles

☐ When updated

These are examples. The point is, designate a timeframe to check training and awareness so they don't fall through the cracks. If by checking certain boxes above you realize your timeframe needs adjusting, then work on adjusting; for example, adjust six months to three months.

You can reduce legal and regulatory risks and the impact of these risks on people when you periodically review your policy in line with new laws and regulations. Keep your people's knowledge relevant. If you want to impress regulators and catch a break from penalties, show them proof of how often and well trained your folks are. Take advice from an auditor (that's me)—I know many organizations get dinged for this reason.

Designate one or two people to handle this, but you'll need your training, legal, and policy teams to help. For a small church, one person can manage the scheduling of periodic training. Most resources in the industry do not address the unique challenges that churches face. The first issue is a smaller budget or no budget at all. The privacy program budget of many corporations surpass what churches can or are willing to invest. The second issue is the limited number of experts. Corporations snag future privacy professionals from colleges before they graduate. In addition, there aren't many experts who are focused on helping churches. I know this because I contributed my expertise to writings and processes that got the industry off its feet. I've served as a privacy advisory board member in the industry. Privacy is therefore a ripe area of opportunity. For the majority of churches, the price tag for training and other resources alone is a discouragement. Large companies and tech companies need privacy experts by the dozen. The money, experts, and relevant information are concentrated there.

Churches need organic and revolutionary resources geared just for them. Since we're discussing training, I wrote this book along with its companion, *Church Privacy 101*, which were designed to align with church privacy courses you could use. I find that people close the learning gap through taking courses and asking questions. I offer such courses, where you'll get tailored awareness, general training, and role-based training on an as-needed basis in both tiny and large packages available to churches. I combine all my specializations and offer flexibility. One benefit is that different church sizes, skills sets, and budgets can partake. The other benefit is the opportunity of having a community of free resources where folks in leadership and members engage and share ideas on church privacy matters with like minds. As with any service your church procures, the privacy training you choose requires a buying decision. Check what you're getting first to see if it meets your needs and is within your budget.

Let's switch for a minute to training in relation to granting and approving access.

Granting and Approving Access to Personal Information

Granting and approving access to personal information should not be limited to a conversation. It should be documented. If a ministry leader feels an individual should have access to the personal profile of all the other ministry members or church members, that ministry leader should not grant the person access in haste. They should justify their decision and have it approved by a higher role in the church. For example, a ministry director can be the objective party who checks and weighs the decision. The point is, make a list so you don't default to instincts and emotional decision-making. I talked about access approval in Chapter 4; I circle back to that point now because you'll need to train church workers to behave accordingly—to know they should have justifiable reasons for granting access and obtain approval from the right authority to let others in their group or teams have access to certain personal information. In big corporations, access control is taught. It needs to be part of your training too.

Incidents

Keep everyone on the lookout for privacy incidents, and teach them to report incidents on time to prevent a data breach. Log data breaches the same way as incidents. In either log, you should include as many details as possible. It's simpler to manage privacy incidents with a table or spreadsheet. Add a column for lessons learned and process changes needed to reduce risks. With a data breach, you need to notify the victims (see Chapter 11). The Bible teaches that love does not keep a record of wrongs in 1 Corinthians 13:5. These records are the exception. Regulators love them. They show you're paying attention to and have a handle on what's happening around you.

Church Privacy Team

Contact List

Incidents can create a lot of chaos and a range of emotions. It doesn't matter the privacy person your church has hired, you must have contact information and alternate contact information for all information management roles in your incident response contact list. Depending on the incident, you might need to contact more than one person. If it's a breach where personal information is lost or disclosed, you may need to contact law enforcement, although this is on a case-by-case basis and depends on what the regulatory authority in your jurisdiction or state decides. How you report up or down your church's hierarchy also depends on how many of the roles your church has. Also, your report might depend on who found out about the breach first. The point here is, have everyone's contact details in one secure place should you need them. You don't need to have all the roles in this table to have a contact list. Only include roles you have in your church. This table is an example. It should represent people with privacy and information responsibilities.

Table 2. Privacy roles

Title	Full Name	Phone	Email
Privacy Coordinator/Manager			
Chief Privacy Officer (CPO)			
Chief Operations Officer (COO)			
Chief Financial Officer (CFO)			
Chief Security Officer (CSO)			
Chief Information Officer (CIO)			
Privacy Expert			
Church Attorney/Privacy Attorney			
Attorney General (your state privacy regulator)			
Police			

In most jurisdictions, depending on the nature of a data breach and the number of people affected, your church must report it to authorities. Inform your staff first so you can work on a resolution while gathering information about the breach. Gather as much information on the breach as you can before reporting externally to authorities. Keep an accurate list of authorities.

Incident Log

Here's an illustration of an incident involving personal information and personal financial information. Of course, not all incidents or data breaches happen online or electronically. No matter where they happen, an incident log is very important.

Table 3. Privacy incident log

Privacy Incident	Date Occurred	Reported By/ To and Date	Risks	Location	Reported To/Date	Status/Date
Lost: Tithing envelopes with credit card information	4/4/23 10:15 a.m.	Deaconess Shirley Gaines Incident recorded by Minister Adam Boyd 4/4/23 12:30 p.m.	Potential ID theft and financial loss	Church sanctuary	Jane Kitts, Privacy Manager James Wise, Sanctuary Police Officer 4/4/23 1:00 p.m.	Resolved on 4/5/23 5 p.m.: personal information undisclosed. Details: On 04/4/23 church treasurer, Rufus Hills, picked up the envelopes behind Shirley as they fell out of the offering basket around 10:15 a.m. Bro. Hills locked them in a safe and forgot to notify Shirley.

You can learn a lot from an incident log. It'll reveal areas that need improvement so you can prevent a data breach. My lesson learned from the above scenario is, maybe Shirley Gaines needs to slow down a bit. What's the hurry? Yours could be that maybe two people should do Shirley's job, or that the collection basket should have a lid. Agreed! Also, if your church has a security guard or police officer, they should walk right behind Shirley on Sundays when she's carrying out her duties. Incident logs inform your decisions and help you manage risks before they become a (costly) breach.

Data Breach Log

If Rufus Hills did not pick up the envelopes behind Shirley Gaines, but a mischievous visitor did and then vanished with your congregants' personal information, credit card information, checks, and cash, that would be a data breach. It would need to be reported, logged, tracked, and investigated (tithers would need to be notified, their credit cards canceled, and their bank accounts and identities monitored). You would do this so that the negative impact on your congregants could be avoided or reduced. That data breach log may look similar to this example.

Table 4. Data breach log

Data Breach	Date Occurred	Reported By/ To and Date	Risks	Location	Reported To/Date	Status/Date
Lost: Tithes and offerings envelopes with credit card information	4/4/23 10:15 a.m.	Deaconess Shirley Gaines Incident recorded by Minister Adam Boyd 4/4/23 12:30 p.m.	Personal ID theft and financial loss	Church sanctuary	Jane Kitts, Privacy Manager James Wise, Sanctuary Police Officer 4/4/23 1:00 p.m.	Unresolved on 4/5/23 5 p.m.: personal financial information disclosed to an unauthorized person. Details: On 04/4/23 around 10:15 a.m. church treasurer, Rufus Hills, hurried to pick up envelopes behind Shirley Gaines as the envelopes fell out of the offering basket, but Bro. Hills was distracted by a man who claimed to be a visitor. The alleged visitor did not know where the restroom was located. The envelopes disappeared after Bro. Hills attended to the stranger.

Privacy Risks to Members and Other Individuals

When privacy is breached, you can expect all sorts of negative impacts. Risks to members/visitors and why individuals may sue include the following:

- financial losses—identity theft
- embarrassment
- reputational damage
- emotional distress
- loss of time—spent trying to clear financial records
- loss of opportunities

Privacy Risks to Your Church

When privacy is breached, your church also has a lot to lose, including the following:

- financial losses
  - lawsuits—individual/class action
  - hefty fines
  - regulatory penalties
- imprisonment
- damaged reputation—negative publicity
- loss of members', visitors', donors', and partners' trust—loss of membership and support
- loss of business operations partners due to the breach/related investigation
- failing an audit/noncompliance

Perform a Risk Assessment of Your Church

Don't let the dreary terminology, *risk assessment*, scare you. You assess risk all the time in your personal life and in church—you just don't think about it that way. In particular, you look up the weather forecast before you leave your home for an outdoor event. If you're like me, when you find out it's going to rain, you want to know what the chances are that the rain will actually fall. If the weather report says 50 to 70 percent, you'll consider this a high probability for rain. The likelihood of rainfall doesn't really stop you from still going out (most of the time), but you'll take an umbrella. That umbrella is your safeguard. It helps reduce the impact the rain will have on you, such as getting your hair, outfit, or shoes wet. It's no different from managing risks at your church, except you need to document your privacy risks and privacy risk assessment. It boils down to identifying potential risks that could lead to a privacy breach, then finding out the likelihood that they will actually happen, documenting your rationale, and applying safeguards to resolve/control the negative impact the risks will have on people's lives. Focus on two activities below.

Assess How Your Church Determines Privacy Risks

- ☐ identify threats (hackers, employee mistakes, system failure, contractor's vulnerability)
- ☐ risk or impact (financial, reputational, legal, opportunity costs)
- ☐ likelihood (the probability that a hacker will attack, an employee will open an email with a virus, or a contractor will be noncompliant if there's no security measure, training, or contractor accountability)

Assess How Your Church Governs Its Risk Management
Risk assessment is one critical part of your risk management efforts. It's not a one-time activity. That's because your church always comes up with a new event, initiative, or project that requires personal information. So risk management is continuous. Try your best to do everything in this book that applies to your church. Every step you take here is a type of risk management. Ask questions if you get stuck.

Church Freelancers, Vendors, Contractors, Gig Workers, and Employees

When you do this, you're managing privacy risks. You can prove you're managing privacy risks when you have checked the following boxes.

Our church has put in place and maintains the following:

☐ a privacy program (privacy processes, procedures, documentation, people/resources, tools, plans)

☐ policies and notices

☐ training, communication, and documentation

☐ privacy compliance assessments

☐ third-party contracts stipulating adherence to privacy standards

☐ implementation plans, breach response plans, and disaster recovery plans

☐ continuous monitoring for obligations and liabilities and ensuring privacy/security safeguards work as intended

☐ disposal and retention plan for personal information (and an alternate backup plan for information)

Action Steps: You've assessed your church's training intervals, contacts list, logging of incidents and breaches, and risk management. The items you did not check are your action items to work on: list them. You have a template you can use to track them. Have you designated someone within your church to handle this responsibility? Jot down your answers.

_____

_____

_____

What's your target date to assign someone to take this responsibility/when will you begin the tasks?
Day_____ Month_____ Year_____

What's your target date to complete these tasks?
Day_____ Month_____ Year_____

What questions would you ask me?

_____

_____

_____

_____

_____

Salaries, Raise Negotiations, and Privacy

Being an employer or buyer of services doesn't give you the absolute right to any personal information you wish to collect. You must have a legitimate or lawful justification for collecting personal information. That's what privacy laws and regulations require. The same applies when you're interviewing candidates for jobs at your church. Be careful about asking questions that violate the candidates' privacy. I teach corporate privacy laws related to employment privacy. Employment privacy is addressed within numerous laws. They protect privacy pertaining to wages, safety, disability, family leave, substance testing, substance abuse treatment, and racial discrimination, among many other concerns. Some examples of these laws in the US are ADA, OSHA, FCRA, EPPA, and ECPA. I list more of these in Appendix B. Depending on where your church is located, your country or state has similar employment laws. Recently, I learned of an incident from a pastor who was negotiating her raise after years of being grossly underpaid. She negotiated based on her value and years of experience. But the church negotiated based on her supposed need. Recalling the experience brought tears to her eyes. She didn't tell the church this, but clearly, it was a violation of her privacy. I've heard many stories like this, and that's usually my conclusion. It's not okay to come out of a negotiation feeling unworthy. It's unfair and illegal to compel anyone (man or woman) to take a lowball offer based on marital status, parental status (how many children they have), how they file their taxes (whether they file as the

Church Freelancers, Vendors, Contractors, Gig Workers, and Employees

head of their household), or their age. Asking privacy-invading questions around these factors in an interview or salary negotiation could get your church in legal trouble.

What do I say to such churches? Here's how you can prevent that from happening. Look at your budget. Never be ashamed of your budget. Realize that negotiation is a healthy business practice. I'm not saying don't negotiate with your candidates. With a little effort, research, and using churchsalary.com, you can gain better insight into the market value of numerous church roles. Once you've done the research, do you need to revisit that budget? You might, and it's perfectly normal. Do as much as you can so you don't end up pushing the burden of proving the value of a role onto your candidates. Doing so could violate privacy. In a multidisciplinary church leadership meeting I attended, someone said that their church used Vanderbloemen's Guide for church staff salaries, raises, and benefits. The guide is based on the size of the church. Not bad. I wrote the title down and looked it up. It appears that Vanderbloemen also offers resources to help boost diversity in church hiring. Their blog at vanderbloemen.com/blog has salary tips for small churches too. It's also worth visiting churchplants.com for a free resource on church compensation. I love their thought-provoking caption: "The only thing more expensive than paying your church staff is underpaying them."

Tip: Once you open your computer, create a file, give it a name, and plug information in it, that constitutes a document. That document can be your plan of what you'll do in what order in a particular situation. Or the document can be your log of what's happening related to personal information issues in your church. For example, nobody can document the process for new members at your church the way you can. It's tempting to dump all the tasks on a privacy expert. If you can capture what you're doing now and improve it, an expert can give it a polish. Finding out what other churches your size are paying their staff won't hurt. This helps you budget for your roles and keeps you from asking privacy-invading questions. If you don't know other churches, research online resources.

Value: Saving money is godly. Logging incidents and data breaches can give insights on new areas of privacy risks that workers should be trained in. In the event of an audit, such documentation is good evidence of your painstaking risk management and due diligence.

Having an accurate budget and negotiating with your staff based on the market value for their role creates a healthy work environment. That means less turnover for your church.

Action Steps: When will you check your budget for roles in your church against the market value so you can avoid asking employees privacy-invading questions? Jot down your answers.

_____

_____

_____

What's your target date to assign someone to take this responsibility/when will you begin the tasks?
Day_____ Month_____ Year_____

What's your target date to complete these tasks?
Day_____ Month_____ Year_____

What questions would you ask me?

_____

_____

_____

_____

_____

The strength of the team is each individual member.
The strength of each member is the team.
(Phil Jackson)

Church Bookstores, Gift Shops, Cafeterias, Gyms, and Clinics

*Procrastination is like a credit card:
it's a lot of fun until you get the bill.*
(Christopher Parker)

The Importance of a Church Bookstore

I am a big fan of bookstores, especially church bookstores. Convenience and selection are big reasons I love them. I can find Bibles, other inspirational books, greeting cards, gifts, and reading accessories. It's also one of the only places on earth where you can find guilt-free chocolate chews with encouraging Scriptures inscribed on them. Speaking of food and treats, this chapter also touches on church coffee shops, cafeterias, bake sales, and fish fries that process credit card transactions. Don't forget your church's online course registration and payment page. You should pay close attention to any church occasion where credit card or personal account or financial information is exchanged for church goods and services. There are privacy concerns there.

Personal Information Collection

Although bookstores operate within churches, they're still businesses, considering money is exchanged for goods and services. You can't procrastinate on your obligation to keep personal information and financial information safe. An online bookstore is the same as any physical commercial bookstore. Some churches have both cash registers and credit card payment processors. These stores may also have members fill out forms to order certain products that require a person's mailing address, email, or phone number for delivery. All church stores collect debit and credit card information unless they're a bookstore at a convent. Convent bookstores that I've been to are different. Quaint. Customers are trusted to leave exact change, make change from the loose cash in a drawer, or make a donation if they wish. There's no collection of personal financial information there. Just cash.

Risks to Personal Financial Information

Credit or debit cards are convenient. Plus, you don't need to agonize over exact change. But criminals can steal personal financial information if the payment system or software used is not properly secured using the same standards of protection that apply to commercial businesses. If the card information is stolen, it could be exploited to defraud your church's bookstore shoppers. Securing your store's website and physical payment system is important. Convenience comes with responsibilities. The church is responsible if it fails to assure that standards are followed. That's a reality you shouldn't ignore.

Vendor Management and Card Payment

Churches use third-party or vendor payment systems to process bookstore, gift shop, course registration, and cafeteria transactions. Vendors provide, maintain, and manage cash registers, credit card systems, and related software. Your church is responsible for protecting its members or shoppers. The church is in charge of controlling and governing security and privacy—specifically, periodically checking to make sure that vendors comply with security standards, update software, monitor vulnerabilities, and fix any weaknesses before criminals and malicious workers exploit them. If your church doesn't monitor the privacy and security practices of its vendors, the church could be liable for the vendors' mistakes. That'd be costly. If personal information or personal financial information, such as credit card numbers, is stolen because of weak security and privacy practices, the church could be blamed. In other words, it's like leaving a baby at a daycare. You pay for the service. You know other parents who leave their babies there. But you don't wait to see what the other parents do. You check periodically to make sure *your* baby is being handled with care. Would you neglect checking because other parents are not checking on their babies? Even if you're very busy, your baby deserves your attention—to make sure the daycare staff are following your instructions and that the baby is not at risk. How responsible is a person who leaves a baby at a daycare indefinitely or never calls to check? What would a court call such a parent? Unfit. Personal information your church has custody of—collected from your members, workers, donors, and visitors—is a baby in the care of your vendors. You need to provide guidance (via policy and contract agreement), check on the practices of your vendors, and monitor them as you would a daycare. How? Require to see security and privacy safeguards they're using and the schedule of how often they run scans and update their systems. Require these as a condition for entering into a contract. Look up their history often—see if they've had a brush with the law.

Chop-chop, let's review credit card industry standards, then assess what your church is doing.

Credit card companies, including MasterCard, Visa, American Express, Discover, and other major credit card companies, require that businesses or organizations (the church included) that accept or process credit cards follow the Payment Card Industry Data Security Standard (PCI DSS). Your members could suffer privacy and financial impact if the standards are not followed. Payment card information can be exposed, putting people at risk of identity theft or fraud. A criminal could open bank or credit card accounts, make extravagant purchases, apply for loans, and set up new utilities or phone accounts with stolen personal and financial information. Plus, your church could face huge legal and regulatory consequences for noncompliance.

Payment Card Industry Data Security Standard (PCI DSS)

PCI DSS is the payment card industry standard for merchants who accept and process credit card payments from their customers. Shortly, I'll walk you through a set of basic checkboxes to assess your church for compliance. Don't shudder at the thought of an assessment. It's quick and assesses whether your church is aware of its privacy risks and is taking some steps toward resolving them and complying with related laws and regulations. At your leisure, browse the PCI compliance website (see the FAQ page in Figure 5 below.)[1] Use this book to log your questions. Learn in bits and pieces. Soon you won't even flinch at hearing the initialism PCI DSS. Isn't that comforting! On that note, let's assess your church.

Figure 5. PCI Compliance website FAQ page

Assess What Your Church Does and Knows about PCI DSS

☐ We're aware that MasterCard, Visa, American Express, Discover, and other major credit card companies require businesses/merchants who accept or process credit cards to follow these standards.

☐ We're aware that our church bookstore processes credit and debit card payments and that the PCI DSS rules apply.

☐ Our church accepts credit and debit cards as a means for members to pay donations and make other transactions.

☐ Our church is aware of PCI DSS standards and the negative privacy impact that can result from noncompliance.

☐ Our church is aware that if we're targeting minors for the sale of goods, e-commerce laws such as COPPA, GDPR, and related state laws apply.

☐ We implement age verification requirements for our e-commerce stores selling age-restricted items; we look into our state/country-specific requirements.

☐ We have a data breach/cyber liability insurance policy for our bookstore/gift store website (see Chapter 15).

☐ We're aware of local, state, and national laws, codes, and requirements related to operating a bookstore and an e-commerce site.

Assess What Your Church Does about Bookstore Staff to Secure Privacy

☐ We've created awareness or trained our store workers on the PCI DSS standards, as the standards are not limited to technology security but rely on humans to be vigilant and diligent.

☐ We've created awareness or trained store workers on the Children's Online Privacy Protection Act (COPPA) and related state laws/regulations.

Church Privacy Team

 Tip: In your contracts with vendors, specify how often you will check on their practices. This way, you don't feel awkward about reaching out and requesting reports.

 Value: You could be fined $5,000 to $100,000 for PCI noncompliance. That's pointless spending you don't have to sweat out. You will earn the trust of your members by complying with privacy standards, laws, and regulations. It's not about what you say but about what you go out of your way to do to protect your members.

Action Steps: You've assessed what your church is doing about payment processing and training the staff. The items you did not check are your action items to work on: list them. Have you designated someone within your church to handle this responsibility? Jot down your answers.

_____
_____
_____

What's your target date to assign someone to take this responsibility/when will you begin the tasks?
Day_____ Month_____ Year_____

What's your target date to complete these tasks?
Day_____ Month_____ Year_____

What questions would you ask me?

_____
_____
_____
_____

Church Bookstores, Gift Shops, Cafeterias, Gyms, and Clinics

Assess How Your Church Handles Payments

☐ Our bookstore uses a card reader attached to a phone/computer to swipe credit or debit cards.

☐ Our bookstore uses a card reader attached to a phone/computer to manually enter credit or debit cards.

☐ Our bookstore uses a cash register (also known as a point-of-sale system) or a smart phone to ring up purchases and scan barcodes.

☐ Our church accepts credit and debit cards over the phone and manually enters data into a virtual terminal.

☐ Our online store or e-commerce is hosted (i.e., a third party controls the shopping cart and payment activities).

☐ Our online store or e-commerce is non-hosted (i.e., payment processing is all part of the church website).

☐ Our online store or e-commerce is a combination of hosted and non-hosted (i.e., data elements are shared from the church's web page with the third party's checkout page).

☐ Our bookstore also accepts and processes physical checks.

If you've checked any of these items, you're responsible for protecting privacy of financial information. In the physical store, does your store use security safeguards, for instance, alarm systems, locks, or passwords? Great. For your online store, do you use a software as a service (SaaS) platform (an out-of-the-box e-commerce platform that requires limited time and technical knowledge to set up)? Typically, they take care of technical maintenance and provide support for your customers should issues arise. The benefit of using certain gateways/platforms and processors is that they take care of PCI compliance because they update their compliance requirements—encryption is included. Storage is cloud-based. It also cuts the cost of hiring a special IT developer to do the setup. A gateway will typically collect the customer information entered, and the payment processor will take it from there and charge their card to get the money.

What payment gateway/platforms and payment processors are out there? These are a few familiar ones:

- Stripe
- Braintree (by PayPal)
- Square
- PayPal
- SecureNet
- WooCommerce (by WordPress)
- 2Checkout
- PrestaShop
- PaymentCloud
- Authorize.net
- National Processing
- Stax
- Magento (by Adobe)
- Helcim
- Cash App
- Google Pay
- Venmo
- Zelle

Church Bookstores, Gift Shops, Cafeterias, Gyms, and Clinics

These are just examples, not prescriptions. Each of these should be evaluated on a case-by-case basis to make sure they provide what suits your church's needs. You should also check any payment gateway/platform you choose for its privacy-preserving value. You'll likely find them talking about this in their privacy notices. If not, contact the company and ask.

Assess Whether Your Church's Payment Gateways/Platforms Have Privacy-Preserving Value

☐ Our payment platform addresses PCI.

☐ Our payment platform addresses COPPA.

☐ Our payment platform takes care of shopping cart functionality and other maintenance, including software updates.

☐ Our payment platform provides a help desk function to address customer complaints and requests.

☐ We've read the terms and conditions and privacy notices of individual platforms/gateways that we use for payment purposes.

☐ Our payment platform facilitates transaction authorization by reconciling personal information from the customer with the bank's information related to the customer.

 Tip: Never relax because a vendor provides you services or products. It's not good business to not have privacy accountability. Privacy laws and regulations require that vendors provide you with information or reports about their practices and that you hold them accountable to high standards. Request the information you need. Also, study their privacy policies and notices, and communicate them to your members, shoppers, and users. It's the church's responsibility to let the users know when collection of personal information is carried out by a vendor under a separate privacy policy. Direct people to the link so they can read the vendor's policy. Regardless of the size of your church, if you have a website, you can afford to take this step. Don't procrastinate.

Value: Knowing about the technologies you use can help you anticipate privacy risks and stay ahead of vulnerabilities. Compliance is also a big win for your vendors.

Action Steps: You've assessed payment gateways/platforms. The items you did not check are your action items to work on and research: list them below. Have you designated someone within your church to handle this responsibility? Jot down your answers.

_____

_____

_____

What's your target date to assign someone to take this responsibility/when will you begin the tasks?
Day_____ Month_____ Year_____

What's your target date to complete these tasks?
Day_____ Month_____ Year_____

What questions would you ask me?

_____

_____

_____

_____

_____

Four Areas Most Privacy Laws and Regulations Spotlight

State, federal, and international laws, regulations, and standards for protecting personal information typically fall into these four categories. To be compliant, you need all four areas to work in harmony.

Assess If Your Church Has Addressed These Areas

- ☐ privacy (preserving any personal and identifiable information about people, including health information that is handled in physical and electronic form)

- ☐ cybersecurity (protecting cyberspace or Internet activities and communications)

- ☐ information security (protecting personal information in digital/computerized form or physical form)

- ☐ financial security (protecting personal financial accounts, bank information, and transactions)

If there are any of the four areas you didn't check, work on those. Best practices, policies, processes, and procedures in these areas have the same general goal: to protect people. When customers key in their credit card numbers/personal information, or provide it on a paper form, that entire process should be protected. These days most transactions are done by electronic means on your website. You need to apply Secure Sockets Layer (SSL) on your website if that's where transactions and entry of personal information take place.

Secure Sockets Layer (SSL)

I know. Secure Sockets Layer (SSL) is big boring terminology. But you will be glad you have it even if you don't like saying it. Here's what SSL does. It provides standard security that protects customers' financial transactions online. Your church bookstore's website is one place where members and visitors conduct financial transactions online. The other place is the website where people register and pay for classes or courses. The same privacy concerns apply. When the customer uses any web browser, such as Safari, Explorer, or Chrome, to access the bookstore's web server, you want their transactions and activities to be protected. By the way, a web server is the system or storage space where the web pages of your website live. That's all I'll say about web servers on this topic. The benefit of SSL is that it gives shoppers the confidence to shop at your bookstore. They'll have the assurance that their personal information and credit card number are safe. SSL helps the customer experience a secure connection without a hacker's interception. Without SSL, a hacker can intercept a customer's transaction and misdirect the customer from your bookstore to a phony web page, tricking the customer into thinking they're entering their credit card information into a legitimate bookstore page.

Assess Whether Your Church Protects Online Transactions

☐ Our church bookstore's website has SSL.

☐ Our general church website has SSL.

☐ Periodically, we ask our web-hosting vendor/provider to check that we still have SSL.

☐ In a browser, our website currently has https:// in front of our church domain name, not http://.

Tip: Call your website host and inquire about SSL and other safeguards that come via website hosting companies. Have this if you collect personal information on your website. Ask about other security measures that can provide additional layers of privacy protection. Small churches with websites have the same responsibility. It only takes a phone call to your site's host. Ask the host what they can offer you. You may have to pay a fee for adding SSL (around $200+ a year depending on your web host). Other hosts add it as a bonus. If your SSL expires, you will need to renew it annually or biannually, depending on the terms.

Value: Once you take care of online financial transactions, you will worry less about the related risks. Some regulators levy fines up to 4 percent of your global annual revenue on top of other penalties for noncompliance. A damaged reputation is definitely a cost as well. Cost savings and fostering trust are the value here.

Action Steps: You've assessed what your church is doing about protecting online transactions. The items you did not check are your action items to work on: list them. Have you designated someone within your church to handle this responsibility? Jot down your answers.

What's your target date to assign someone to take this responsibility/when will you begin the tasks?
Day_____ Month_____ Year_____

What's your target date to complete these tasks?
Day_____ Month_____ Year_____

What questions would you ask me?

_____

_____

_____

_____

_____

The Value of Applying Secure Sockets Layer (SSL)

There are a variety of benefits to using SSL. I'm highlighting a few here.

Customer Trust

Customers can tell if you have SSL. Here's a telltale sign when they're shopping on your church bookstore's website. Look at your browser when you visit your bookstore online. Instead of seeing the URL http://synaguetempleoftroychurch.org/bookstore, customers will see https://synoguetempleoftroychurch.org/bookstore. That *s* after the *http* means *secured*. Meaning the site is encrypted. It makes a huge difference when shoppers are deciding if they should trust or shop your site. For privacy reasons, customers prefer websites that have security or a safe connection.

Search Engine Rankings

If you have SSL, search engines such as Google Search will give you a high rating when people search for your site. You'll even see a tiny padlock in front of your website address or URL when it displays https:// in a browser. It's a competitive advantage for businesses. Customers will choose your website over another because they feel safer shopping on your site.

Prevention

When hackers try to intercept or eavesdrop on a customer's transaction to steal financial information, what they hope to do is get in the middle of the process and redirect your customer to a phony web page. The unsuspecting customer won't even notice what's going on and may start plugging their credit card and other personal information into a bogus web page form. The attacker will steal the information. The criminal could drain the customer's bank accounts as a result of having access to their financial and personal information. With SSL, they're unable to intercept the transaction at your church bookstore. This also applies to online giving and giving kiosks located in church hallways. SSL can protect against perpetrators who try to intercept or divert credit card transactions to their camp to defraud your donors and members. While that is important, SSL alone is not sufficient for compliance. SSL, or encryption, is only one of many requirements of PCI DSS. Other PCI DSS requirements include risk assessment and documentation, system log management, physical and technical access to cardholders' information, regular system updates, vulnerability, and scans, among others.

Other Considerations for Your Church Bookstore's E-commerce Site

Keep these other considerations in mind when evaluating your bookstore's e-commerce site.

First Impression

Your bookstore should have a website privacy notice that is unique to the activities of the bookstore (this gives customers, regulators, media, investigators, and other interested parties a glimpse of your privacy practices). Your notice should inform customers of your commitment to protect personal information and the personal financial information you collect. I went over how you should create that (in Chapter 4).

Church Bookstore Shoplifters

I'll never forget an analogy that Tony Messer of Global Sign SMO Internet Group shared: hackers are the shoplifters of the Internet realm. In the physical store, you have cameras, and the bookstore has a lock and an alarm system of some sort. Why can't you do the same when selling online? Online shoplifters can leave you with more liability than the physical shoplifter, so don't relax because your bookstore is online. Have you ever been worried about shoplifters? Tighten security and privacy in both realms.

Privacy by Default and Privacy by Design

Privacy by default means that when a person uses a technology product or service to create an account, their account profile information and the personal messages or content the person uses the service or product to create is not exposed to the public. This also means that the manufacturer cannot capture and use the personal information as they please. The person who is the owner of the account has the control. It is up to that user to change their settings to "Public" if that's what they choose to do. Most manufacturers or applications do not set user accounts to "Private" by default or privacy by default. This applies when you create a Facebook, Instagram, Twitter, LinkedIn, WhatsApp, or any account on a platform or app that allows you to interact with others. The privacy setting should allow the user to choose what they want. Check your account next time you log in.

Privacy by design means that organizations proactively incorporate privacy when they're designing products, services, or processes. They consider the privacy of personal information that their products or services will collect or use. Also, they design in such a way that products, services, and processes automatically preserve the privacy of the users even if the users take no action to protect privacy themselves. It's a baked-in approach to protecting privacy rather than an afterthought. Do your church's products, services, and processes consider privacy?

Some privacy laws require that organizations apply these two concepts to their products and services. To technology companies, these concepts taste pungent, like black coffee or Brussels sprouts. It requires a little more work to protect customers. It's not what these companies desire. They prefer personal information, which tastes sweet, like cake, because they can sell it. I used the word *companies*, but your church is also accountable the moment it collects personal information. Maybe you collect information through your e-commerce or online bookstore, or maybe you have an event coming up that requires registration. You should anticipate how privacy will be protected before you start. Apply ways to protect privacy or safeguards as you update existing processes. Don't rely on manufacturers or service providers to protect your visitors' or members' personal information. You can apply these two concepts in the broader context of your church's activities or church business.

Assess How Your Church Handles Privacy in Your Bookstore

- ☐ Our online bookstore uses a vendor-provided and vendor-run e-commerce site, cash registers, and credit card processing devices.

- ☐ We've read the terms and conditions about who is responsible for routine security and privacy maintenance of our e-commerce site.

- ☐ We understand what we are responsible for and what our vendor/contractor is responsible for, including making sure the following are carried out:

- ☐ running vulnerability scans on our e-commerce site

- ☐ fixing weaknesses or deficiencies on our site

- ☐ receiving software and applications updates and applying them to our platforms

- ☐ checking to see when software, services, and applications are due for updates

Often, manufacturers find out later that the bad guys have figured out a clever way to bypass the security safeguards they'd applied in technology products. That's where updates or patches come into play. Patches block technology security holes that hackers could easily exploit to get in and steal information. You do not need to buy new software or products to stay secure; just make sure you update your applications so these holes can be closed without delay. Manufacturers typically alert licensees that their software needs an update and provide access to download it. Scans help you discover if there are attacks on your computers or systems. Also, they check whether there is malicious software planted by a hacker who's just waiting for the right opportunity to attack.

Tip: Watch out for *default* settings in services or products. Change the defaults to your preferred privacy or security settings right away. Manufacturers use anti-privacy default settings that make it easier for them to guzzle up personal information as soon as you start using their products or services. Do your part. Assign someone to look at every app, software, and device you buy or sign up for. Know how they collect personal information. Locate the privacy and security settings. Reset them to limit excessive data collection. It doesn't take a whale of a budget or a platoon of privacy experts to take this simple step. Call the manufacturer. They'll walk you through how to reset their product or services to protect privacy.

Value: Taking these steps helps reduce weaknesses in technology products, services, and processes that criminals, manufacturers, employees, contract workers, and other unauthorized parties can manipulate to steal personal information. It will cut down the exposure and misuse of personal information and lessen liabilities.

Action Steps: You've assessed what your church is doing about personal financial information and payment privacy in your store. The items you did not check are your action items to work on: list them. Have you designated someone within your church to handle this responsibility? Jot down your answers.

_____

_____

_____

Church Privacy Team

What's your target date to assign someone to take this responsibility/when will you begin the tasks?
Day_____ Month_____ Year_____

What's your target date to complete these tasks?
Day_____ Month_____ Year_____

What questions would you ask me?

_____
_____
_____
_____
_____

Church Gym

Church gyms are remarkable if they have vending machines. That is, if vending machines at your gym have sports drinks, protein drinks, and snacks that are designed to help you recharge post workout. Don't be shy if you like those vending machines. I do.

Depending on your state or country, if people pay a membership fee to exercise or participate in a fitness program at your church's gym, strict federal or national privacy laws about health care may not apply to your gym. However, in some jurisdictions, personal health information is considered sensitive. In the US, the other name we call this type of personal information is protected health information, or PHI. If your gym starts offering services that are charged or billed to health insurers, your church gym could be stepping into playing with the big boys and might be held accountable in the same manner as hospitals, insurance plans, and their business associates, including billing companies and similar health-care-related organizations.[2] Services that may trigger these laws at your gym include the following:

- physical therapy

- dietician services

- health assessment and other wellness services, including alternative health services

These services require additional personal information than gym membership alone. If you're sharing this information with the medical community—hospitals, insurance companies, or their partners—you may need to consider if health information laws apply to your church's gym. The first step is to inventory your services. What are your gym services? Pinpoint what you offer that may fall into the above three categories. Next, which health entities are you sharing information with? Are members and visitors using their health insurance cards to cover their bills at the gym? That would mean you're sharing information with health insurance plans. In the US, the federal law, the Health Insurance Portability and Accountability Act (HIPAA), may apply. If it does, no sweat. It's not the end of the world, but you do need to be responsible about how you protect PHI. HIPAA was not created for gyms, but the type of health information you collect and who you work with can trigger accountability. Create a spreadsheet and name all the services you offer. Indicate what types of personal information and PHI you collect from gym members, for example, full name, contact information, demographic information, insurance card information, health condition, treatment or treatment plans, lab tests, test results, medications, medical history, spoken records, physical records, and digital records. You can't protect what you don't know. That's why these initial steps are important. Document how you store the information too and have a certified professional assess your gym. Take these steps one at a time. We'll take a look at more action items shortly.

Church Clinic

Some churches have a clinic. It's convenient when someone gets hurt or falls sick on the premises. An acquaintance of mine once reacted negatively to a medication while we were attending a class at a church. She rushed to the clinic. Whew! The nurse there saved the day. Church clinics see kids and adults of all ages, which means they collect some level of medical or health information to better serve visitors, members, and workers. On-site clinics may be exempted from certain aspects of health-care regulations that govern larger health providers and their partners. But, since some clinics collect personal health information and medical records, they do need to ensure they meet privacy and security requirements similar to other health-care organizations. Also, a patient still needs to sign a release for their records from the church clinic to be shared with other health-care providers. This is an area in which a privacy expert could offer help and make recommendations based on your unique situation or services.

As I mentioned earlier, your church needs to conduct an inventory. Document the services offered at the clinic. What types of PHI are collected or handled? What is shared outside the church and with whom? To protect PHI, HIPAA may have several requirements, depending on if their rules apply to your clinic: you'll need to have privacy and security policies, have processes and procedures for handling PHI, train workers on proper handling of PHI, perform a periodic risk assessment, apply encryption to PHI, and manage access to computers that process PHI.

Health Fairs

A health fair is an occasion where you could encounter mouthwatering professionally cooked veggie burgers. An occasion where your breathing could become irregular as you watch a dietician use granulated sugar to demonstrate the amount of sugar you guzzle down with everyday beverages ranging from Pepsi, Coke, and Mountain Dew to Gatorade, Vitamin Water, and Arizona iced tea. That's my recent memory at least. A health fair is an informal community event that offers interactive health education, awareness, and medical screenings to attendees at little to no cost. Health education could include screenings of weight, blood pressure, skin cancer, cholesterol, and hearing. The personal health information that's collected varies. It depends on your jurisdiction, especially in the US; not all health fairs are regulated under health-care laws. Health fairs that are hosted by hospitals or health networks are likely insured and sponsored. Either way, if your church is hosting the health fair, you still need to do your homework and ask all the right questions. This is another area in which a privacy expert can offer help and make recommendations based on your unique situation or services. Again, always start with an inventory. If your church is hosting the health fair, ask the organizer(s) which services the health fair will offer, what types of PHI will be collected or handled, and what will be shared outside the health fair and with whom. It's not an awkward question to ask what they are doing to be compliant with HIPAA and other health information requirements. Request evidence of compliance with the same requirements.

Protecting Health Information

Just as privacy is part social, part physical, part psychological, part legal, and part spiritual, so is health. It needs adequate protection. Personal health information protection is not limited to a church that has a health ministry. Any church interested in individuals' health and well-being should also care about privacy. Penalties for noncompliance with protected health information rules can easily go up as high as $1.5 million depending on the situation or the violation. That said, let's assess how your church is doing.

Gym Services

Identify what services your church gym provides to members or visitors. Creating a list of all the services you offer is a helpful practice so you don't leave out anything. Describe these services in your document. List types of personal information you collect for each. Note the extent of personal information your members need to provide to access your services.

Assess Your Gym Services

- ☐ Members pay for membership: they show up, show ID, exercise, participate in fitness classes, change, and leave.

- ☐ Members receive physical therapy.

Church Privacy Team

☐ Members receive dietician services.

☐ Members receive wellness services, and we conduct health risk assessments.

☐ Other: _____

☐ Other: _____

☐ Other: _____

If you're offering more than access, fitness equipment, space, or a class at your gym, health-care laws and regulations might apply. See compliance action items below.

Assess Your Church's Progress with Protected Health Information (PHI) Requirements

This checklist is what your church should do if HIPAA applies. It may seem long, but don't fret. A list will help you discover items you need to start considering.

☐ We conduct data inventory and mapping of personal health information we process.

☐ We perform a risk assessment on the information.

☐ We implement training appropriate to the requirements for handling personal health information.

☐ We allow individuals to give express consent before giving away their personal health information.

☐ We have a process for data retention and for deleting personal information per patients' requests.

☐ We implement encryption, Secure Socket Layer (SSL), and other network security measures to be certain that health data is not intercepted, disclosed, altered, or stolen.

☐ We partner and collaborate with health insurance companies and other entities covered by the GDPR and HIPAA.

- ☐ We ensure our compliance also meets international standards such as the GDPR and a national standard such as HIPAA.

- ☐ We make sure our email hosting and marketing vendors/third parties do not send out communications to our patients/gym members without their express consent.

- ☐ We specify security and privacy requirements in vendors' contracts.

- ☐ We implement appropriate physical controls to secure paper and electronic access to personal health information.

- ☐ We're aware of and have confirmed any exceptions to the regulatory requirements or rules.

- ☐ We're aware of the risks of hefty fines and penalties for noncompliance.

- ☐ We have a plan, a process, and procedures in place to notify individuals of data breaches.

- ☐ We've consulted with a health-care privacy compliance expert and/or a lawyer.

- ☐ We limit use and disclosure of personal health information to authorized use and disclosure.

On-Site Clinic

Assess What Your Church Does about Privacy Related to Your On-Site Clinic

- ☐ We have a document that identifies who runs our church clinic, whether it's our church or an external organization.

- ☐ We check to see if there are any compliance exceptions granted to on-site clinics in our jurisdiction.

- ☐ We research legal and regulatory requirements that apply and document them.

- ☐ We conduct periodic reviews of the requirements.

☐ We've created/maintain a data retention policy.

☐ We've created/maintain a privacy and security plan.

☐ We document all security and privacy safeguards that are used to protect health information.

☐ We incorporate related action items from all the sections in this chapter.

☐ We have a health-care compliance expert/privacy expert whom we consult periodically.

Health Fair

Know the type of organization facilitating and collecting the health information. An organizer of a health fair could be a hospital, insurance plan/company, a health-care network, or other entities. Even if you have an independent organization running your health or fitness center, if the church's name is associated with the fitness center, the law expects you to do your due diligence and confirm that personal information requirements are met, or else your church will risk its reputation. Some small churches may have members who are pharmacists or other medical professionals and volunteer to give free flu shots to other members. This happened at a small church I attended. This activity requires personal and health information to be exchanged. If it's happening at your facility and on your clock, you assume responsibility when you approve the activity. Find out how personal information is going to be handled—whether it's on paper or in a digital form. A free and convenient service is good, but ask questions.

Assess What Your Church Does about Privacy before Hosting a Health Fair

☐ We confirm the organization has a notice on the purpose of collection and how personal health information will be used.

☐ We confirm the organization has a notice on security measures that are implemented to protect health information.

☐ We confirm the organization has a notice on how information will be shared and with whom.

☐ We confirm the organization has a notice on retention policies.

☐ We confirm the organization has a notice on how information will be accessed and by whom.

☐ We confirm the notice is publicly available on their website and provided to us (the host) by email or postal mail.

☐ We confirm an agreement exists, is signed, and addresses the responsibilities of the church and of the organizer.

Tip: With health fairs, when the discussions begin, don't try to ask the questions verbally during a meeting. Make a list of the items you wish to ask about, then send questions by email. Specify they should respond via email by a required date. Doing this creates a record demonstrating you're doing your due diligence and that they either answered or didn't.

Value: Protecting personal health information reduces risks and any negative impact on members. It'll nurse trust in your church community. A church health program that is open to the public is a gigantic community outreach opportunity. Any services offered where your church's name is known by the recipients of such services will be perceived by the community as a trusted activity. Applying privacy practices makes your gym, clinic, and health fair trusted activities. These practices will keep your reputation unblemished.

Action Steps: You've assessed what your church does about privacy in your gym and clinic and before hosting a health fair associated with your church's name. The items you did not check are your action items to work on: list them. Have you designated someone within your church to handle your health privacy responsibility? Jot down your answers.

_____

_____

_____

What's your target date to assign someone to take this responsibility/when will you begin the tasks?
Day_____ Month_____ Year_____

What's your target date to complete these tasks?
Day_____ Month_____ Year_____

What health fairs will your church host this year? List your ideas (e.g., nutrition, diabetes awareness, mental health, heart health, or work-life balance fair). Are privacy considerations part of your planning process?

_____
_____
_____
_____
_____

What questions would you ask me?

_____
_____
_____
_____
_____

*The fear of the Lord is the beginning of knowledge,
but fools despise wisdom and instruction.*
(Proverbs 1:7)

7

Church Leadership, Counseling, and Mental Health

*Success in management requires learning
as fast as the world is changing.*
(Warren Bennis)

Authority Abuse

People in leadership roles, such as priests, ministers, pastors, bishops, and elders, among others, play the role of spiritual father, mother, or confidant, and members look up to them. It's easy to cross the line with spiritual parenting or shepherding when you're not careful about violating people's privacy. One example is openly blasting or dishonoring someone's privacy under the guise of spiritual counseling or rebuke. There are times when it is biblical to bring a church member's behavior in front of one or two other witnesses, and sometimes the entire church (Matthew 18:15–17), but constant privacy violations will not make a member feel peaceful, nor can you win them over. It's spiritually toxic. But you can prevent this.

Be transparent about your sharing practices before someone divulges information about their personal lives or personal experiences to the clergy or leadership. You read about onion rings in Chapter 2. Does your church have an onion that controls the sharing of personal information obtained during counseling? You should. Share only with the people who are in that onion and on the appropriate ring. This particular onion should have counselors and therapists, among other professionals—professionals who can advise the clergy or leadership on the direction to take. The discussions within this onion do not need to identify the individuals being counseled. Some ministries are headed by individuals who are specialists—for example, mental health ministry, prison ministry, food distribution, women empowerment, couple's ministry, special needs ministry, crisis support, and grief support. These facilitators should be members of an onion related to counseling. But not everyone in this onion will be privy to the same amount of information, so pay attention to the rings as well.

Members should have a general idea of how personal information is shared when they join the church. It's as important as showing members the church's organizational chart, financial reports, and different ways they can give their tithes. Do you have reasons for why your church shares personal counseling information or related information with each person within the onion? Use the same criteria from Chapter 2. Be up front. Privacy principles, laws, and regulations call for transparency. Don't give anyone a sense of privacy if you're not going to honor their privacy needs. Remember, this is not just about formal pastoral counseling. It's also about impromptu conversations you have with members. Someone may approach you at the church picnic and share a serious, personal story. Tell the person how you share information before they delve too deep into their personal details. Trust is a decision. Give them information to help them make an informed decision.

The crux of this is, people need to know what to expect. It's the only way they can have opportunities to ask questions and make good choices for themselves. Privacy principles, laws, and regulations recognize giving someone a choice as a good privacy practice. It's ethical. It's also spiritual to choose or exercise free will. So don't pull the wool over your sheep's eyes just because they need your help. Sharing information is not always bad; it depends on the situation. And in those unique situations, people need to be made aware that there's no absolute privacy. Lay out your purposes for sharing so members get it.

Assess How Your Church Protects Privacy of Pastoral Meetings/Counseling with Members

- ☐ We're transparent with each member about how we handle privacy before we engage them in private conversations about their private life.

- ☐ We do not share counseling information with any member about other members.

- ☐ We do not share counseling information with other clergy or leaders outside the church. If the situation requires additional expertise that our church does not have, we will discuss other resources with the person, and we will let the person decide.

- ☐ We do not share counseling information with other people involved in the problem or issue.

- ☐ We do not share personal information with counselors within or outside the church unless the person consents to allowing our counselors to collaborate on a proper solution for their situation.

- ☐ We do not share counseling information with all members and/or mention names to illustrate a sermon or lesson other members should learn.

- ☐ We do not mention names or describe a person's situation in a way that members can figure out the person who sought counseling.

- ☐ We do not share counseling information in conversations with church workers who are not involved in helping solve the problem and do not have a need to know the personal information.

Again, here are the things you should never do:

- fail to be transparent with members about how your church shares counseling information and why

- fail to remind individuals about how your church shares information when people seek informal counseling, advice, or call on a member of the clergy or leadership

- fail to protect the names of people you're counseling when you're speaking with others

Don't use analogies that make it possible for other members to identify the person you're talking about. Don't share counseling information with the entire congregation or staff. Don't share counseling information unless the person being counseled expressly authorizes you in writing to speak with others in the church—including with people involved in the matter, other pastors/leaders or counselors, church members, and church workers. Give the counselee a chance to consent to or decline how you will handle information. Don't speak with a member of the clergy at another church using identifiable descriptions of the person you're counseling.

If the individual does not consent to sharing, don't share. Don't involve the person's immediate family, relatives, or friends if the person did not give permission for the disclosure. However, the individual should understand and consent that if they express a desire to hurt themselves, a family member, or a child, the church will involve other professionals for safety reasons. If the behavior is harmful and life-threatening, you should share counseling information to protect others who are directly linked to the issue. Doing so protects others from harm.

A church should not be a place where anything goes. You need order—a plan, rules, processes, notices, and consent. "For God is not a God of disorder but of peace—as in all the congregations of the Lord's people" (1 Corinthians 14:33). Peace and order do not make your church less spiritual. They make it super spiritual.

As Dr. Roger Barrier said, "Pastors have a responsibility to their parishioners to provide them with protection, security, and care. If they violate this, pastors leave themselves open to lawsuits."[1] Recently, I've learned of a godly man who was turned down for a leadership role, not because of what he did, but because his wife is careless with members' privacy. His church understood the potential privacy risks and liabilities. They were unwilling to accept them. The church thought it was more important to protect people from getting hurt. If that church is reading this, I want to say, thanks for being such a great example. But what's next? The wife needs help and so do other members who are not seeking leadership roles but are equally careless with other members' private information. Will you have experts periodically come to your church to create privacy awareness? Will you create a privacy policy and make it available to all your members? Will you recommend privacy books and courses to your congregation? These are your leadership responsibilities.

Misusing the Mic

Having control of the microphone gets leaders in trouble all the time. Leaders can abuse their pastoral or clergy privileges and easily influence others negatively without thinking about the consequences. It happens when a leader shares more than is necessary about a church member or members just to make a point that the person is wrong or that the leadership disapproves of the person's ideas or views. Church members have coined the terms *spiritual abuser* and *abusing pastor*. The Bible, on the other hand, calls that *corruption* and *falsehood*. "Let no corrupting talk come out of your mouths, but only such as is good for building up, as fits the occasion, that it may give grace to those who hear" (Ephesians 4:29 ESV). "Therefore, having put away falsehood, let each one of you speak the truth with his neighbor. . . . Be angry and do not sin; do not let the sun go down on your anger" (Ephesians 4:25–26 ESV). Here's what I say: don't let the mic rise up on your anger. This really boils down to control.

Mic misuse doesn't happen everywhere, but one example is a leader trying desperately to gain approval or support of their congregants after a church member disagrees with a decision the leader made or proposed. It's common practice for such leaders to fight back or bake their opinion into the sermon and deliver it in such a way that'll help them win back the congregation's support or loyalty. Sharing identifiable descriptions of the personal life of the individual who has a different point of view and portraying the person as disobedient is a popular tactic. That's how personal information spreads to people who do not need to know the private details about another member. The person may leave their church after they realize their private life is out in the open. But sometimes when you look closely at the situation, you can see that the member wasn't insubordinate and the leader was quick-tempered (see Titus 1:7–11 to see how both should behave in such matters). That's an example of what people generally call spiritual abuse.

Accountability

Accountability is good for leaders. In church, members may have different points of view than their leadership. Some express those views directly to their leaders to the betterment of the church and everyone involved. Of course, every church needs feedback and different perspectives to thrive. Sometimes the feedback might be seen as criticism, rebellion, or insubordination, or it can be taken personally, when it's really a difference in perspective that should be encouraged. The leadership may think a good solution is to isolate the person they perceive as the critic. The next move might be to speak against the person to the congregation or, more cleverly, preach a sermon on their stance against the person's views. Some sermons sound like the preacher's personal problem with another person in or outside the church.

Your leadership mustn't agree with all the feedback it gets. You do have to find a way to handle different perspectives without fostering a culture of me/us versus them or shaming members through sermons, meetings, announcements, or letters. Breaching privacy when you should be preaching/teaching can attract legal issues—such as slander or libel. Learn to disagree fairly. Never fight an individual or a group of members through the mic or from the pulpit because you have a larger influence. It doesn't solve issues to have the last say. Rather, you'll slip across privacy lines you shouldn't have crossed. It's godlier to be kind than right.

Answer the questions on the following checklist to evaluate what you include in your messages. (For weekly use, you can download this free checklist from www.ChurchPrivacyBookSeries.com to use when preparing sermons, lessons, or other messages.)

Assess Your Message, Lesson, Sermon, or Meeting That Uses Personal Information

For every analogy you use that identifies a person and their personal experience or personal life—in your message, lesson, sermon, or meeting—evaluate it with the following questions:

- What am I planning to say about this person?

- Will my words reveal the identity of a person or group of people?

- How will what I say help the hearers?

- How will what I say impact the person or the people it's about?

- How will what I say solve the problem?

- How could what I say be used by people who are not in the church but are privy to the information?

- Could I make my point without mentioning the name, place, or time the issue happened?

Church Leadership, Counseling, and Mental Health

- Will what I say win the person over and allow us to have a better understanding, or will it drive them to take legal action?

- Is it worth using the church's hard-earned resources, time, and good name to defend slander or libel?

Assess How Your Church Is Assuring Privacy Compliance

☐ We've created a form with these questions and made it available to our preachers, teachers, presenters, and ministers in paper format.

☐ We've made the form available digitally on our intranet and we send it via email.

☐ We've included the message evaluation step in our privacy policy/rules.

☐ We know a privacy professional we can contact if we have questions.

Action Steps: You've assessed how your church protects privacy of pastoral meetings/counseling with members and what your church does about privacy in your sermons, lessons, messages, meetings, and other communications. The items you did not check are your action items to work on: list them. Have you designated someone within your church to handle this responsibility? Jot down your answers.

_____
_____
_____

What's your target date to assign someone to take this responsibility/when will you begin the tasks?
Day_____ Month_____ Year_____

What's your target date to complete these tasks?
Day_____ Month_____ Year_____

If you are a leader or support one, how can you help them take privacy seriously regarding their messages?

_____
_____
_____
_____
_____

What questions would you ask me?

_____
_____
_____
_____
_____

I've learned that people will forget what you said, people will forget what you did, but people will never forget how you made them feel.
(Maya Angelou)

Let's Talk about Sex

Have you ever observed a situation where someone who exposed a sexual misconduct was ostracized and gaslighted, and the one who allegedly committed the misconduct escaped the fire? It typically doesn't take long to see that the alleged offender has position, power, and influence. I was advising a pastor on a different matter. Then I changed the subject to examine an area of privacy concern we'd never discussed—sexual misconduct and privacy.

I said, "The devil's tactic is creating in people a tendency to hide after a sexual misconduct. Your church and my church are not immune to this tendency."

"So it's like when Adam and Eve hid from God after eating the fruit of good and evil and their eyes were opened and they realized they were naked," the pastor replied.

I nodded in agreement. "And it's also like when David went above and beyond to hide his sexual sin. Remember, the prophet Nathan pretty much clipped David's wings by reminding David that he had no right to privacy on the matter. By hiding his sin, David accumulated more sins to cover the first sin. But when David penned Psalm 51 in repentance, his heart changed." I recited verse thirteen to the pastor: "Then I will teach transgressors your ways, so that sinners will turn back to you" (Psalm 51:13). David pled for forgiveness so he could teach people who found themselves in the same predicament, the people who learned of his sin, and the ones who were deeply affected by his sin. As a result, those people could return to God. Like David, we need to be truthful about misconduct and let God use it to teach and change us and others. All it takes is one person to hide a misconduct, and the entire community suffers (Joshua 22:20).

Have you or your church leadership ever hidden the sexual sin of a leader as a gesture of loyalty to that leader rather than investigating the complaint? Have your members ever supported such a leader out of fear or for their own self-preservation? Or have you ever hidden someone's misconduct to protect the reputation of the church? God doesn't need you to protect his reputation. David realized that. Instead, you need to save your community like Joshua did with Achan. Take responsibility by taking proper steps to investigate the problem. Create a process ahead of time to investigate sexual harassment or other misconduct so you can arrive at a fair and timely solution. Your community will heal quickly as a result. Hiding a misconduct is not privacy.

"True, hiding, dismissing, or silencing a known misconduct is not privacy—it's false loyalty. As a church, our number one loyalty should be to God and his commandments. When we become aware of the misconduct, we are to address it with courage so that justice is achieved, correction is made, and all parties involved can be restored in peace,"* the pastor elaborated.

That's good teaching. I couldn't have explained it better. Do likewise in your church.

I recently attended a women's leadership meeting hosted by Jo Saxton, the global leadership coach and founder of Ezer Collective. As Jo coached about seventy-plus women in attendance, her discussion touched on a teaching pastor, Danielle Strickland, who resigned her leadership position to take a stand with a victim of abuse. The victim was allegedly silenced by the church's process or lack thereof. I learned Danielle maintained that she was doing this for her church, not against her church. Wow! It takes selfless courage to stand down so your church can take notice of abused/neglected members and take their needs more seriously. I'm not privy to the type or extent of abuse here. But I do know for sure that you need a policy that addresses abuse, misconduct, and harassment. You should have fair processes and procedures. This situation is a typical example of why you need to address misconduct and restore your members before it's too late. Also, properly handling people's personal information or details during such a process is critical. Otherwise, you'll violate privacy and do more damage than good.

This reminds me of whistleblowers. They make for interesting discussions in corporate privacy courses that I teach. Corporations have whistleblower policies and related investigations for a reason: so people with more power, influence, and connections cannot escape accountability for their misconduct. Meaning, they can't silence, retaliate, or fire the employee who brings unethical conduct to light. The organization protects the whistleblower. That's because the whistleblower's report of the issue is for the greater good of the organization in maintaining the core moral values, ethics, credibility, and legal obligations to people both in and outside the organization. Have you ever asked yourself why you don't protect victims or complainants of misconduct in your church in the same way that corporate organizations protect whistleblowers? How many churchgoers do you know who left a church

---

* See Leviticus 19:15, Philippians 2:4, 2 Timothy 3:16, 1 John 1:8–9, and Ephesians 4:3.

after they revealed a misconduct? I know many. How many have left because their misconduct was revealed about them at church? I know tons of them.

Both the complainant, or whistleblower, and the alleged offender need protection—that is, privacy protection. Privacy is very important during an investigation. Both parties could be hurt emotionally and more if privacy is not adequate.

- Does your church have a sexual harassment or misconduct policy?
- Does your policy require protection of the privacy of the complainants?
- Does your policy require protection of the privacy of victims who are minors?
- Is your policy supported by a procedure or process about how to intake complaints?
- Is your policy supported by a procedure or process for investigation?
- Does your policy designate a contact person or group (with their email and phone number) who will follow up with the complainant?

If you have these types of policies, how do you make your members, workers, visitors, and youth aware that these policies exist? I've observed a parent almost pull out her hair frustrated that her church didn't have an organized process for handling a sexual harassment situation involving her son and an older youth.

Indefinitely covering up a sexual offense and a sexual offender is not privacy. While in the US many corporate whistleblower policies place much emphasis on protecting the whistleblower, in some countries the emphasis is about protecting both parties. Why protect the alleged offender? Most churches ask me that. The protection is only for a time, for investigative purposes. *Fairness* is a privacy principle. It makes sense. Keep in mind that someone could be falsely accused. So why announce to everyone before you investigate? Also, investigation is not about making the victim feel worse than they already do emotionally, mentally, spiritually, physically, or otherwise. It takes courage to speak up. One sure way you can make matters worse is to defend the offender before you hear out the complainant or before you ask meaningful questions. Don't be too quick to vouch for someone's innocence. Last time I checked, the devil can enter anyone anytime (Luke 22:3) provided their mind and heart are receptive at the moment.

Another way of making matters worse is asking the wrong questions or asking with a sarcastic tone. For instance, "Did they actually touch you or mention your name when they said . . . ?" Another is using private information against the victim, for instance, "Haven't you had this type of issue at another church before?"

Harassment can be verbal or physical or involve indirect gestures or requests. It doesn't always involve touch. For the purposes of this book, let's stay on point. That is, privacy can be violated in many ways. Empathize first. Be kind. Be fair. Don't spread it.

If you provide an intake form online, in person, on paper, or over the phone, have safeguards that'll protect personal information on those forms. Decide ahead who in your leadership should handle complaints. Think *onion*. Make onion rings (see Chapter 2). Don't you need to protect the core values of your church? This is a perfect opportunity.

Tip: You can disagree but remain faithful and committed to someone's privacy. Don't assume immunity from liability. Let privacy be the default when disagreeing. Your actions, good or bad, take the name and mission of the church with them. Hiding complaints rather than addressing them will do the same. The best and cheapest action is to designate a person to handle the areas of concern discussed in this chapter.

Value: Unity. Healthy disagreement done in harmony and peace is better than being right. Avoid spiritual abuse, and take advantage of any chance you get to preserve the bigger picture of the church's calling. Promote unity.

Further Reading 1: After I penned this book, I stumbled upon David Middlebrook's article "Pastoral Confidentiality: An Ethical and Legal Responsibility."[2] But it's so relevant, I couldn't pass up the opportunity to add it as a recommended reading. I like Middlebrook's thoughts on the duty of loyalty: maintaining confidentiality even when it's not in your best interest as a member of the clergy. He does a great job laying out the moral and legal obligations of the church with regard to confidentiality.

Further Reading 2: I also treasured Ken Behr and Dale Hudson's practical discussion on confidentiality regarding church workers who work with children. Both leaders detailed examples of information people in the church community share privately that the church shouldn't keep confidential. You will benefit from reading their article titled "Church Confidentiality Policy: What's Appropriate in Children's Ministry."[3]

Action Steps: How are you going to start putting together a complaint process? How about starting with a specific phone number or email address where people can contact your church about misconduct or privacy violations? Jot down your answers.

_____
_____
_____

Who could you delegate investigations to?

_____
_____
_____
_____
_____

What's your target date to assign someone to take this responsibility/when will you begin the tasks?
Day_____ Month_____ Year_____

What's your target date to complete these tasks?
Day_____ Month_____ Year_____

What questions would you ask me?

_____

_____

_____

_____

Why People Need Counseling and Privacy

Why do people go to therapists? Why do they need a counselor? They're looking for someone they can trust. Someone who understands that their privacy is important. Someone who will listen without judging them. Counseling helps people improve their health, make sound decisions, reconnect with God, and experience transformation in their lives—in the areas of marriage, parenting, other relationships, career, finances, lifestyle, recovery, and well-being. In some cases, churches have professional counselors in-house. In some large and small churches, the preacher or clergyperson does the counseling. In other cases, churches refer their members to external counselors or groups. Many churches do a great job of providing different levels of counseling. Overall, trusted people, therapists, and counselors recognize that privacy is required.

Sometimes well-intentioned people want to glide into a counseling role because they're gifted in encouraging others. Often, we are the closest thing to a therapist or counselor that someone in need has at their disposal. I get that. However, being a member of the clergy, a ministry leader, a long-standing member, a volunteer, or an employee is not a qualification to become a counselor or therapist. Keep that in mind. Qualifications must be earned in the right way. If you don't have the proper training or certification, and you don't do this for a living, you're not a true therapist, counselor, or health professional. I'm not saying you need certification to help someone in an emergency situation or crisis. Even if you're called to counseling, adequate training that addresses how to handle discreet issues is crucial. Do it lawfully and in a way that will benefit the person you're helping instead of distressing them because you didn't know how to handle the situation. Be honest; if people at your church tend to overshare personal information about one another, let professionals handle this.

No matter our education level in counseling, whether at church or in college, we all get to hear some of the same matters that licensed professionals listen to all day. The difference is, we may not be handling these issues the same way or the right way as professionals do. If confidentiality and privacy are not respected during counseling, it creates senseless risks. The counseling may appear to be working, but it won't last if trust is not in the equation. People need to feel safe, confident, in control, and peaceful when sharing. That's privacy.

Licensed counselors and therapists study rules about handling personal information. They know the law and professional rules in a way the rest of us don't. People who are not professional counselors may not take confidentiality and privacy as seriously because they are not being paid, lack proper training, or may not sense any direct consequence for breaching privacy. Imagine if you worked at a hospital: would you throw around personal health information about patients so freely like you might do in your church after you counsel someone? You wouldn't. At work you'd fear the consequences. That said, let's look at what your church does.

Assess What Your Church Is Doing about Counseling Privacy

- ☐ We have a counseling policy/code of conduct.

- ☐ Each type or level of counseling has a defined goal, criteria, procedures, steps, outcomes, and level of expertise required.

- ☐ All workers with counseling responsibilities or *counselor* in their title have received appropriate training.

- ☐ All counseling refresher training includes topics on how to correctly handle personal information taken on paper forms, orally, or via electronic communication in addition to other personal information that people share.

- ☐ All counselors adhere to personal information rules and code of conduct.

☐ We guard against counseling relationships becoming inappropriate or romantic.

☐ We incorporate best practices and resources provided by counseling associations.

☐ All counseling candidates and existing counselors take additional privacy training to make certain they can apply good privacy principles.

☐ We require that people in any counseling role take specialized training, have supervision, and have ongoing professional development.

☐ We do what's in the best interest of the client's privacy; even if our views differ, it's no reason for us to violate their privacy.

☐ We understand that our decision about counseling depends on the level of counseling we have at our church.

☐ We do not let the lack of resources push us to give counseling roles to our members without equipping them to protect privacy and avoid creating situations that attract liability, negligence, and malpractice.

☐ We understand that in situations where the law may require a counselor to share information to protect the person we counsel or others, we will disclose information. For example, we'll share with law enforcement.

☐ We have processes and procedures that guide us on what to do if we receive a court request for information about an individual we're counseling. We involve our legal counsel.

☐ Our legal counsel periodically checks laws in our state for guidance.

Tip: Anyone with the title of counselor needs to read your privacy policy about counseling each time they get ready to counsel someone. They should let the person know that their personal information is going to be handled in line with the policy/code of conduct. You should include that in your privacy policy under the counseling section.

Value: Boost members' confidence and trust. Privacy has a culture-building value for both counselors and members.

Action Steps: You've assessed what your church is currently doing. The boxes you didn't check are your action items: list them below. Have you already designated someone within your church to handle the responsibility of ensuring that all counselors (volunteer or professional) maintain privacy? Jot down your answers.

_____
_____
_____

What's your target date to assign someone to take this responsibility/when will you begin the tasks?
Day_____ Month_____ Year_____

What's your target date to complete these tasks?
Day_____ Month_____ Year_____

What advantages do you think your church will provide members if privacy is taken seriously during counseling?

_____
_____
_____
_____
_____

Church Privacy Team

What questions would you ask me?

_____
_____
_____
_____
_____

Mental Health: What People Are Saying Versus How They Are Doing

Doesn't everybody always seem so perfect on Sundays? Or at least they look perfectly fine when they arrive at church. They are laughing, hugging, and worshipping. They look like people without a care in the world. When you say, "Good morning, how've you been?" people will respond, "God is good," "I'm trusting him," or "I'm blessed." Very few people say, "I'm sick," "I'm depressed," "I'm really traumatized by what happened to me this week," or "I'm suicidal, and I have a good plan to end my life as soon as I get home." The truth is, people's lives are not as perfect as they may seem. Sometimes people don't speak honestly because they believe nobody will really listen. They think everyone's life is perfect except theirs. That perhaps nobody cares or really wants to know about their situation. As a result, they think it's best to protect themselves from being hurt by other people's reactions to their personal issues. They fear their private issues will be spread around.

For many people, interaction with others only happens in the sanctuary, on Sundays, or when serving in a ministry. The Bible says you should not neglect the habit of meeting with others in fellowship, "not giving up meeting together, as some are in the habit of doing, but encouraging one another—and all the more as you see the Day approaching" (Hebrews 10:25). Through fellowship, you lighten somebody else's load. So you're supposed to make time and make it a habit, pretty much taking your Sunday morning exchanges of pleasantries to another level. Fellowship opens doors to building friendship, encouragement, and confidence—the assurance that someone needs to feel so they can trust you with protecting their privacy or dignity when they share their mental health issues.

Listening for and Observing Mental Health and Respecting Privacy

It is important to listen to others and be a good observer. I used to think I was a great listener until a speech communication course I took during my undergraduate studies debunked my belief. I also thought I was a good observer until a tragedy happened—our ministry facilitator's young nephew committed suicide. When the director of one of the ministries I served on assigned me to write about mental health, I laughed in disbelief like Sarah (Genesis 18:12). I knew nothing about mental health. I turned around and said to God, "Are you serious?" A couple of days later, I was enrolled in an all-day mental health training. My jaw dropped when I found out how uneducated and misguided I was about mental health. That and what a terrible listener and observer I was. I also learned I was horrible at preserving mental health privacy. We are all like that sometimes. But now we can work on changing that.

Making Observations

What exactly are you observing and listening to when you interact with someone? When you observe someone long enough, you may notice personality changes, even for someone you don't know well. As you listen, you may sense they're anxious, confused, or afraid. You can discern a lack of motivation, lack of focus, weight loss or gain, sadness, and sluggishness. If they're a church worker, they may be calling in sick more than usual, missing deadlines, and resigning from jobs more often than not. Maybe you notice a drastic change. For example, someone is not as well dressed as they used to be. They don't care about their looks and have lost enthusiasm for their appearance. Or you've noticed a typically chatty person becoming very quiet and withdrawn. Maybe you notice, or someone tells you, that they're drinking alcohol more than normal or using other substances to suppress feelings of hopelessness or stress. Someone may also be giving away their prized possessions because they're planning to end their life. There are plenty of signs that show something may be wrong with another person.

Mental health issues manifest in different forms and severity. Some are more noticeable than others. But they're all very private to the person who is experiencing the issues. This is not only true in the church community but everywhere. Church members and visitors are not quick to share their mental health struggles. They have a good reason. Privacy. They don't want to be hurt by how people might react or what people might say even if they don't intend to cause any hurt. This is where your church can help meet people's need for privacy. Respect and preserve the privacy and dignity of the person who opens up about their mental health. Give the person the confidence they need to get treatment privately even if they choose resources outside your church community. Getting church members educated is important. Try offering a mental health seminar or workshop. If you're a small church, you can secure a free virtual workshop. Among other lessons, learn that there's a difference between someone who has mental illness and someone who shows corrupt, evil, or immoral behavior. The former is an illness, and the latter is a choice, for example, the naked man who cried out at the top of his voice day and night, cut himself with stones, and lived in tombs (Luke 8:27) versus the thief on the cross (Luke 23:40–41). Mental illness in any form is not a sin; it's a health concern. Never call corrupt or immoral behavior mental illness.

Mental illness is not a convenient insult or joke. We've all done it—called someone who doesn't have any mental illness retarded, mental, mad, loony, psychotic, or depressed because they acted in a way we found unacceptable or annoying. Jesus' family did the same to him. They called him crazy (Mark 3:21). It's fine to disagree, but it's never okay to disrespect. We live in a world where people use mental illness as an insult even in the church. Do you know anyone who uses certain words when describing those they disagree with? Others label others mentally ill as an excuse to manipulate the person into doing what they want. Some people invalidate anything good a person does or even the truth they tell. They tell others that the person is mentally ill. By doing this, they cause others to lose respect for the person or not take the person seriously. These are just a few of the many reasons a person would keep mental illness to themselves. "Love must be sincere" (Romans 12:9); "Love your neighbor as yourself" (Matthew 22:39).

People guard their mental health information to prevent being misjudged, discriminated against, or embarrassed or even losing their job or reputation. Given the stigma that society attaches to mental health problems or disabilities, assess how your church helps prevent serious emotional distresses related to privacy concerns.

Assess What Your Church Is Doing about Mental Health Privacy

- ☐ Our church helps members understand mental health without attaching a stigma.

- ☐ We make members and workers aware that mental health issues are common.

- ☐ We make members and workers aware that mental illness can happen at any time to anyone from all walks of life. Mental health doesn't depend on how great a person's life looks on the outside or their age, gender, ethnicity, or socioeconomic status. People such as Job, David, Jacob, and Elijah experienced mental health challenges.

- ☐ We make sure members and workers are aware that a mental health issue should be taken seriously and handled respectfully. We protect personal information that people share about their mental health.

- ☐ We make sure members and workers are aware that depression can be caused by or triggered by different factors, including traumatic events (e.g., death, divorce, miscarriage, job loss, or business loss) and health issues.

- ☐ We make sure members and workers are aware that people should be treated with respect whether they have mental health issues or we suspect they may have mental health issues.

- ☐ We make sure members and workers are aware that information about people's mental health or behavior should be protected whether in oral or written form; otherwise, we risk hurting people.

- ☐ We make sure members and workers are aware that if they discuss information about the person with others, they can cause that person to be misjudged and stigmatized, and it is a violation of the person's privacy.

- ☐ We have designated specific people to handle mental health information and the right professionals to be involved to help people in mental health crises.

☐ We train our workers and volunteers about different scenarios, how to respond in a respectful way, how to get additional help to support the person, and when to call hotline phone numbers.

☐ We train our workers and volunteers on questions to ask or not ask when someone is in a mental crisis.

☐ We teach our workers and volunteers that a person might choose to testify in church about their condition, but it shouldn't be forced. We don't use their testimonies as permission to reveal more information about their condition.

☐ Honoring and respecting privacy is about giving back control to the individual. We allow the person to control what they want to share, how much they want to share, where they want to share it, and with whom they want to share it.

☐ We allow the person to be the first to ask for prayer in church so they can give the amount of detail they desire.

For the items you haven't checked, make those your action items to discuss, and incorporate them into your policy, training, awareness, notices, and communication plan. Also, make resources available to people. Realize you're not equipped or always available to solve mental health crises or problems.

Helpful hotlines include the following:

- National Suicide Prevention Lifeline 1-800-273-8255

- Boys Town National Hotline 1-800-448-3000

- Other_____

- Other_____

- Other_____

- Other_____

Helpful Bible passages you can use to communicate to your members how to care for those with mental health issues and their personal information include the following:

- Be pure, peaceable, gentle, full of mercy, without partiality, and without hypocrisy (James 3:17).
- Speak the truth (Proverbs 12:22).
- Sit in silence (Job 2:13).
- Bear one another's burdens (Galatians 6:2).
- Other_____
- Other_____
- Other_____
- Other_____
- Other_____

Tip: A church that attaches a stigma to mental health will likely create a culture that fosters the same. Health information is sensitive information and must always be handled with caution. The Onion Model can come in handy here. Not everyone has a need to know or can handle this information without passing judgment. Nonprofit mental health organizations are always looking for opportunities to create awareness on this topic. Look up a few in your locale. Invite these organizations. For starters, try https://www.mentalhealthfirstaid.org/about. You don't need a big budget to do this. Providing snacks will be sufficient.

Value: Protecting mental health privacy shows your church cares about people's mental health needs. The church earns trust in return and provides a solace for those struggling with mental health challenges.

Church Privacy Team

Action Steps: You've assessed what your church is currently doing about mental health privacy concerns. The items you did not check are your action items to work on: list them. Have you designated someone within your church to handle this responsibility? Jot down your answers.

_____

_____

_____

What's your target date to start revising or creating rules of behavior regarding mental health and to communicate resources to your members, volunteers, employees, and other workers?
Day_____ Month_____ Year_____

What's your target date to complete these tasks?
Day_____ Month_____ Year_____

You have learned in this chapter that people are often hesitant to share what is going on. How might your church encourage members to better trust one another?

_____

_____

_____

_____

_____

What questions would you ask me?

_____

_____

_____

_____

_____

Those who trust in themselves are fools,
but those who walk in wisdom are kept safe.
(Proverbs 28:26)

8

Small Church Privacy Challenges

Success is the sum of small efforts, repeated day in and day out.
(Robert Collier)

Benefits and Challenges of Being a Small Church

"Small churches are not a problem, a virtue or an excuse."[1] This quote by Karl Vaters is a reminder that the size of your church is irrelevant to the quality of ministry it should offer. "Just because your church is small does not mean you can't do good ministry. There's no single command to the New Testament church that can't be accomplished by a small church."

Churches are like schools or hospitals. There are small, medium, and large versions. You can be an exceptional teacher or excellent student in a small school. You can have a successful major surgery regardless of the size of the hospital. I've been to all types of churches with different flavors—style, ambiance, size, name, location, order of worship, people, niche, and approach. But they all have one mission: to teach the Bible and see lives saved and transformed. To achieve this mission without legal headaches, churches need to pay attention to the authorities, rules, and regulations. Like schools and hospitals, if churches can't protect people's personal information while carrying out their mission, they're bound to hurt people and find themselves in legal battles.

It's a blessing to be part of a small church community. The warmth and family atmosphere are inviting. Among other perks, visitors don't get lost in the crowd. New members are showered with attention, enabling them to settle in easily.

Don't Compare Yourself to Others

Megachurches may have a lot of resources and a larger lawn, but the grass isn't necessarily greener there. At least, not all of it. There are dry brown spots. The view depends on which direction you're looking from. Small churches don't have the complexities that bigger churches have: more people to manage, higher bills, larger events, a number of services to accommodate more people, more parking lot traffic, and a dozen police officers for every service for security reasons. Imagine how much personal information megachurches collect on a weekly basis from people in all their departments and ministries. People have to fill out forms for almost every gathering they wish to attend. Lawfully collecting, storing, sharing, and using personal information can be very complex in a large church. Although it's more complex for big churches, small churches are not off the hook.

You might argue that your church is too small to add privacy protection responsibilities to your already full plate. Or you may believe that the church never had to worry about privacy and security in the New Testament or in its entire history. I disagree. In the Old Testament, Rahab honored the privacy of Israel's spies after identifying who they were. She didn't sound an alarm to alert her neighbors. She protected them from their enemies by hiding them on her roof. She then diverted their enemies to search for the spies where she knew they wouldn't be found. Those enemies are equivalent to hackers today. The spies and Rahab entered into a nondisclosure agreement (Joshua 2:14). I know Rahab was glad. The spies felt safe. Peace at last!

In the New Testament, Saul of Tarsus persecuted Christians. He depended on leaked information to trace, monitor, and arrest believers. Some Christians fled. They relocated. Some lived together in secret communities to escape arrest and persecution. They kept their whereabouts and meeting places private. They hid their identities. For this reason, Ananias was afraid to meet Saul and pray for him in Damascus. He was afraid that welcoming Saul into their community meant he would be compromising the privacy and security of all the believers who lived there or had escaped to Damascus. Saul was not trustworthy. The Saul they knew was a malicious hacker. He went door-to-door, breaking in, invading, intruding on people's private spaces, and persecuting them because of their beliefs (Acts 9:10–15). Today, privacy laws prevent such intrusion and discrimination and give individuals the right to worship freely without persecution. Privacy is a life-or-death situation, as it was for those Christians in Damascus.

If you collect personal information from anyone in your church, you need to be concerned about privacy. If you collect personal information via your website or your phone, you need to be concerned. Feeding God's sheep (John 21:17) goes hand in hand with taking care of and protecting the sheep (John 21:16) from bears, lions, and wolves.

Being Small Is Not a Defect

At nine years old, I was the youngest and tiniest kid in boarding school. Although there was no other student by the name of Grace, everyone added a distinct identifier to my name. They called me "Little Grace." I felt the smile in people's voices; they said it as if they were saying, "She's so tiny and cute." I took pleasure in being my teachers' and classmates' pet. But then again, I wanted to be just plain *Grace*. The *cute* part I liked. *Little* not so much. Then I heard my mom say some encouraging words to someone: "Being small is not a defect." That stayed with me even after I was not so small anymore. What I am suggesting is that you be the best small you can be—injecting privacy zest into your smallness will help you do that.

When I learned about Zacchaeus' story (Luke 19:1–10), it resonated. Later in life I read about famous short people in the US. I stumbled upon the accomplishments of Robert Reich, the economist. Reich is a former Rhodes scholar who served as the US Secretary of Labor under four US presidents. People were quick to make jokes when the four-foot, ten-inch-tall Reich had to stand on a box to give him extra height behind a podium. "At least I stand firmly on my platform," Reich retorted.[2] Mom was right. Great things can come in small packages. That includes great and sound churches and ministries. Stand firmly and implement excellent privacy on the platform on which God has placed you.

No Substitute for You

When I started my career in information security and cybersecurity, there were few women. That hasn't changed much. For years I've been the only female in teams made up of guys. When we traveled on missions to conduct physical security inspections or audits, I was the one who was assigned to climb into tiny and delicate spaces. Sometimes I went under floors or into ceilings to inspect communication wires while the guys secured the ladder—ready to catch me if I came crashing down. Every time the team needed to physically access a space they couldn't enter, I'd hear whispers: "No, that won't work. We need someone with smaller fingers. Where's Grace?"

We had to think on our feet like burglars. On many occasions, I felt like Oliver working for Sikes in Charles Dickens' epic novel *Oliver Twist*. One day all was going well until we needed to figure out if the space under a fence was big enough for a human being to wiggle under to gain access to a highly secured federal government facility. Upon hearing about this James Bond-like mission, I put my foot down.

"No, thanks."

"What's the problem? You'll fit," my team lead yelled.

To his surprise, I responded, "I'm allergic to grass. Use a measuring tape instead." That caused some stares mixed with groans of disappointment. A measuring tape wasn't as much fun. My team relished the ninja effect I gave the mission. Here I was with big guys who at the moment wished they were as tiny as me to accomplish this feat.

As a small church, your God-given ninja effect for the kingdom of God cannot be substituted. There are certain experiences a big church cannot deliver as well as you can. Privacy and trust can be added to those experiences you excel in. What vision has God given you? To become a large, mega, or gigachurch? Or to thrive as a small church? I don't know. What I can tell you is, little is much when God's in it. If you start small, implement a privacy and data protection plan and strategy, and invest time, as you grow bigger, it will get less expensive, less overwhelming, and less intimidating. These efforts will cover you if anything goes wrong. How? Unlike me, I can tell you that criminals are not inhibited by allergies. They're determined to get the job done, both physically and digitally. Criminals don't like to do more work than they need to. A church is an easier target for them than a corporation. To data thieves, small churches are like low-hanging juicy mangoes.

Your resources are low. Options are fewer. Your ability to network with other small churches to share knowledge, privacy solutions, lessons learned, and strategies (as big churches do) might be minimal. I feel you, but don't despair.

Small Churches Perish Too for Lack of Knowledge

Have you ever been to a house church? Having attended many small churches that launched from someone's living room as well as the ones in spaces that could hold thirty to one hundred-plus members, I quickly learned that a lot of small churches operate as silos. Even as they grow into medium-size churches, they don't interact with others or network with other churches as large churches do. Leaders are too inundated with attending to members' needs; they hardly retreat to go elsewhere and learn new information. This is not at all sustainable. I read an article written on the Baptist News website. The article pointed out that seminary graduates avoid small churches. I am not saying leaders without formal education are not doing a fantastic job leading in small churches. They are. But because new graduates prefer big churches, small churches often fall behind on relevant knowledge, information, and trends.

Not being in the know with relevant concerns leaves small churches with wide knowledge and management gaps. Karl Vaters states that small churches make up most of the churches in the world. He estimates that more than 90 percent of churches have under two hundred members, while more than 80 percent have less than one hundred.[3] In other words, more than one billion Christians worship in a small setting. Your church may be really small, but it is still significant. And there are more small churches than big ones. The good news is, you'll no longer fall behind on privacy trends. This book helps you gain relevant knowledge needed to close your learning gap on data privacy. Here are your action items:

Find Experts

You probably have a few questions at this point, such as, do you need to hire a lawyer, secure insurance, or hire a few privacy experts? It depends on your situation. But I'd say, get a few freebies first. This book is a start. Read through *Church Privacy 101* and this book to help you identify what you're doing now. Sign up for a course and consult an expert later.

You will likely need to hire someone at some point. Not all great privacy experts are lawyers, and not all great lawyers know privacy. Privacy is a specialty. Don't get tricked. If someone wants to help you with privacy, ask for proof of expertise and verify their privacy certification and experience. Get references. Make sure the person has specifically handled privacy, not cybersecurity, information assurance, information security, or IT. Otherwise, you'll just be exchanging money for hours. That would be a waste of church funds.

Do the same with a lawyer—make sure they are specialized in privacy. Also, you can't have a good, meaningful conversation with a privacy lawyer if you don't know what you're talking about. My three books will prepare you so you don't get taken. These books will help you get better value from the expert when you have a thirty-minute consultation with them in the future. These books will prepare you to think quickly and ask meaningful questions. A lawyer cannot have a meaningful solution for you unless they know how privacy works and have experience advising other organizations. Get proof of the lawyer's expertise in this area—make sure they have privacy certification. This is a blossoming field, and there are no pro bono lawyers waiting around anywhere to help you. All the more reason you should use every opportunity to learn and apply what you can now. That way no one overbills you. And if you think they are, holler and I'll help you assess the situation.

Find More Helping Hands

Next, you need people. Members of your church who volunteer can add value to your privacy practices. Some of the best volunteers are students. If you don't have many students, this presents an opportunity to offer internships to students from nearby universities or colleges. You don't have to hand the students access to any of your precious data. But they can help you get organized using this book. They can interview you and other key people and help you with inventory. They can even help develop some of the documents I've mentioned in this book.

In which programs or fields of study are these students? At local universities, computer science, technology, data science, and cybersecurity departments can let you know if they have a data privacy curriculum. Students from these disciplines need work experiences to parade on their résumé. Giving students this opportunity is a win-win. Post an announcement with the school. You can also post an announcement at a larger church than yours. Always verify that the students are enrolled at the university. Get references from their professors.

Avoid Costly Mistakes

Resources aside, as a small church, you'll make mistakes. Big mistakes. You don't believe me? One Sunday, someone in charge of handling the money at a church I started visiting discreetly took the money to her car and hid it there—to deposit at the bank after the church service. She set her keys on an empty chair near her purse in the back of the sanctuary. Her bunch of keys mysteriously disappeared. Her car was ransacked during worship. I wasn't shocked because it's common for churches to easily put blanket trust on people—even visitors and strangers. I've done it too and learned. What was my advice? Install steel storage lockers. For around $160 to $200, one or two lockers can hold more than ten bags and several bunches of car keys for the small number of members.

Data Traders and Criminals Love Small Churches

Here's another big mistake: new faces may want to use the church's laptop or desktop computer. You may say, "Just let them use it. It doesn't cost us anything to help these visitors." Say that if they want to use the restroom. Computers? No. Don't underestimate what a person can do on your device in under three minutes. Take advice from the ethical hacking ninja, once I gain access, I can hit three thousand devices in minutes. Even more, think about personal information that can be easily traded on the Internet. Suppose someone loses their wallet containing cash or a check, and the wallet is picked up and stolen. Their photo ID, home address, driver's license, and Social Security card are worth more money than mere cash or a check. This information can be used to financially exploit the victim indefinitely. In the long run, the person whose personal information is stolen can lose more than the value of the cash or check they initially lost. Protecting personal information is worth the effort.

I've seen small churches raise money to replace equipment because of this mistake. Anything hooked up to the church's network is vulnerable when one piece of equipment is vulnerable. One device is one too many. This can be avoided. In one small church, computers were damaged by viruses and other types of malicious software. How did it get to that? Adults and children asked to use church computers for personal activities. Unsupervised, they downloaded and used apps that opened the door for a slew of malicious software. In an effort to build membership, small congregations often feel that saying yes to people's every request is a warm gesture and part of making people feel comfortable enough to return and join as members. Don't count on it. Cash, checks, information, and equipment if lost or mishandled is problematic for a church of any size.

Trusting the Wrong People and Things

Karl Vaters, a small church pastor for more than forty years, admitted to similar situations happening to his church several times. They trusted the wrong people, and money was stolen as a result. After reading Vater's blog post "Small Church Finances," I made a note to reach out to Karl and say, "You've done a phenomenal job discussing learning this lesson the hard way. But it's from the perspective of a security and financial problem. What about privacy?" This was a great article.

How did he reduce risks and the negative impact on his small church and its members going forward? He did what this book is teaching you now. Know your valuables. Identify the threats—people (members, visitors, employees, volunteers, contractors), unsecured storage, and technology flaws. What risks do these present to personal information and your devices? Identify where you're vulnerable; for instance, you're vulnerable because you don't have a plan, rules, or privacy processes. Be intentional about reducing the negative impact that the risk of doing absolutely nothing may have on your members.

A Plan Will Save Money

Remember, people have entrusted you with their money and personal information. Don't risk losing that trust. Develop a plan. This book is your plan. Come up with strategies to make that plan a reality. You have checkboxes throughout this book. Spend less money to make your plan work rather than more money to recover from disaster when the unthinkable happens. Don't be penny-wise and pound-foolish. I recall this remark that global business and motivational speaker James Malinchak made at a live virtual event: "I've never met anyone with a money problem, only people with priority problems." Prioritize. Unfortunately, this sometimes holds true in church. In my industry we have a saying: "You can't protect what you don't know." Again, know your information assets. Inventory your privacy practices. Be in the know about what's valuable. Valuables are not limited to cash and checks. Personal information is valuable and costly when compromised.

Privacy Consciousness

Karl's story made me realize he is privacy conscious even though he doesn't articulate it that way. Karl said he was tempted to crack a joke at Justin Bieber's expense to get laughs during his Sunday sermon. But Karl had a change of mind—after some self-examination. While reviewing his sermon notes, the joke stopped him in his tracks. He paused and examined it closely. Karl asked himself this question: "Would I tell that joke about someone who was in the room to hear it?" His answer was, "Not a chance." Besides, Justin Bieber was rich, but he was just a teenager. What Karl previously saw as a casual joke was going to be directed at someone God made in his own image, a real human being. Karl concluded that the joke was cruel. He said it taught him to see everyone as God's image-bearer—regardless of fame or economic status.[4] As a privacy advocate, my response was a resounding, "Amen! Preach, Karl!"

Privacy is a real human need even if you've never met the person. As a church, you should respect people's privacy. Manage personal information properly to protect all image-bearers including members, visitors, donors, event attendees, workers, and famous people, among others. In Chapter 7, I discussed sermons and messages and offered some exercises you can use to examine analogies and jokes in your sermons, remarks, and messages.

Be careful what you say about people unknown to you, even in jest. Avoid laughing, preaching, or praying at their expense; these are behaviors that can heap distress on their reputation and provoke rumors. This is a privacy issue even if the person is famous/rich. You may suppose that they should have thick skin, but the reality is that they are humans in need of kindness. Privacy is kindness. I encourage you to read *Church Privacy 101*, as it explores these issues and more. My Five-Part Test will change you for the best, even in a small church.

You're Too Busy for This!

Suppose you're a preacher or minister of a small church of fifteen members. In addition to midweek Bible study and preaching on Sunday, you're making rounds between two hospitals to attend to two sick church members. You haven't eaten all day. You haven't slept well. You're stretched thin. An attentive church member who lives just a couple of miles away invites you to stop by and help yourself to some herbed turkey wings and roasted potatoes to help you recharge. "You can catch a little power nap here in our visitor's room," they add. It's an offer you can't refuse. You hop in your car and promise to be there in no more than ten minutes.

But you don't get there in ten minutes. Not even in two hours. You collide head-on with another car while trying to pass a slow-moving vehicle. You didn't mean to hurt anyone. You're unharmed, so you pray for the folks in the other vehicle. You even go and check on the people in the other car.

If you have your driver's license and have been driving for a while, you know it's safe to say that accidents are unintended. And it doesn't take an ambulance hauling off several injured or dead people from the scene for the accident to be considered serious. One mistake is all that's needed to impact the life of someone, such as another driver or pedestrian.

Here's what the police will say: You broke traffic safety rules on a two-lane street. You tried to pass a slow-moving vehicle by going into the other lane where traffic was going in the opposite direction. In other words, you misused the lane. You didn't pay attention and didn't stay within the speed limit. After the ambulance takes the other driver off to the hospital, your auto insurance agent returns your call. They conclude based on your story that it was clearly your fault that someone got hurt and two cars were damaged. Neither the police nor the insurance agent will say, "No worries, you're stretched thin, trying to help people, and you didn't mean to hurt anyone. You're too busy to be held accountable."

Privacy Regulator

Similar to traffic laws, when you violate privacy laws, a privacy regulator won't accept your excuses. If people were hurt because of you, you face the consequences. It's no different when the privacy authority, regulators, and data protection authorities come on the scene of a privacy accident or data breach. You were tired, you were overworked, and you were trying to do what was right. Regardless of your small church size and your good intentions, you're at fault. First, you didn't collect personal information within your lawful limits (similar to the lawful speed limit). Second, you misused information just because you could (you repurposed another lane against safety rules). Third, you didn't secure or preserve the privacy of the people you collected personal information from—it's on your unencrypted laptop in the back seat of your car, a place that is so convenient for a thief to access and defraud the person the information belongs to—(other people were injured because of your negligence). The related privacy breach here is about the negative impact of your decisions or indecisions on people who trusted you with their personal, financial, or health information.

Over-Accommodating

From a data privacy view, these are the disadvantages of over-accommodating. You compromise your health, time, and resources. That means you help people, but you also hurt them. The goal here is to help people in a way that nobody gets hurt and the law is not broken.

How can you accomplish that? Use simple tools. Whether you use a Mac computer with programs such as Pages and Numbers or a Windows computer with their Microsoft cousins, Word and Excel, you're ready to go with these basic office tools. Good privacy practices start with creating documents. This book suggests what to create. These inexpensive documents will help you manage a privacy breach. A handful of committed members can get this started.

Give Away Multiple Hats

Start thinking about who to assign to the trust roles even if you only have five committed members. Members of small churches wear multiple hats anyway. Add one more: privacy leader. Give your members a role description (with their name on it) even if it's one paragraph. Get some ideas from Appendix A for that. Allow people to grow naturally into these roles. The early church or house church was skilled at developing effective leaders due to their organic approach to nurturing and affirming people's roles and growth. That said, privacy in Paul's day was a matter of life or death. It's important to note that these were ordinary people, not formally trained privacy advocates, data protection officers, lawyers, or seminary graduates. Yet each leader managed privacy like a pro to save many lives, both physically and spiritually. So can your church.

Privacy Assembly

Schedule informal meetings, a maximum of thirty minutes to start. But call the meeting what it is, a "privacy meeting." You can get fancier than that with names, but make sure *privacy* is in it. Gather once a month to chat so your members can be committed and held accountable for learning about privacy and applying it. Draft and file your meeting notes. That didn't cost you too much, right? It's doable. Privacy practices don't have to be complicated or expensive.

The Value in Being Small

Your small church is healthy. Small has its advantages. Your value in the body of Christ is unique and phenomenal with regard to whom you serve and how you serve. You are to the body of Christ what I was to my mission team—the small hands, small fingers, and agile and slender body that could squeeze through spaces other team members couldn't. That's what your small church is in the kingdom of God. Applying good privacy practices is doing good ministry. Similarly, I tell corporations that doing good privacy is doing good business. It reduces legal and financial risks, amplifies trust, and prevents people from getting hurt.

Assess Your Church's Privacy Practices

- ☐ We have a leader or facilitator who is committed to fostering and maintaining a privacy culture.
- ☐ We schedule regular privacy meetings to discuss privacy concerns and risks.

Church Privacy Team

☐ We include the word *privacy* in the job/role title of our privacy leader.

☐ Volunteers/members/children/visitors do not use the church business computers.

☐ We keep up to date with news about data breaches involving apps that our church uses.

☐ We have a policy that prohibits leaving documents containing personal information in our cars or on our desks.

☐ We check our teachers and preachers to ensure sermons and lessons are not slanderous or libelous.

☐ We discuss strategies and plans to help our church demonstrate that we are privacy-centric and trustworthy.

☐ We have a process to evaluate why we entrust particular roles to certain people.

☐ We require people who have keys to church offices to sign an agreement to safeguard access entrusted to them.

☐ Our privacy leaders stay abreast of state, federal, and international laws and regulations.

☐ We consult privacy experts periodically for guidance.

Tip: Beyond the primary leader of the church, identify someone else in your church who is already a good influencer. Someone who motivates people, loves to lead projects, and people enjoy working with. Provide the person with the three books in my privacy series, and discuss the books with them in the context of your church. Tell the person why you've selected them and that you need someone to lead in this area. Make an announcement to your church that you've appointed this person. Preach a sermon on privacy. I have tons of ideas for you in *Church Privacy 101*. Use the contact information on the back of this book if you need help with that. When you preach your privacy sermon, please share the points you covered. That'll make my day, and I'll have a gift for you.

Value: Even if you have a membership of as few as five people, appointing someone will free up more of your time to handle other church concerns. You'll support the person in charge and provide oversight. Others will joyfully buy in and do what the person says. Your small church will experience a surge of privacy culture that you can sustain.

Action Steps: You've assessed what your church does to ensure privacy is maintained. The items you did not check are your action items to work on: list them. Have you designated someone within your church to handle your privacy responsibility? Jot down your answers.

_____

_____

_____

What's your target date to assign someone to take this responsibility/when will you begin the tasks?
Day_____ Month_____ Year_____

What's your target date to complete these tasks?
Day_____ Month_____ Year_____

What opportunities are you throwing away because you think your church is too small?

_____

_____

_____

_____

_____

Church Privacy Team

What questions would you ask me?

_____

_____

_____

_____

_____

A small church is not an excuse for doing less-than-excellent ministry.
(Karl Vaters)

9

Children

A person's a person, no matter how small.
(Dr. Seuss, *Horton Hears a Who*)

The privacy of a child's personal information is a bit different from the privacy of the personal information you collect from adults. A child cannot make an informed decision about their personal information. They don't understand the consequences of their decisions or choices. If you promise a child something sweet and exciting, they'll cooperate and give you personal information about them or their family. It's illegal to ask a child to consent to the collection of their personal information. Asking children for more personal information than is necessary is also illegal. Children's online privacy laws recognize that a child may willingly give your church's website personal information. A child may also be willing to give permission for you to use their personal information for any purpose. But it is illegal to collect personal information from children even if they give it willingly. Laws/regulations do not hold children legally responsible for giving you permission. Rather, adults or organizations are accountable for accepting illegal consent. For example, TikTok was fined $5.7 million,[1] and YouTube was fined $200 million[2] for violating children's online privacy.

A child or minor is anyone under thirteen or sixteen years of age depending on the jurisdiction. Regulators levy some of the highest fines on violators of children's online privacy. The Children's Online Privacy Protection Act (COPPA), GDPR, and many federal, national, state, local, and provincial laws protect children's privacy online. The government is not out to punish businesses or your church with the hefty fines and penalties. This is how it protects children from online predators of all kinds including, but not limited to, tech companies who wish to spy on children or learn personal information about their parents. The government is also protecting children from abductors and child sexual abusers, among others. These perpetrators cannot excuse their actions with illegal consent they might have obtained from children. All website owners, including your church, should know the rules associated with processing children's personal information online and offline. More parents are paying attention to websites these days, and they're typically the ones who sue or escalate their complaints to both state and federal authorities.

Collecting Children's Personal Information

These days, Sunday schools, nurseries, and children's programs require parents to provide personal information about their children and themselves. This puts more privacy responsibilities on the church.

There are many intake forms to complete. Of course, we want to know who the parents and guardians are in case of an emergency, that is, if a child gets sick or suffers injury. Churches collect information including a child's full name, physical address, birthday/age, health issues, care requirements, medications, and parents' phone numbers and email addresses. Sometimes parents have to leave food and advise the caregivers about the details of the child's diet. Then there are children with special needs. Different situations require additional personal information.

Most times when children are signed up for any church activity, their parents' information is also recorded. In case of an emergency, parents need to be contacted right away. If the parent is unavailable, an alternate point of contact listed by the parent can be alerted. I don't know how much personal information your church collects about children. You should create a standard for collecting a child's full name, home address, birthday/age, health conditions, and care requirements as well as caretaker information such as parents' phone numbers, email addresses, marital status, custody information/guardianship, and emergency contact. Do you need to collect everything I just listed? No. These are examples. But you should document your justification for collecting any of these different elements of personal information. If you can't justify it with a specific purpose, don't collect the information. Identify and document how you secure the information from the point of collection to the actual use and storage of the information. Designate specific people to collect children's personal information. It's not every volunteer's or member's job.

Child Caregivers

It's best to create a standard or policy for hiring church childcare employees and approving volunteers to work with children and children's personal information. It's a huge responsibility and requires a lot of trust. Examine those who work with children and those who support these workers. Ensure they receive periodic privacy awareness and training.

Importance of Collection

It's risky, but it's important to collect personal information. Teachers or child caregivers need information to better care for and protect kids. But collecting does not mean over-collecting. Collect the minimum of what's needed. If you can't align the information with a need, don't collect it. This is not only personal information about children but their parents' also. It's best to obtain parental consent before you collect personal information directly from children.

Church Websites and Children

As I mentioned earlier, depending on your jurisdiction, some laws or regulations require parental consent to collect information about children under thirteen or sixteen years of age. It's a good business and privacy practice to address children's privacy in your website privacy notice. The General Data Protection Regulation (GDPR) and US laws require this. There are consequences for noncompliance, which include hefty fines and penalties. Controlling the behavior of people who work in your church's nursery, children's Sunday school, and other children's ministries is crucial because your church is responsible for the privacy of children in your care. If privacy is violated, parents could sue. Likewise, regulators could crack the whip on the church. That said, grab a drink, and let's assess what your church is doing about children's privacy.

Church Privacy Team

Assess Your Church's Privacy Practices and How They Protect Children

- ☐ We review how we collect, store, use, share, and dispose of personal information about children.

- ☐ We research the laws about how children's personal information is to be collected and protected.

- ☐ We check that our children's privacy policies, rules, processes, and procedures meet legal and regulatory requirements.

- ☐ We train childcare workers/volunteers who are in contact with children about our acceptable behavior and policy.

- ☐ We keep phone cameras and other cameras away from children unless it's part of an official church presentation or production.

- ☐ We don't snap photos and post them on social media no matter how cute or adorable the children are.

- ☐ We don't tag kids in photos without the express consent of their parent/guardian.

- ☐ We get a signed parental release for children's photos, images, or videos before we post or publish them.

- ☐ We provide notice to parents about how personal information we collect about children will be used—the purpose, the length of time, and who will have access. The primary purpose for collecting the information is safety so that the parent can be easily reached in case of emergencies.

- ☐ In the notice, we inform parents about how we secure the information and protect their children's privacy.

Tip: Make sure everyone reads the policy on handling children's personal information and children's privacy. It takes just one person to make a mistake, and it takes just one child or parent to escalate the violation and draw public and regulatory attention to the church. Vet people before they work with children or obtain children's personal information. Check your website to see if you comply. Don't ask children personal questions on your website or ask them to sign up for events without first getting parental consent and involvement. For further reading, I recommend "Children's Online Privacy Protection Rule: A Six-Step Compliance Plan for Your Business."[3] This is great content that the Federal Trade Commission (FTC) puts up. You may not be under FTC's jurisdiction, but you are under the jurisdiction of other regulators and need to know this information and how to use it.

Value: Creating these protections reduces liability to the church and promotes cost savings and trust. A COPPA violation can cost anywhere from $30,000 to $5.7 million in fines. Check children and teen privacy laws in your state. Even though your church is not a business, not nearly as large as certain companies, and not under the FTC's supervision, your state may apply similar rules to your church when it's in violation of children's privacy rights. Learn from the mistakes of TikTok, YouTube, and other businesses.

Action Steps: You've assessed what your church is doing about children's privacy. The items you did not check are your action items to work on: list them. Have you designated someone within your church to handle this responsibility? Jot down your answers.

_____

_____

_____

What's your target date to assign someone to take this responsibility/when will you begin the tasks?
Day_____ Month_____ Year_____

What's your target date to complete these tasks?
Day_____ Month_____ Year_____

Church Privacy Team

What can you teach your children's Sunday school teachers and nursery workers about privacy?

_____

_____

_____

_____

_____

What questions would you ask me?

_____

_____

_____

_____

Anything that's human is mentionable,
and anything that is mentionable can be more manageable.
(Fred Rogers)

Part Three
Church Communication and Technology

10

Cybersecurity, Website, and Applications

If you spend more on coffee than on IT security, you will be hacked. What's more, you deserve to be hacked.
(White House Cybersecurity Advisor Richard Clarke)

Cybersecurity and Data Privacy

Cybersecurity is not the same as privacy—or information security or IT. Some folks confuse them. They're all cousins, so people use the terms interchangeably, just like when I tell someone my name is Grace and they call me Joy. They're both biblical virtue names, and they're both one-syllable words. But joy and grace have different meanings. It's the same with cybersecurity and privacy.

Cybersecurity is about protecting information or exchanges of information in devices and systems that are connected to the Internet. That's any information. It's not like privacy, which protects only *personal* information. Cybersecurity protects communications, transactions, and any information that people create or share over the Internet—that's any information transmitted through a computer, electronic device, or a computer network, such as the network of computers that church employees use to carry out church work. Cybersecurity cares about confidentiality and integrity of information moving back and forth on the Internet, and in doing so, it helps protect people's private lives and dignity.

We all share personal information on the Internet. Do we? We log in to our bank accounts online, renew our driver's license online, log in to employee benefits online, pay bills online, give offerings and tithes through payment apps, check in to doctors' appointments, arrange food delivery via DoorDash, share rides through Uber or Lyft, and the list goes on. We even create profiles with banks and other websites that we do business with. This is why cybersecurity is important to protect that personal information and those transactions. Cybersecurity protects the Internet path or route to make sure the information that's being created or transmitted gets to the destination safely. It makes sure somebody else is not illegally listening to or stealing online exchanges. But one could also do some of these activities offline—on paper or via other electronic means that do not use the Internet. Where's the protection for that? Glad you asked. That's where cybersecurity ends and information security kicks in.

Cybersecurity Versus Information Security

- Cybersecurity doesn't protect printed information; information security protects information in paper and electronic forms.

- To protect paper and electronic information, information security also deals with protecting the physical buildings and computers or devices where information resides.

- Information security protects any information from unauthorized alteration and disclosure and from being made unavailable to authorized persons who need the information to do their jobs.

- Cybersecurity protects digital personal information on the Internet or in cyberspace.

Both protect *any* information, not just personal information. But what are the IT (information technology) folks doing if cybersecurity, privacy, and information security have all these responsibilities? Glad you noticed. They're not watching *Days of Our Lives* or scouting out the best deals on Amazon. They have their work cut out for them. As their name implies, they're responsible for making sure information technology is designed and works as intended, and that systems, equipment, networks, and services interconnect and are interoperable to help people exchange information and conduct different digital activities. If all of these unique disciplines work well together as they should, personal information is protected in digital form, cyberspace, and also in physical form. That said, let's look at action items.

Church Privacy Team

Assess What Your Church Is Doing about Cybersecurity

☐ Our church has a cybersecurity policy.

☐ We create roles and responsibilities for those workers who need to have access to personal information.

☐ We train people and discuss how workers can safeguard and protect confidential personal information online.

☐ We require that workers change their passwords periodically (e.g., every six months).

☐ We use encryption to protect email communication and documents.

☐ We change factory or default passwords on our computers and servers.

☐ We use antivirus, intrusion detection, intrusion prevention systems, and firewalls to protect our computer network against unauthorized activities.

☐ We secure our Wi-Fi network with the same standards as our main network to prevent hackers or malware from accessing our network.

Assess What Your Church Is Doing about Information Security

☐ Our church has an information security policy.

☐ We train people and discuss how workers can safeguard confidential and personal information online and offline.

☐ We have an acceptable-use policy so workers know which computer uses are unauthorized, illegal, or inappropriate.

☐ We update our software.

☐ We apply antivirus protection and scan for vulnerabilities.

Cybersecurity, Website, and Applications

- ☐ We encrypt information.

- ☐ We apply physical security (e.g., security guards, door and window locks, badges, and alarms).

- ☐ We monitor and correct our workers' bad behavior or poor decisions during computer use.

- ☐ We back up data to an alternate storage location so that if information and/or devices are destroyed, we can recover them.

- ☐ We have a business continuity plan.

- ☐ We have a disaster recovery plan.

- ☐ We have access control management to give workers only enough access necessary to do their jobs, not to all the information in our systems and network.

- ☐ We make sure any form of physical personal information is shredded or disposed of in a lawful manner so dumpster divers are unable to rummage through the garbage or recycle bins and steal personal information.

Tip: Use technology and physical safeguards but focus on changing people's behavior. You do that by exposing people to the rules of behavior and the acceptable use policy. Require that they sign off after they've read and understood it. Do the same for your privacy policy. Having a plan, policies, and procedures for how your church handles cybersecurity, information security, and privacy shows good information governance on the part of your church's leadership. Create a document you can call your plan, stay with that plan, and be sure to update it.

Value: Your members can hold each other accountable. The more people are aware of privacy, the more they'll notice noncompliant behaviors. Peer accountability breeds a strong privacy culture.

Action Steps: You've assessed what your church is doing about information security and cybersecurity. The boxes you didn't check are your action items: list them below. Have you designated someone in your church to handle this task? Jot down your answers.

_____
_____
_____

What's your target date to assign someone to work on these tasks/when will you begin the tasks?
Day_____ Month_____ Year_____

What's your target date to complete these tasks?
Day_____ Month_____ Year_____

What questions would you ask me?

_____
_____
_____
_____
_____

Effectiveness of Apps for Team Collaborations

Salvation is full and free. But you can't say that about free apps. You pay without realizing it. Your members' payment transactions are their personal information, as are their conversations and other interactions. Of course, you don't consider that when you sign up for and use WhatsApp, other Facebook apps, Skype, StarLeaf, Microsoft Teams, and a variety of Bible apps. You think about the conveniences. True, online apps are an effective way to communicate, collaborate, and learn. There are thousands to choose from. They're often made by brands you recognize, making these apps an attractive way to get work done. They're free, or so you think. But they invade privacy. They gather personal information about you and your members.

Research shows that 9 percent of popular apps downloaded from Google Play are linked to websites that can invade your privacy and sell your information.[1] How do you know which apps respect privacy? That can depend on where you download them from. You should download apps from app stores that are transparent about their privacy practices and give you privacy options. For example, Apple's App Store screens app developers' privacy practices. The vast majority of apps they allow in their store are privacy-friendly, but still, you must be very careful about what you share online or store in your apps and devices, especially on your phone. It's important that you keep your personal information and the information collected by your church secure. It's not only external apps you download onto devices that are of concern. Your operating system (Microsoft Windows or Apple iOS) comes with a caravan of apps from the factory. Have your IT staff uninstall the nonessential apps. Take a look at Microsoft Windows, for example—does your church really need Disney's Magic Kingdom? Candy Crush Soda Saga? Xbox? Seriously, on church computers? Let's peek at Apple iOS. Does your church device need Watch, Stocks, Find My, or Compass? Remove these apps and hide any app the manufacturers don't allow you to remove. Your phone also has several built-in apps. They're not just sitting there. They're grabbing any personal information on you that they can. You should remove the ones you don't need.

Apple tells you which built-in apps you can delete. Microsoft does the same. Use the search function on their websites to search "uninstall or remove apps." Don't be afraid of technology; control it. Privacy is about control. Make technology work to your advantage. Do the same for every new phone or computer you buy for the church. Don't assume any device you unpack from a box will be 100 percent loyal to you just because you paid for it. Technology doesn't work that way. Make it what you want it to be. You have a responsibility to protect the church and the community you serve.

Personal Identifiable Information (PII)

Don't put yourself or others at risk. The apps you use every day can put your church at risk. This means you have a responsibility to protect all personal identifiable information (PII). Different privacy regulators have their own definition for personal identifiable information or any information that identifies a person. Always remember to check the regulator's definition. For example, the Information Commissioners Office is the privacy regulator in the UK and describes PII as "information that relates to an identified or identifiable individual."[2] What identifies an individual could be as simple as a name or a number and could include other identifiers such as an IP address or a cookie identifier, just to name a few.

Although the Federal Trade Commission is not a church regulator, I like what it says to any business or organization out there about personal information: "This information often is necessary to fill orders, meet payroll, or perform other necessary business functions. However, if sensitive data falls into the wrong hands, it can lead to fraud, identity theft, or similar harms. Given the cost of a security breach—losing your customers' trust and perhaps even defending yourself against a lawsuit—safeguarding personal information is just plain good business."[3] Take the word of a regulator, privacy is a serious concern.

You're Only as Strong as Your Weakest Link

Making sure the people within your church understand what is expected of them in terms of privacy and security is one matter, but what about the external companies, vendors, and partners you work with? What are they doing to keep church information secure and assure privacy? Make sure you're aware of what the vendors and partners you work with are doing with personal information. You need to find out which tools or apps they use so you can ensure that they're mindful of the risks and are taking a secure and diligent approach. Ask as many questions as possible to evaluate their awareness and compliance before you hire them. Ask questions throughout your business relationship. Periodically check their privacy practices and look at their policies. Check if they train their employees on security and privacy best practices. Keep in mind that some of the costliest data breaches in the world were possible because hackers successfully exploited vendors' weaknesses. You should also treat apps like vendors. So double-check your vendors.

That said, grab your beverage, and let's learn how to stay secure with online apps.

Seven Simple Steps to Stay Secure on Online Apps

Most apps will ask for some type of personal information to allow you to use them. This is okay, but it's important you are mindful of what is being asked. Educating members and workers increases security and privacy overall. Follow these seven steps to be certain the apps your church is using are secure:

1. Understand your responsibility to protect your own and other individuals' personal identifiable information (PII).

2. Check the app's privacy policy, its privacy history, and what it does with your data (even its cookies policy). Has this product experienced a data breach or been involved in a security incident in the past? That'd be a red flag. Has it been investigated by regulatory agencies? For what? What was the outcome? Has it been on the news or called out by industry watchdogs such as the Electronic Frontier Foundation (EFF) on privacy violations? Don't underestimate app or product reviews online.

3. Don't use an app to share information about yourself or your church that isn't necessary.

4. Check that you have permission from the individual who owns the personal information before you share it on an app. For instance, a member may use WhatsApp but may not want their personal information sent via the app.

5. Make sure to check you're using the highest privacy settings on the app.

6. Do regular housekeeping of your data or information in the app—delete information when no longer needed.

7. Keep records of which apps you use and what you use them for so others in your church can easily track the apps being used and only use approved apps. See the simple template/form. Create or customize a similar table to fit your needs.

Manage Apps, Collaborative Software, and Services

The apps I've listed below as examples in the template are not recommended apps. There are millions of apps out there. These are just examples of apps that may be familiar to you. The point is, start organizing and evaluating the strengths of their privacy features or the absence of privacy features. You don't need privacy expertise to start evaluating the specific apps that you use. Check the apps' privacy notices and terms of use. Read privacy-related articles about these apps.

Table 5. Applications, software, and apps assessment

App Name	What We Use This For	Reviewed By	Risks Identified	Configured & Risk Reduced By	Approved for Use By	Date
Zoom	Bible studies Ministry meetings Small group fellowship Sunday school	Ed Sparks Alice Franks Tolu Abrams	(1) No encryption (2) Zoom bombing	Liz Perez	Ruth Boaz	4/5/23
Skype						
StarLeaf						
Microsoft Teams						
WhatsApp						
GroupMe						

Dropbox						
Cash App						
Google Pay						
Stripe						
Venmo						
PayPal						
Zelle						
Yammer						

Collaborative Apps and Services for Managing Church Worship Services

There are several apps you might be using right now or will be using in the future for worship services, records management, collaborations, people management, events, donations, and electronic giving, among other things. They all work and do their job similarly and uniquely. But remember, keep a list of church-approved apps using something similar to the template I've provided. Privacy is paramount. Your privacy policy or rules should stipulate that your staff only use apps that have been thoroughly researched and approved. Below, you'll find examples of different church management tools that help with the collaboration of worship services and meetings. They perform great. But you need to consider each software from a privacy perspective when deciding to buy and when using them. Having data is important when making privacy decisions. You need information to do comparison shopping. Let's look at a church management tool called Planning Center as an example, then we'll look at Servant Keeper.

Planning Center

Planning Center has flexible tools that offer a convenient and efficient way for churches of different sizes to plan worship services and event check-ins for visitors, attendees, volunteers, and members. They also work well for church meetings, workshops, and classes. Attendants can complete a check-in using a laptop, tablet, or phone. The apps also offer self-check-in where attendees can scan an entry pass or barcode from their mobile phone.

You may choose any of their tools. What's important is that you know where all that personal information (full names, home addresses, email addresses, ages, birthdates, membership profiles, and credit card transactions) goes after it's all said and done. Do you know who to ask and what to ask? Remember, I said that having information is important for privacy decisions.

Questions Your Church Should Be Asking Any Church Planning Software Manufacturer

Key questions: Where does all that personal information go? Where is it stored? How is it protected? Who is responsible: the church or manufacturer? What legal and regulatory obligations do the church and the service provider or manufacturer share? I already know the answers, but you need to know them too. Planning Center's privacy notice tells you they're not responsible for the personal data you collect from your church attendees. What does that mean? That's another way of saying that you initiated the collection of personal information; they didn't. They're just helping you process what you collect. They have some responsibilities, but the bulk of the responsibilities are on you. That means your church better have a good plan for protecting and managing the personal information you collect through their products or services. Their privacy notice says they don't sell information they collect from the church. They also share all the legitimate reasons they need to collect certain information. Their notice includes a link to their security practices, which includes how they protect credit card payment information, and what they will do if a data breach occurs on their system.

Planning Center Customer Service

Privacy is an important decision. It's always good to get in the habit of contacting a manufacturer or service provider who has a lot of personal information of your members and visitors. It was grueling trying to find a phone number on their website or to ask specific questions. When I finally did, I couldn't get a real person on the line. You're limited to their physical mailing address and filling out a form with your personal information if you want to reach them or ask questions.

Servant Keeper

Servant Keeper is another church management app. Like Planning Center, it offers customized event management, ministry communication management, accessible members directory, group management, and more. What should you do with Servant Keeper? Ask the same key questions we just went over in the Planning Center section.

Servant Keeper Customer Service

Servant Keeper is similar to Planning Center. The notice on their website provided a physical mailing address, email address, and phone number. A real person came to the phone. I mention this because customer service may be better with any provider once you sign up. But it's best to use a company that will respond to you quickly when there's a data breach. This applies to all apps. The quality of their product/service matters, and you need information to make timely management decisions. For Servant Keeper, you also need their privacy notice. For their privacy notice, scroll to the bottom of the homepage under "About Us." Are they transparent about their privacy practices? Read what they say.

Cookies

Servant Keeper's website will offer you cookies. Don't panic. Don't salivate. Whenever you see a banner about cookies on any website, that means you'll be tracked. On the bottom of Servant Keeper's web page is a little banner that says, "Cookies & Privacy Policy." That's not the privacy notice, nor does it lead to one. Rather, it's an option for you to opt out of cookies. If you click that banner, please don't click the "Accept" button. Click "Cookies Settings" and then uncheck the little square box to the right of "Non-Necessary," then click on "Save & Accept." By declining, you're opting out of unnecessary cookies that track you and collect personal information about your behavior, choices, and preferences on the website you visit. Certain cookies can track what you view/buy while visiting that site and long after you leave that website and go to other websites. Declining means they can't use information about your online activities and target you with ads. Declining nonessential cookies is a habit you want to form because you'll see cookies banners a lot online, not only on this website. After reading their privacy policy and coming up with questions, ask those questions. You can ask about cookies also. The following assessment is useful even if you already have a software similar to Planning Center or Servant Keeper.

Assess How Your Church Handles Privacy through Church Management Apps/Software

☐ We look for the privacy settings and other capabilities we can tweak.

☐ We look for app functionalities that run automatically and that can grab personal information and turn them off/disable them.

☐ We read about the product closely and search online to see what other users don't like.

☐ We find out what the media is saying about it. How are the reviews (pros and cons)?

☐ We research to find out if the manufacturer's practices are ethical. What are regulators saying about the manufacturer—both good and bad?

☐ We research to find out if there are any pending lawsuits or if there was one in the past.

☐ If we choose to use the app, we include it in our app spreadsheet so we can track updates.

☐ We document the dates of the app's updates we apply, as some security and privacy risks can be fixed when we update the software.

☐ We teach church members what we learn so they can exercise prudence when they use apps. For example, we let members know a camera is on when certain apps are on—people should be dressed, and personal conversations/other private activities should be avoided.

☐ We change or tweak settings to what makes us feel comfortable or assures us that personal data is protected. For example, the settings we check in Zoom include the following: general, audio, video, recording, and advanced features.

Cybersecurity, Website, and Applications

☐ We're aware that all apps, software, and platforms have settings that preserve privacy.

It's wise to trust, but verify and validate privacy on every app or software you use. Think like the military. Don't use any communications device or software you didn't make yourself without checking potential holes or open doors in it. Don't just accept an app because other churches are using it. Dissect it. Evaluate it for yourself.

Tip: When you find an app you are interested in, don't use it before doing some research. Your first move is to find all the open privacy doors and close them. The best approach I recommend to small churches is that they leverage their youth. Remember the quote in Chapter 4: "Tell me and I forget. Teach me and I remember. Involve me and I learn." Large churches can also take this approach. Think about the value of what you're teaching the youth by involving them in this task. Recruit teens and younger members to form a review board for apps so they can inform you and others about navigating privacy features on apps. To you, evaluating apps may seem daunting. I know. To the youth in your church, it's fun. So what's stopping you from giving them something fun to do, an awareness, and empowerment. Read the Terms and Conditions and the Privacy Policy of each app. Only download apps from trusted app stores that screen out apps that steal personal information. For example, instead of just searching on the Internet, go to Apple's App Store and download the app you're interested in. The App Store has been cracking down on apps that illegally take your personal information.[4] Aren't you grateful for that?

Every three months, go through your devices—laptops, desktops, tablets, and phones—and delete apps you're not using. Many device manufacturers know me for that. When I'm unsure if I got rid of all the unnecessary apps, I'll call for help so I can get rid of anything that's left.

Value: If people can apply privacy on their own electronic devices, they're more likely to apply the same care with church-related personal information. That's a win-win for your members and your church.

Action Steps: You've assessed what your church is doing about collaborative and management apps. The items you did not check are your action items to work on: list them. Have you designated someone within your church to handle this responsibility? Jot down your answers.

_____
_____
_____

What's your target date to assign someone to take this responsibility/when will you begin the tasks?
Day_____ Month_____ Year_____

What's your target date to complete these tasks?
Day_____ Month_____ Year_____

    Go through your phone and electronic devices right now. Research online and record how many of the apps on your devices have privacy-related risks. Identify and write the risks you discover. Communicate this to others in your church.

What questions would you ask me?

_____
_____
_____
_____
_____

Bible Apps

Since I am always on the go, having a handy digital Bible means I don't have to carry my five-pound student study Bible from New York City to Seattle and Iceland to Brussels. It's a blessing. (By the way, what are you reading in the Bible today?) To be honest, sometimes I like to touch and feel my Bible no matter what apps or sites are out there. Besides, I'm an enthusiastic notetaker. Ever since I discovered it wasn't a sin to write in my Bible, the pages of my Bible have experienced a lot of my handiwork. Red ink. Highlighters. Pegs. Rubber bands.

Whenever someone gives me a fresh new Bible (like a church in Denmark did as a welcome gift), I rejoice. A Bible is an essential item on my travel packing list. But it's hard to pack a Bible when I'm trying to travel light or avoid extra luggage fees. Bible websites are a gift from heaven. As a privacy geek, I start each use with prayers for protection. I besiege heaven for privacy grace. You can't see it, but some Bible website providers are scraping your personal information and allowing others to pay to watch your every move and serve you ads. They're hoping you will spend money while you're trying to consume the Word of God.

How does "keep your lives free from the love of money and be content with what you have" (Hebrews 13:5) sound when you're reading the Bible online, and in the corner of the web page, your eye catches a pair of comfortable Crocs you've been hoping to get? What if the ad shows up miraculously on your screen with an invite to get 30 percent off? Should you pull out your credit card and snag up the sale or focus on studying your Bible? That's the Bible Gateway site for me. Temptation awaits every day. No privacy. I did my research and fled to Bible Hub. No ads. Or so I thought, for a while. Until one day a Godiva chocolate ad popped up at the very bottom of a chapter I was reading. I couldn't make the connection. But I was certain it had to do with being tracked and targeted because of previous online searches and websites I'd visited. I couldn't read the last verse without scrolling past assorted dark and milk chocolate.

Many Bible apps don't belong to churches, nor are they wholly controlled or owned by faith organizations. Ponder that. There weren't ads when I first started using certain Bible websites. Now I can't control the ads. My privacy is important when I'm reading the Word of God. If I want the level of shopping distraction these sites offer, I might as well drive to Macy's, Bloomingdale's, Neiman Marcus, H&M, or Home Depot and study the Bible there while taking advantage of deals. Even better, I might dash into Walmart where I can actually watch the prices drop as I read and put on a happy face. But that's not the experience I crave. I really don't want to shop and study the Bible at the same time.

Once, I was enjoying an article about the Pharisees who tried every trick question they could come up with as a setup to get Jesus arrested. They tried every controversial topic imaginable. I read the part where Jesus answered their question about divorce. He said, "But it was not this way from the beginning. I tell you that anyone who divorces his wife, except for sexual immorality, and marries another woman commits adultery" (Matthew 19:8–9).

I decided to look up this Scripture online. I tried Bible Gateway. But anytime I went to Bible Gateway, a collage of the nation's top three divorce attorneys would pop up. Do you see any connection there? This was not a harmless annoyance. I was tracked. Fine. You won't lose sleep over a collage of the nation's top divorce lawyers following you all over the Internet. But what if the cookies were used to profile you and adjust prices of products when you visited an online store so you ended up paying more than other shoppers for the same merchandise? What if cookies picked up on your medical and financial information, and as a result, when you shopped for insurance or credit, you were denied? Would you find cookies invasive then? Ads created from the data gathered by cookies target people based on their online activities. They pick up any personal information that their tracker can glean from the websites you visit. Also, the content or topics you search for online can be tracked. Who knows what else they take.

The gospel is free, but some organizations that serve you Scriptures online will not dish out the gospel for free. You've got to pay with your personal data, by being tracked and followed with ads. Keep that in mind the next time you read the Bible online! That said, let's get moving. We'll assess how your church handles the Bible apps available on the market.

Assess Free Bible Apps Your Church Uses

The point of this assessment is not for you to use the specific app$ here. They're examples of free Bible apps. If you use these apps, add them to your list of apps and examine them for privacy. The goal is to create a list or spreadsheet. Which apps do you use? Again, to preserve privacy, it's best to download Bible apps from reputable app stores—for example, Apple's App Store. Apple provides their shoppers with very useful information about the privacy practices of the developer of each app in their store. As the user, you have this pertinent information on hand before you download any app. With these apps, you also have privacy preferences. For example, you can opt out of the app's tracking functionality. Don't let apps track the activities of your phone or device. Make members aware.

Our church uses these free Bible apps:

☐ The Bible App (formerly known as YouVersion Bible App) (www.bible.com or www.youversion.com)

☐ Bible App for Kids (YouVersion) (www.bibleappforkids.com)

☐ Bible by Olive Tree (www.olivetree.com)

☐ Bible.is (www.bible.is)

☐ Fast Bible app available in app stores

☐ Blue Letter Bible (www.blueletterbible.org)

☐ SermonAudio (www.sermonaudio.com)

☐ Other_____

☐ Other _____

☐ Other _____

Assess Free Bible Websites Your Church Uses

Again, the goal of this assessment is for you to make a list of what you use and evaluate the websites. The lists are not prescriptions or endorsements, just examples.

☐ Bible Hub (www.biblehub.com)

☐ Bible Gateway (www.biblegateway.com)

Church Privacy Team

- ☐ King James Bible Online (www.kingjamesbibleonline.org)
- ☐ The Kings Bible (www.thekingsbible.com)
- ☐ Other_____
- ☐ Other _____
- ☐ Other _____

Assess Paid Apps Your Church Uses

The point of this assessment is not for you to use the specific apps here. They're examples of paid Bible apps. If you use these apps, add them to your list and examine them for privacy.

- ☐ NeuBible (www.neubible.co)
- ☐ Jesus Calling Devotional (www.jesuscalling.com)
- ☐ Fighter Verses (www.fighterverses.com)
- ☐ Other_____
- ☐ Other _____
- ☐ Other _____

Assess Your Church's Ongoing App Privacy Practices

- ☐ We research Bible app options.
- ☐ We note which are free and which require payment, and we compare privacy benefits by examining privacy settings/choices.
- ☐ We check to see if each app's website has cookies (which could grab personal information and track users across the Internet especially on their desktop or laptop).

Cybersecurity, Website, and Applications

☐ We don't use an app until we know what type of cookies it has or if we can turn off unnecessary cookies.

☐ We check if an app manufacturer's or developer's reputation is low or if they've had issues with regulators—past or present.

☐ We examine the privacy issues manufacturers or developers are being hammered for violating.

☐ We create an inventory of apps and rank them by usefulness and privacy effectiveness.

Tip: Invite some members to give feedback on or share personal experiences with the Bible apps they've used. Find out which privacy issues they have identified and which apps they prefer and why. I love this exercise. I'm always sharing, and people are always reaching out. I learn a lot from others too. Good word of mouth is beneficial regardless of the size of your church. Frequently, if an app costs a little money, chances are it's better secured to protect your privacy than free apps. I personally prefer to pay for apps when I have the choice.

Value: Members will feel included in creating a privacy-sound app resource list that will benefit all app users in your church. It helps create privacy awareness in a way that's personal to members. At the same time, this exercise organically fosters a vital church privacy culture. Educating your members shouldn't just be during a church service or meeting. Actions speak louder and can save money. Your church's privacy statement or policy alone cannot accomplish this. Getting practical and actionable with privacy activities and resources speaks volumes on the church's privacy stance as a whole.

Action Steps: You've assessed what your church is doing about Bible apps. The items you did not check are your action items to work on: list them. Have you designated someone within your church to handle this responsibility? Jot down your answers.

_____

_____

_____

Church Privacy Team

What's your target date to assign someone to take this responsibility/when will you begin the tasks?
Day_____ Month_____ Year_____

What's your target date to complete these tasks?
Day_____ Month_____ Year_____

What Bible apps will you now discontinue using and why?

_____
_____
_____
_____
_____

What questions would you ask me?

_____
_____
_____
_____
_____

Amateurs hack systems; professionals hack people.
(Bruce Schneier)

Church Email, Social Media, and Cameras

Passwords are like underwear: you don't let people see it, you should change it very often, and you shouldn't share it with strangers.
(Chris Pirillo)

Church Email

Data criminals can sneak into one email, land on a computer, and then pull personal information or files from the entire network of computers. That's easy—considering they just need one of your workers to open a malicious email, click on a link, open an attachment, or download a malicious software. The results can be devastating.

Through email, church computers can be infected with viruses or worse. All connected devices can black out and go down. The network can become incapacitated to the extent that normal church business activities are interrupted. Personal information of members and visitors can be stolen, and there is no telling what the thieves will do with it. Obviously, that devil would use stolen information to carry out his agenda to steal, kill, and destroy lives (John 10:10).

According to the 2017 Verizon Data Breach Investigation Report, 66 percent of malicious software linked to data breaches made their way into the system through email attachments.[1] Who receives emails and opens email attachments for your church? Employees, contract workers, and volunteers, among others. This human mistake of opening email attachments from untrusted sources opens doors for hackers to move in and attack church computers and networks. You may not see the threat with your physical eyes, but when you open a malicious attachment, it installs a multitude of mischievous software onto your computer. The virus could spread to other computers and systems that interact with a single computer. The spread is called an *infection*.

Don't just depend on common sense. Your staff needs help and reminders. Damages resulting from email mistakes cost millions of dollars to address. This is where good awareness and training come in. Church workers need to know how to spot malicious emails. Criminals target certain types of workers. For example, whaling attacks target the big fish such as the pastor/minister, bishop, treasurer, or financial officer—people with authority or those who have approval authority over church funds. Others target the medium and small fish depending on the goal of the attacker. Leadership, support staff, and contract workers all need email privacy training and reminders so they'll pay close attention to their email activities and use good judgment.

Since employees' and workers' errors are common causes of data breaches, regulators have a history of penalizing organizations for not properly training their workers. It'd be best if you could demonstrate you've done your due diligence. What better way to show accountability than starting with your specific email practices and training. It's cheaper than paying the penalties for a data breach. I'll talk about the costs in the next chapter.

That said, grab your drink and let's work on a few email privacy items.

Assess Your Church's Email Privacy Practices

☐ We don't open emails if we're unsure of the sender.

☐ We don't leave our free personal email account (Yahoo, Gmail, Hotmail, or Verizon.net) open all day on church computers.

☐ We don't open attachments from unknown or unsolicited senders. Viruses may be embedded in the attachments.

Church Email, Social Media, and Cameras

- ☐ If a known sender's email address looks strange, we call and confirm before opening their email. Chances are it is spam and viruses may be embedded in the email.

- ☐ Everyone knows the procedures to follow with a suspicious email.

- ☐ We log out of email accounts when we're not using them.

- ☐ We're careful with sites we visit on church devices.

- ☐ We're aware and stay aware of the consequences of not taking the above actions and more.

Assess Preventive Safeguards Your Church Uses

- ☐ Our church has blocked high-risk or dangerous websites and requires that people not visit certain sites because of the capability of those sites to glean information or transmit malicious software onto our church computers.

- ☐ We use virtual private network (VPN) technology to secure Internet connections and communications when working remotely.

- ☐ We have an antivirus program installed and updated as necessary on all church devices.

- ☐ We apply updates as soon as they are available from the manufacturers of our licensed products. For example, we ensure that operating systems and applications for Windows and Mac devices are current.

- ☐ We block the ability of people to download unapproved software or apps on our computers.

- ☐ Our computer network is scanned periodically based on defined intervals.

Assess Your Church's Training and Awareness

- ☐ We create awareness on how personal information could be stolen from our networks and computers. We offer preventive measures.

Church Privacy Team

☐ We train individuals on the warning signs to look for and how to report suspicious activities and potential problems.

☐ We periodically hold training specific to email security and privacy.

Tip: Email privacy and cyber hygiene training/awareness are must-haves. If your privacy expert offers training, snatch it every quarter. This will keep your people on their toes. They'll learn about many red flags to look out for when communicating via email. Another way to keep people aware is by using posters about information privacy. Place the posters in fellowship halls, office spaces, kitchens, and other general areas where members hang out in the church building.

Value: Everyone will remain observant and alert about minimizing privacy risks. Privacy violations and data breaches discovered by members will be reported to leadership in a timely manner and addressed expeditiously to minimize risks.

Action Steps: You've assessed what your church is doing about email privacy, online safeguards, and training/awareness. The items you did not check are your action items to work on: list them. Have you designated someone within your church to handle this responsibility? Jot down your answers.

_____

_____

_____

What's your target date to assign someone to take this responsibility/when will you begin the tasks?
Day_____ Month_____ Year_____

What's your target date to complete these tasks?
Day_____ Month_____ Year_____

What questions would you ask me?

_____

_____

_____

_____

_____

Social Media

At the end of the day, social media is really about personal information. It identifies a person and is linkable to an identifiable person. So much data is linkable to a person even if they don't intend it to be so. Privacy is about choices. Don't force members to engage with the church via a particular social media platform. Don't use social media as the only way they can participate in services, ministry, or receive pertinent information. Diversify your communication mediums.

Facebook, YouTube, WhatsApp, Google, Twitter, and Other Social Media

Churches are evolving and increasing their reach. Most have expanded beyond domestic to international territories to share the gospel via more technology. For example, social media has allowed churches to enlarge their communities and raise funds with minimal financial costs. So how can this be a disadvantage? Well, ignorance of how technological tools function increases privacy risks. Protecting privacy is a legal, regulatory, and moral obligation. Social media platforms have had frequent brushes with the law because regulators understand that while their services are free and convenient, the privacy of their users can easily be jeopardized, and this is a critical concern.

Regulators in the US, as well as those globally, penalize social media and tech firms for privacy violation instances such as the following:

- not giving an accurate privacy notice on what personal information they collect

- not respecting users' privacy settings or choices

- monitoring, tracking, and recording users' every move and behavior without consent

- not deleting information that should have been removed per a user's request

- selling and sharing users' personal information to data brokers without consent

- not properly training their staff to avoid mistakes that could put privacy at risk

- engaging in illegal marketing—targeting users without consent and children without parental consent

You may be thinking that these corporations (Google, Facebook, Twitter, and other technology firms) are arguably larger than most churches. Correct. They're gigantic. And one can see how easy it would be to violate privacy principles. However, you should pay attention to their errors more diligently. Proverbs 22:3 says, "The prudent see danger and take refuge, but the simple keep going and pay the penalty." These corporations bring to light errors that you should learn from and prevent. Although unintended, their experiences with the law allow you to see how regulators handle privacy violations and the privacy principles they take into account. I identify tech firms so you know that every business makes privacy mistakes, which can serve as learning opportunities for other organizations. Now your church is equipped with this book to avoid their costly mistakes. The law gives the consumer privacy rights and wants to make sure your business, together with these tech platforms, preserves your members' privacy and ensures it's not violated. I highlight four social media apps or platforms below as examples. So grab a snack and let's look at action items your church may need to work on.

What Is Your Church Doing with Facebook?

Facebook is a social media platform where people go and connect with friends, look for past acquaintances, converge with strangers who share similar interests, and connect with people they know in their community. The whole idea is to network. For some churches, this is a perfect place to regroup. Facebook also owns WhatsApp and Instagram, and the parent company of Facebook is Meta.

☐ Our church has a Facebook page.

We use Facebook for the following:

☐ ministry events

☐ prayer

☐ studying

☐ sharing information

☐ other _____

☐ Our church encourages people to engage in our Facebook community.

☐ We've assessed the privacy risks of using Facebook.

☐ We've identified the privacy precautions people should take (and parents should take).

☐ We've created a list of privacy precautions people should take before they create an account or engage on Facebook.

☐ We place this list on any correspondence we send to our church community and mention it during verbal announcements related to our Facebook community.

☐ We are aware that on July 24, 2019, the Federal Trade Commission announced that Facebook would pay the largest civil penalty by any organization anywhere ever in a privacy case (a $5 billion settlement), that it is the largest civil penalty the FTC has ever imposed on a company, and that it's one of the largest penalties the US government has settled in any kind of violation.[2]

☐ We're aware that in 2018, Facebook was fined $11.3 million by the Italian regulatory authorities for misleading consumers about how it uses personal information.[3] And in 2021 WhatsApp was fined $3 million over data sharing.[4]

☐ We follow privacy violation news so we can better use caution with tech platforms and inform our church community to do the same.

☐ We understand that Facebook is a business for profit; we're in this for the people we're called to serve and protect. We are responsible for informing our members.

What Is Your Church Doing with YouTube?

YouTube is a video-sharing platform. You can upload just about any video to YouTube to share with the world. YouTube can also stream live events as they unfold, which makes it perfect for church services and events. People in mini, mega, and gigachurches can watch YouTube videos and live stream from any location in the world. Streaming services are perfect for evangelism and outreach and are just outright convenient. You can invite anyone to your church. It doesn't matter where they live. Just send a link, and they're there, especially people who are really shy about being around church crowds. It works. Just so you know, Google owns YouTube.

☐ Our church has a YouTube account or channel.

☐ Our church holds a YouTube Creator Award—for subscription popularity.

We use YouTube for the following:

☐ ministry events

☐ prayer

☐ studying

☐ sharing information

☐ other _____

- ☐ Our church encourages people to engage in our YouTube community.

- ☐ We've assessed the privacy risks of using YouTube.

- ☐ We've identified the privacy precautions people should take.

- ☐ We've created a list of privacy precautions people should take before they create an account or engage.

- ☐ We place this list on any correspondence we send to our church community or mention it during verbal announcements related to our YouTube community.

- ☐ We are aware that on September 4, 2019, the FTC announced that Google and its subsidiary YouTube would pay a record $170 million to settle FTC and the New York Attorney General's allegations that the YouTube video-sharing service illegally collected personal information from children without their parents' consent.[5]

- ☐ We're aware that regulatory authorities came down hard on YouTube because the collection was illegal. YouTube did not get parental consent or permission to collect information on children. The company made millions of dollars off of children. YouTube violated COPPA. This law protects anyone under the age of thirteen from being targeted, monitored, and served ads—some of which are not age appropriate.

- ☐ We're aware it was the FTC's largest fine on any company for violation of the COPPA rule.

- ☐ We follow privacy violation news so we can better caution members about tech platforms and inform our church community to do the same.

- ☐ We understand that YouTube is a business for profit; we're in this for the people we're called to serve and protect. We are responsible for informing our members and employees about privacy.

Church Privacy Team

What Is Your Church Doing with Twitter?

Twitter is a social media platform that allows you to share short messages with a predefined number of characters, images, and videos. Those messages are called tweets. Your followers can engage with the content you share by reacting with symbols (emojis), by posting replies, or by retweeting/resharing the content with their own followers. Elon Musk owns Twitter. He is the founder and CEO of Tesla.

☐ Our church has a Twitter account.

We use Twitter for the following:

☐ ministry events

☐ prayer

☐ sharing information

☐ other _____

☐ Our church encourages people to engage in our Twitter community.

☐ We've assessed the privacy risks of using Twitter.

☐ We've identified the privacy precautions people should take.

☐ We've created a list of privacy precautions people should take before they create an account or engage.

☐ We place this list on any correspondence we send to our church community or mention it during verbal announcements related to our Twitter community.

☐ We are aware that on December 15, 2020, Irish data protection authority slapped Twitter with a fine of 450,000 euros (roughly $547,000) for not reporting a data breach in a timely manner and that the breach exposed almost 90,000 EU users' private messages to the public.[6]

☐ We're aware that around August 4, 2020, Twitter disclosed that it may be facing a fine from US authorities in the estimated amount of $150 to $250 million for using phone numbers and emails to target users with ads.[7]

☐ We follow privacy violation news so we can better use caution with tech platforms and inform our church community to do the same.

☐ We understand that Twitter is in business for profit; we're in this for the people we're called to serve and protect. We are responsible for informing our members and employees.

What Is Your Church Doing with TikTok?

TikTok is a social media app. It's unique from other apps I've discussed here because it allows users to create short videos roughly fifteen to sixty seconds in length, which are quick and perfect for sharing and engaging with people on any social media platform. You can get creative with the video and add music, graphics, and text right on the app. The possibilities are endless. TikTok is owned by ByteDance, a company in Beijing, China.

☐ Our church uses TikTok.

We use TikTok for the following:

☐ ministry events

☐ prayer

☐ sharing information

☐ teen/youth activities

☐ other _____

Church Privacy Team

- ☐ Our church encourages people to engage with TikTok.

- ☐ We've assessed the privacy risks of using TikTok.

- ☐ We've identified the privacy precautions people should take.

- ☐ We've created a list of privacy precautions people should take before they create an account or engage.

- ☐ We place this list on any correspondence we send to our church community or mention it during verbal announcements related to our TikTok use both personally and for church activities.

- ☐ We are aware that TikTok is run by owners based in China and some personal data gathered or generated from US users is stored in China. US officials did not have a clear answer from TikTok regarding cross border transfers of US users' data until mid-2023.

- ☐ We're aware that a number of regulators are concerned about the data collection activities of TikTok.

- ☐ We're aware that the US once considered banning TikTok because of privacy concerns that TikTok might be a surveillance tool for China.[8]

- ☐ We're aware that in 2019, the FTC slapped TikTok with the highest civil penalty in the amount of $5.7 million for violating children's privacy.[9]

Tip: Review why regulators fine these social media platforms and pay attention to the apps and services they offer. There are articles all over the Internet. You'll discover what regulators are also expecting from you as an organization. What these corporations are fined or penalized for indicates practices your church might be held legally responsible for. Keep on top of new developments. Some churches push WhatsApp use on members and visitors and have no idea about the latest privacy concerns with the popular app. In January 2021, WhatsApp's latest controversial privacy policy and terms of use forced users to share a significant amount of personal data with Facebook against their will.[10] Search online to find out the latest privacy breach news on any platforms or apps you use. In small churches, delegate this research role to a student or two. This step costs nothing but a few minutes of your time.

Value: Take the responsibility of finding out about risks and warning members about privacy invasions and abuses and deceptive and unfair practices.

Action Steps: You've assessed your church's awareness about social media and popular apps. Items you didn't check are your action items going forward: list them below. Have you designated someone within the church to handle privacy on social media? Jot down your answers.

_____
_____
_____

What's your target date to assign someone to take this responsibility/when will you begin the tasks?
Day_____ Month_____ Year_____

What's your target date to complete these tasks?
Day_____ Month_____ Year_____

What questions would you ask me?

_____
_____
_____
_____
_____

Cameras

The first time I experienced a camera in my church was in 2013. I hated it with a passion. I understood that the church intended to extend its reach so more people could have an opportunity to hear the gospel. But I still hated it. I especially don't like cameras in church while I'm immersed in worshiping and praising. I always find a seat behind or far away from the cameras.

Like many people, church is my escape. It is my spiritual spa. I can express myself in this organic space of worship without stopping to think of who is around me or watching me. Worship is personal. During worship, many supernatural things happen inside and outside of you. You are being transformed as you switch from the physical to the spiritual terrain and back in total surrender. It feels more peaceful when you're not being watched. That's where privacy comes in. When I'm plugged in to worship, being watched by others is tough for me. Worship is not a performance. I never want it to be. Cameras sometimes disrupt the flow and authenticity of the sacred moment. While I survive, it still feels unnatural. There are certain times I don't mind the cameras as much, such as when I'm immersed in an Easter production, because every moment is so spiritually engaging that I forget the cameras are there. Everyone is different on how they adapt. Should churches get rid of cameras? It depends on how and when they're used. Let's unpack a few scenarios.

Sunday Service

Sunday services are one of the key church events where cameras are used. For many churches, especially mega and gigachurches, cameras are the norm, as services need to be broadcast to satellite campuses in different parts of town or other regions. I've attended services at such campuses. There are benefits, such as making in-person services available to more people and cutting fuel costs and vehicle emissions. But you do need to be considerate if someone wants to avoid cameras. Don't make the person feel bad. Let them choose.

Cameras are not limited to large churches, however. Even churches of less than twenty members are streaming their services to the world. Years ago, recorded worship services did not show many close-ups of the audience. The main focus of the camera was on the preacher. That style has changed now—and has its benefits and drawbacks. Yet the human need for privacy remains.

Church Email, Social Media, and Cameras

Meetings and Bible Studies

I've been invited to many Bible studies and church meetings that were broadcast live. Sometimes I've held back on my participation or didn't ask certain questions because I felt inhibited by the presence of the cameras. I found I'm not the only one who feels this way.

Although I'm uncomfortable with cameras, I admit that from the perspective of an auditor, videos of church business meetings are more credible than written meeting minutes alone.

Honoring Choices

Generally, people who do not wish to be on camera will identify the cameras in the sanctuary and choose to sit out of view. But not every member or visitor knows they have that choice, so it's best to inform everyone. Utilizing ushers to meet people's privacy needs can be helpful. They can assist camera-shy attendees with finding a seat out of view as well as help those who desire to be seen on camera. Yes, those people exist. It's all right—it's a choice. And it may be about timing. Being on camera may be peaceful for someone one Sunday and not on another Sunday. The church's duty is to accommodate people the best way it can. Mercy is a requirement (Matthew 9:13).

And then there is this possible scenario: someone may walk into the sanctuary and disturb the peace of the service or violate members' religious privacy and freedom because the perpetrator knows the cameras are there. For instance, they may behave wildly or violently on camera with the intention of going viral. In this instance, you will have to take appropriate action, such as calling the police.

Expecting the Unexpected

Anything can happen in the sanctuary at any time. In some churches, most of the events (such as baptisms and dedications) are predictable, but in other churches, spontaneous and unpredictable events can occur such as healings, prophesies, and prayers. The Holy Spirit hasn't updated his privacy policy on this. Somehow the Word of God (whether spoken, read, or sung) is active and powerful and does unscheduled and unsearchable things on camera. How do you protect privacy then? Keep cameras at a reasonable distance. Focusing the lens on every facial and emotional expression and related detail is not important. If someone falls prostrate at the altar, the priority should be to make sure their unguarded state is covered. I once witnessed a woman who was so overwhelmed with gratitude while testifying that she was cancer free for the fifth time that she laughed, wept, ran around the pulpit, and eventually dropped to the floor in total surrender. The camera immediately turned from her to focus on the reaction of the whole church cheering and fighting back tears. I cried like a baby. That was privacy and transparency at play in that scenario. Her transparency emboldened all of us, but those watching on camera didn't need to see her skirt lifted out of place and her thighs exposed.

Sometimes culture plays a huge role in how we handle unexpected situations in church. But when it's all said and done, privacy is an individual's need regardless of culture. And it's not just your church staff that should take precautions but your members also.

The Intimacy of the Moments

Intimacy is one reason why people go to church. In the middle of a song, someone may walk to the altar and decide to receive salvation or rededicate their life to God. On other occasions, they may wait and respond after the sermon is preached or the gospel invitation to accept Christ is extended. As an altar volunteer, a church worker who assists people when they make this move, I've heard people confess, "I was resisting going to the altar at first, but somehow I found myself beginning to walk toward it." They felt the intimacy of the moment and were drawn by the Holy Spirit to step up. Making sure people feel safe to do as they're led by God's Spirit is key—that's why we must guard their privacy and handle them with respect.

Healing and deliverance happen that way too. In some churches, healing scenes are similar to the healings described in the book of Acts. Even in modern times, people are healed on the spot, and they're on camera testifying the next minute. It's similar to the epileptic boy and others Jesus healed publicly (Matthew 17:14–21). That power to slay evil can even begin to work when we're worshiping and praising God in songs or prayer. Remember when singing broke chains in prison in Acts 16:25–26? (It would have been nice if that were video recorded. But, of course, there were no cameras then.) How and when God chooses to heal isn't up to us; we can't put restrictions on God. We just need to be sure not to ignore people's privacy and dignity.

Should You Turn Off the Cameras?

People whose hearts are convicted to come down to the altar do so for prayer needs, to rededicate their lives to Jesus, to restore their fellowship with God, and more. Should cameras be turned off for the invitation? Some people don't like cameras. I've heard some clergy give congregants the option of coming forward after the official invitation when cameras are off if the person is more comfortable doing so. This gives individuals the option to escape the spotlight. Some may argue you need to respond to an invitation publicly in front of witnesses. Joseph of Arimathea accepted Jesus' invitation in private (John 19:38). There may have been witnesses but only those who mattered. I know Joseph would not have liked church cameras. Neither would Nicodemus, who secretly visited Jesus (John 3:1–21). In this story, we don't see Jesus asking him to come back in the daytime for a bigger audience or more witnesses. My observation begs the question How many witnesses do you need? One? Two or three? We don't know. But certainly not the entire universe. Whatever you do, the bottom line is that you offer a notice and choice that will help someone to comfortably respond to the gospel rather than not respond at all.

Privacy-Sensitive Servers

Members who are trained to encourage others and share the gospel almost at the speed of a race car mechanic are called altar counselors or sanctuary volunteers. In my case, as I mentioned earlier, I'd go to the front of the sanctuary to help people who came forward. Cameras are unavoidable when you're involved in supporting others during church services. Outside of a general church service, I've seen a maid of honor pass out during a wedding ceremony, a pregnant woman faint, a guest at another church event experience a violent stroke, and a choir member black out while cameras were on. The good news is, these events weren't on the same day; plus, the people mentioned here were all okay in the end. I've relished observing the selfless, privacy-preserving actions of many photographers, videographers, and sanctuary volunteers who denied the in-person and online audiences the pleasure of seeing someone's personal mishap on camera. We need more of these types of privacy-sensitive church servants.

Hold my hot cocoa for a second. Let's assess what your church needs to work on.

Church Privacy Team

Camera Responsibilities

The church has the obligation to use cameras responsibly and strategically. If an embarrassing situation happens, it's kind to avoid pointing that out for everyone who's streaming the service or event to see. A church worker once confided in me about why she discouraged cameras recording all the pews in her church. "People work nights: they come straight from work tired," she explained. "Sometimes they sit in a section far from the cameras." In other words, cameras shouldn't broadcast people dozing off a little. Agreed. Which is why some people find relief by worshipping from home without cameras panning over everyone.

Assess What Your Church Is Doing about Providing Privacy Awareness to Your Media Team

- ☐ Our media team has a strategy meeting about using cameras and takes into consideration the privacy impacts.

- ☐ Our media team discerns and respects certain occasions and sections of the church where people may not want to be on camera.

- ☐ Our media team is trained to discern situations where people might be hurt emotionally because they were captured in a vulnerable state on church cameras.

What Happens Publicly Stays Private

When people come down to the altar in front of the entire congregation, we counsel them privately to protect their privacy while we determine where they stand spiritually. We protect what they share. We don't document those conversations, only their spiritual decisions. Recording decisions means checking boxes that apply to their decisions; for example, they came to the altar to request prayer, they're accepting Christ, they desire baptism, they wish to join/rejoin the church, or they make other decisions. Personal contact information is also recorded on the same intake form that's kept in church records for follow-up. Reflect on how your church handles this aspect of personal information collection and handling. Now that you're privacy savvy, what can you improve?

Church Email, Social Media, and Cameras

Assess How Your Church Notifies Attendees about Privacy before They Approach the Pulpit for Help

- ☐ Our church lets attendees know how much we value their privacy during church services.

- ☐ Our church has a notice in the bulletin or service program and announcements stating that information collected or decisions made during an attendee's one-on-one with an altar counselor is not audio recorded or published.

- ☐ Our church has a notice in the bulletin or service program and announcements stating that personal confessions of sins made during an attendee's one-on-one with a counselor are not audio recorded or published.

- ☐ Our church lets attendees know that in certain circumstances where what they share about themselves or others indicates that their lives or someone else's life is in danger, our church will share some of that information with a professional who can help the individual and others involved, including children.

Private Moments

Again, consider Joseph of Arimathea, the secret follower of Jesus, and Nicodemus, among others who met with Jesus privately at night. With his divine nature, Jesus could see through people like chiffon. Jesus knew their hearts and was okay with it. He was merciful and sensitive to their needs, not chiding their faults. He never condemned the private moments or meetings. Imagine if Jesus had said, "No way, meet me at the next Sermon on the Mount or forget it!" If he did, we would not learn about Joe and Nick today. Is your church sensitive to privacy needs? Does your church accommodate members such as Joe and Nick? Privacy doesn't mean zero people around; it could mean a select group or limited set of observing eyes. That's what Joseph and Nicodemus needed, and Jesus granted and respected their need. With that said, let's assess your church's sensitivity to people's privacy needs.

Assess How Your Church Handles Spiritual Expressions and Decisions

- ☐ Our church gives attendees the choice to respond to the gospel/rededicate their lives to Christ off camera.

- ☐ Our church gives attendees the choice to request prayer off camera.

- ☐ Our church gives attendees the choice to experience baptism off camera.

- ☐ Our church gives attendees the choice to request membership with the church off camera.

Pressure

Whether you're an usher or a volunteer in another ministry role, don't pressure anyone who wants to sit in the back. Cameras may be a church trend, but not everyone is comfortable on camera. Maybe they are comfortable most of the time, but a particular morning, afternoon, or night can be different. There's a day like that for everyone. I wish that every day was an easy day, but that simply isn't the case. Privacy is about timing, the place, and who is around or observing. Your easy day or morning is not somebody else's. So it's best to respect them if it's not the right day or moment for that person.

Let's assess your sensitivity to privacy needs.

Assess How Your Church's Ushers Handle Privacy Choices

- ☐ Our ushers are instructed to be flexible with people who prefer to avoid the cameras.

- ☐ Our ushers are instructed to let people know about certain sections in the sanctuary that are within the lens range of the sanctuary cameras.

- ☐ Our ushers are instructed to let people switch to certain sections that are not covered by the cameras.

> **Tip:** Not all truths should be published. Whether you collect facts directly from someone on or off camera or via other means, it's never a good idea to repeat everything a person says if it's not relevant or needed or if consent is not given by the person. The person might be a stranger you'll never meet again, but you must respect their privacy regardless. Be flexible and understanding with visitors and members who want to avoid cameras.

Church Email, Social Media, and Cameras

Value: Good privacy practices in all situations motivate your workers, volunteers, and members to do the same. You build a culture of privacy not by what you say but by what you practice, even if the person you do it for has no idea.

Action Steps: You've assessed what your church is doing about cameras, ushers, and privacy. The items you did not check are the action items you'll work on: list them. Have you designated someone within your church to handle this responsibility? Jot down your answers.

_____

_____

_____

What's your target date to assign someone to take this responsibility/when will you begin the tasks?
Day_____ Month_____ Year_____

What's your target date to complete these tasks?
Day_____ Month_____ Year_____

Do you think all services and events need to be recorded? Give your reasons for why or why not below:

_____

_____

_____

_____

_____

Church Privacy Team

What questions would you ask me?

_____

_____

_____

_____

_____

*The way of fools seems right to them,
but the wise listen to advice.*
(Proverbs 12:15)

12

Church Bulletins, Directories, and Announcements

Complete honesty is not the same as full disclosure.
(Ron Brackin)

Church service bulletins, programs, directories, and announcements of personal matters/events are all well-intentioned, but criminals and opportunists love any information that's available and vulnerable. Churches should not publish a bulletin or directory or make announcements without giving thought to members' privacy. Ask people what works best for them and give them some choices. A choice is one of the key principles of privacy. Find out what information people want to withhold. This way, you're less likely to violate privacy and will reduce risks and liabilities as a result.

Church Bulletins

As a first-time visitor at a church, I received a Sunday service bulletin. It came with the personal information of members. I had in my very hands a list of church members who needed prayer for their situations. There is nothing inherently wrong with prayer requests. But I could tell that a number of members were sick and lived alone. Their addresses, phone numbers, and health conditions—among other items of personal information—were listed. I started to imagine all the consequences of making this information available to all who walked into the sanctuary. Someone could show up at the door of these members to attack those members, and they wouldn't be able to fight back. Someone could open an online account or profile with all their personal information. Armed with physical addresses, anyone could have these helpless members' postal mail forwarded to a PO Box in the middle of nowhere and use their identities to commit other crimes or defraud them. Certainly, if I could think about these scenarios during the sermon, anyone else could do the same and act on them. I totally lost track of the sermon that Sunday. I can't remember what the preacher talked about for forty-five minutes because I was imagining these criminal possibilities. These are not figments of my imagination. Pay attention to your local news: these crimes happen more often than you think.

The following Wednesday I met with the leadership of the church with my copy of the bulletin bearing scribbles of all the advice I had to offer about paper and digital bulletins or QR codes. At first note, everyone saw the danger. We worked it out, and a few new privacy processes were underway. Just like that! Would your church respond with such expedience and grace if I showed up and pointed out a few risky privacy infractions?

The information I saw in the bulletin was not for everyone's eyes. Personal details such as these should be limited to a particular ministry or to the church secretary. If a church member desires to visit someone on the prayer list, they should call the designated person or ministry for the details. Otherwise, those who are shut in are exposed to dangers such as robbery, identity theft, identity fraud, and even death if their personal information falls into the wrong hands. It's everyone's responsibility in the church to protect privacy. Privacy is safety.

Stating medical conditions in the Sunday bulletin should only be done after receiving the express consent of the individual. The church leadership should keep in mind that the sick person may feel obligated to share with a church or ministry leader. They may not know that they're not obligated. So make those privacy decisions available and known to everyone in your church. I've seen health conditions, full names, phone numbers, and hospital names and room numbers in church bulletins. It's unacceptable. Some churches group the sick members by their health issues (for example, surgery, cancer, mental health). This is irresponsible and inconsiderate and could put someone in serious physical danger. Creating this content is lawful if the individual gives consent. However, consent is not protection. You can protect your members if you only make this information available to verified and trusted members upon request. That's protection. Empower people to share, but protect them.

Sharing personal information with everyone who walks into the church is not okay. Here's an example of a bulletin that's unacceptable:

SUNDAY BULLETIN

PLEASE REMEMBER
- THE SICK
- THE SHUT-INS

WITH
- PRAYERS
- VISITS
- CARDS & OTHER ACT OF KINDNESS

NAMES & ADDRESSES

Mrs. Charlese M. Hann 197 Till St., Arlington, KS 66083

Mr. Roy Harlan 697 Pine Grove Ave., Apt#30, Augusta, KS 60887

Ms. Regienne-Ann Hugh Senior Home, 54 Elm St., Room G11, Burdett, KS 60123

Mrs. Harriet H. Martin Balsam Wood Terr., Arlington, KS 61789

Mr. Rufus Non 15009 Towne Center Ave., Apt#938B, Augusta, KS 61887

Ms. Ella Crawford-Gene Manor Home, 50 Mangrove Rd., Room E9, Burdett, KS 60148

Mrs. Hannah H. Forester 33 Eastern St., Arlington, KS 65987

Mr. Chris Sanders 909 18th Ave., Apt#407, Augusta, KS 60881

Ms. James J. Giles Senior Home, 54 Elm St., Room G11, Burdett, KS 67123

Mrs. Winnifred R. Goodman 111 West Gate St., De Soto, KS 60987

Mr. James Giles 339 Mazda Ave., Apt#15, Canton, KS 60718

Breast Cancer

Ms. Mercy Q. Bash Burdett Home, 51 Capitol Heights St., Room G11, Burdett, KS 60123

Mrs. Kimberly Johnson 14 Dallas St., Arlington, KS 61982

Work Injury

Mr. Mildred Pearson Cole 12 7th Ave., Apt#247, Augusta, KS 60887

Ms. Daisy A. Miles Canton Senior Home, 4 Elite St., Room 44, Canton, KS 60123

Heart Surgery

Mrs. Alexis Q. Cooper 456 Central Ave, Fort Scott, KS 60981

Mr. Nathaniel Watson 9 North Ave., Apt#300, Caney, KS 70857

Ms. Hazel L. Lucas Main Assisted-Living, 1000 K St., Room 5, Burns, KS 70123

REMEMBER THEM IN YOUR PRAYERS.

Figure 6. Sunday bulletin example

These are not real names—I changed the names and addresses but left the original format. This is a sample of a bulletin your church should *never* pass around to service attendees, whether in paper or electronic form. Not everyone needs to know this much information about the shut-ins and the sick. It may be well-intentioned, but it's unfair to state their full name, address, apartment number, hospital room number, or health condition.

Prayer Announcements

Making generic verbal announcements is okay. Church members know they can inquire privately if they need the details. However, I have found a disturbing trend. There are church members who are not enthusiastic about praying for others unless they learn or discover as much as possible about the situation. Worse, when they discover it, they spread the personal information but still forget to pray! This is unfair if the person needing prayer is unwilling or uncomfortable with sharing the details with everyone. Some people can readily speak about personal issues, while others need more time, control, and preparation. People are different. Not only do your members need prayer, but they also need the package I call PAP—prayer and privacy. Remember that when you handle their prayer needs.

Directories

The same goes for congregations that still publish church directories. These booklets should not be placed at the sanctuary entrance or foyer under any circumstances. A directory is not a handout. Visitors have no business getting a copy of the church directory. Instead, give visitors the preacher's business card with the main church phone number. If you have more than one minister, give them both business cards. If a member decides to share their phone number with a visitor, that's their decision. A visitor shouldn't be in the church for two weeks and already have the directory of all the members. Noooo!

The level of personal information people provide for the published directory should be flexible. Give people options. Offer the use of initials and last names instead of full names. Addresses should be optional too—maybe provide mailing addresses instead of residential addresses. The directory also shouldn't be on an online portal where access is not properly controlled.

The directories I've seen included the following:

- full name

- home address

- phone number (landline and mobile numbers)

- birthdate (adults' birthdays with month, day, and year included)

- anniversary (if a married couple)

- children's names and birthdays (month, day, and year included)

Church receptionists and secretaries should avoid referencing the directory when providing information to a stranger regarding other church members. Again, safety and privacy are key here.

Here's a real story. Yana moved from Ukraine to the US for college and had an awful experience with church directories:

I lived with a family in the US. They'd known my mother since I was a baby. After escaping many of the man's attempts to sexually assault me, I got admission to a school in another city several hours north and moved. What a relief. I was confused about how to tell my parents. I got settled in the next city, found a church home I liked, and was very involved in ministry.

I did not know that the man had been looking for me in churches, as he knew I was a devout churchgoer. He called several churches around the city and found one where a reverend confirmed he knew me and that I was worshipping at his church. The man asked where I lived, and the person went in the church directory and gave him my address. It was my old address. He connected with the people there. Not sure the lies he told the church, but they fell for it. They gave him information about my workplace. Nobody thought to call me about this stranger. The man called my workplace, and the receptionist transferred the call to my voicemail. He harassed the people at my workplace to find out my schedule and said he was coming to visit me. My job declined his requests and informed me.

He connected with other people in my church. He was shown where I sit on Sundays. The man came and harassed me in my church. The next time I spoke with someone who knew him, I found out this same man had called my previous school and had also talked to people I knew, asking for information about me. I was disappointed at my church, to say the least. I didn't feel safe in church. I was afraid to complain because I knew people might think I was paranoid. I stopped updating my contact information in the church directory. What if this obsessed man had had a gun? What would the church have told my parents or authorities if I had gotten hurt? I left and went to another church. At the next church, I wasn't listed in the directory, but they didn't handle privacy well there either.

Like Yana, many members' privacy is violated in this way, but nobody notices, and the person feels awkward complaining. More on this in *Church Privacy 101*.

Similarly, I had an elderly friend who lived in a gorgeous assisted-living apartment. When I visited, she confided that many elderly and sick tenants were attacked and robbed because they thought a legitimate visitor was at their door. The residents opened their doors to let the visitors in. *How did they get past the receptionist?* I wondered. You never know what the criminals told the receptionist in order to gain access to the assisted-living facility. Maybe they said they were someone from church or showed a bulletin just like the awful one I just discussed. The receptionist believed them. It was very upsetting to see my friend so frightened.

Assess How Your Church Handles Bulletins

- ☐ We have a church bulletin that's distributed during Sunday service to attendees.
- ☐ We distribute bulletins through the following mediums because we do not include personal information:
- ☐ social media
- ☐ paper at the sanctuary door
- ☐ email

Church Bulletins, Directories, and Announcements

☐ website/app

☐ online portal

☐ text

☐ other_____

☐ We do not use the following elements of personal information in our bulletin.

☐ We do use the following elements of personal information in our bulletin (check all that apply):

☐ full name

☐ mobile phone

☐ home phone

☐ address

☐ relatives

☐ email

☐ photo

☐ birthday

☐ anniversary

☐ health information (for example, condition, diagnosis, and treatments)

- ☐ We use first names.

- ☐ We use first names and last initials.

- ☐ We give notice to explain how the personal information will be used before we publish the bulletin.

- ☐ Members have the choice to decline being mentioned by full name.

- ☐ Members can choose a verbal mention.

- ☐ We are aware of the risks that can result from over-disclosure of personal information, including identity theft, physical danger, stalking, harassment, and illegal marketing.

Assess How Your Church Handles Directories

- ☐ We have a church directory.

- ☐ Our directory requires approval and an authorized account in order to access it.

- ☐ Our directory does not sit in a general area that's open to all church attendees.

- ☐ We do not use the following mediums to distribute our directory: text, social media, email, or website.

- ☐ We do not make it mandatory for members to be included in the directory or provide us with the following: physical address, children's/relatives' personal information, photo, birthdate, and anniversary.

- ☐ Our members may choose to provide full name, phone (we don't specify what type), email, and mailing address.

- ☐ We provide a privacy notice to explain how the personal information will be used and the risks of providing the information to us.

- ☐ We are aware and include in our privacy notice the types of risks that can result from the disclosure of personal information, including identity theft, physical danger, stalking, harassment, and/or illegal marketing.

Assess How Your Church Handles Announcements of Personal Matters/Events

- ☐ We deliver announcements of upcoming activities, events, fellowships, gatherings, weddings, funerals, births.

- ☐ We make personal announcements within small groups, not during general church services.

- ☐ We ask members' preferences before delivering the announcements through the following mediums: text, social media, paper, email, website, verbal, and video.

- ☐ The type of personal information we use in verbal, digital, and printed announcements depends on the member's preferences.

- ☐ We give a privacy notice to explain how the personal information will be used.

- ☐ We are aware of and include in our notice the types of risks that can result from the disclosure of personal information, including identity theft, physical danger, stalking, harassment, and/or illegal marketing.

Tip: It's always best to ask an individual or family what they prefer before listing or announcing personal information. Don't think about what the church has always done. Accept that some traditions need to go. Think about people's real needs. If you feel someone needs visitation, keep the detailed address information with a designated person/ministry so members can request the information. That way, you can vet and track who requests the details.

Value: Privacy saves lives. A choice or having a say empowers people. Privacy is not only about information that is leaked or stolen. It's also about what a person feels peaceful about sharing and how many people they feel comfortable sharing that with. You'll reap long-lasting, trusting relationships with your members if you give them peace and empower them.

Action Steps: You've assessed what your church is doing about bulletins, directories, and announcement privacy. The items you did not check are your action items to work on: list them. Have you designated someone within your church to handle this responsibility? Jot down your answers.

_____
_____
_____

What's your target date to assign someone to take this responsibility/when will you begin the tasks?
Day_____ Month_____ Year_____

What's your target date to complete these tasks?
Day_____ Month_____ Year_____

What can you personally do to protect the privacy of the elderly and vulnerable?

_____
_____
_____
_____
_____

What questions would you ask me?

_____

_____

_____

_____

_____

The wise are cautious and avoid danger;
fools plunge ahead with reckless confidence.
(Proverbs 14:16 NLT)

13

Prayer Requests, Hospitalizations, and Funerals

Church is not an organization you join; it is a family where you belong, a home where you are loved and a hospital where you find healing.
(Nicky Gumbel)

Prayer Requests

Technology opens the door for prayer requests to be done virtually. The privacy issue is that most times the technologies used by churches for these conveniences are not wholly owned, operated, and controlled by the church. Whether prayer requests are sent through your church's social media account, text messages, emails, or radio programs, privacy issues are the same. Websites such as Hillsong, Joyce Meyer, The Potter's House, Lakewood Church, and Vatican News (to name a few) have prayer request functionality. The concern is not what the ministry does with a person's personal information and experiences; it's what the third parties who run the web services do with the information. Trust me, Pope Francis doesn't track you and study your behavior, but others do.

When you look at most church websites, there is a button for prayer requests. Most influential Christian speakers do the same on their sites. Christian radio stations play a huge part in keeping people encouraged and prayed for around the clock. Some have prayer request forms online. Pretty cool! But you do not need to know all the personal details about someone to pray for them. When the answers come from heaven, you don't need to match the answers to people's names. All this is done for you.

"We do not know what we ought to pray for, but the Spirit himself intercedes for us through wordless groans. And he who searches our hearts knows the mind of the Spirit, because the Spirit intercedes for God's people in accordance with the will of God" (Romans 8:26–27).

The Spirit has people's last names too. Take it from me. You don't need someone's last name to intercede for them. That said, let's unbox prayer requests and privacy-related action items.

Assess What Your Church Is Doing to Assure Collection Limitation

Privacy protection is needed for prayer requests. Rule of thumb? Little is much. Keep it simple and short.

- ☐ We practice collection limitation and do not request additional information, because it creates more opportunities to reveal personal information.

- ☐ We provide a notice to people at the top of the form indicating that to protect privacy minimal information is okay.

- ☐ We limit the number of words that the fields in our online prayer request form can take so people don't divulge too much personal, financial, or health information.

- ☐ We provide examples of how to draft a good prayer request.

- ☐ We ask people not to divulge other people's personal information in their prayer requests, such as full names or workplaces.

Assess What Your Church Is Doing to Extend Guidance During In-Person Prayer Meetings

- ☐ We ask people who request prayer in person to keep their requests brief.

- ☐ We understand that people can be quite emotional when giving prayer requests and it's their way of letting out steam. If someone needs to say more, we ask if they'd like someone they can talk to, and we follow up.

Church Privacy Team

- ☐ We do the same for testimonies. We help and guide people so they don't say more than they need to or are comfortable with sharing.

- ☐ We put a note on our form saying that more personal information isn't necessary for prayers to be answered.

- ☐ We don't require a first and last name for anyone to request prayer vocally or in written form (via our website or by text messages).

Assess What Your Church Is Doing about Including Emails in Prayer Requests

- ☐ We do not require that visitors or members give their email address when requesting prayer through our website form, paper form, or via text message.

Assess What Your Church Is Doing to Set Prayer Categories

- ☐ We assign prayer topics to choose from such as the following: general, well-being (includes emotional, mental, and physical health), relationship, spiritual growth, education, career, business, job, finances, and parenting. Requestors can choose any of these categories without needing to expound.

Assess What Your Church Is Doing to Assure Fairness

- ☐ We understand that sharing a lot of information might help the person offload some pressure, but it doesn't help in other ways. If this information is accessed by a malicious individual, it could be used to violate the privacy of the person who shared the personal information. That violation can be in the form of unsolicited advertising, exposure of their private affairs, or the use of that information to steal identity.

- ☐ We practice fairness and understand that it's an important privacy principle. We have the requestors' privacy interest at heart and are always looking for ways to safeguard them.

Prayer Requests, Hospitalizations, and Funerals

For every prayer request you receive, the person making the request needs two things: prayer and privacy. I mentioned earlier, in Chapter 12, that you should deliver PAP (prayer and privacy). Privacy means respect. Delivering PAP is respect.

 Tip: Minimize the information you ask for on prayer request forms. For example, if your form allows a thousand characters, cut the amount down to one hundred characters or less. People don't need a paragraph to explain a prayer request. For online forms, it takes five minutes to make this type of change. If your church is not big enough to have an in-house IT department, get your web designer to adjust the forms.

 Value: You'll earn more trust when people realize you're protecting them from themselves. It's okay to earn trust brownie points.

 Action Steps: You've assessed what your church is doing about prayer requests. The boxes you didn't check are your action items moving forward: list them below. Have you designated someone to handle the privacy responsibility for prayer requests? Jot down your answers.

_____

_____

_____

What's your target date to assign someone to take this responsibility/when will you begin the tasks?
Day_____ Month_____ Year_____

What's your target date to complete these tasks?
Day_____ Month_____ Year_____

How might you pray differently for requests in order to respect privacy?

_____

_____

_____

_____

_____

What questions would you ask me?

_____

_____

_____

_____

_____

Hospitalization: Privacy Even during Sickness

Sometimes a church member must undergo a medical operation or procedure. Other times, someone becomes ill and lands in the hospital. This can be a very trying time for families and friends. Although patients tend to appreciate a little cheering up in the form of flowers, cards, and visitors, not everyone from your church should show up—not even if the preacher wants everyone to. Just imagine if all the members decided to crowd the hospital after Sunday service; it would be very uncomfortable—for the visitors, the patient, and the other patients at the hospital. Your church is obligated to encourage sensible choices when it comes to hospital visitations.

Of course, there are brethren who just want to offer support, but privacy and safety are still paramount. Patients should not have to worry about nosy strangers showing up at their bedside, especially those who have nefarious intentions. The sensitive details of the patient should be kept private from the general assembly because the church's duty is to protect its members.

Patients are not obligated to disclose their medical information even if they are under pressure to divulge it. Many of us struggle with saying the two-letter word *no*. It's hard to say it to our loving church family. But the earlier the patient lets their church know that they're in the hospital, the better.

Just because the patient restricts visitors doesn't mean you can't show the person love after they have returned home. Genuine and caring people should still be there, loving, hugging, and planting pecks on the patient's cheeks when the patient is ready to receive the love at home or when they return to church fellowship.

That said, let's take a look at what your church is currently doing.

Assess What Your Church Is Doing to Help Members Who Are Patients

- ☐ We have a policy on privacy that addresses hospital visitation and also lists privacy options for the patient.

- ☐ We encourage patients to decide about visitors as soon as they can and request that the hospital visitors' desk allow no visits except from close family if that's what the patient wishes for privacy reasons.

- ☐ We encourage patients not to respond to every text or inquiry from the outside, including from the church. It is important to us that they relax peacefully and get their treatment.

- ☐ We assign a point of contact to communicate with the patient or their family and then update the church.

Assess What Your Church Is Doing about Member and Clergy Visits to Hospitals

- ☐ We make visiting rules available to members who desire to visit another member in the hospital.

- ☐ We require that members first inquire within the church to learn the wishes of the patient.

☐ We believe visits are more meaningful when we respect the patient's wishes; after all, our goal is to preserve their dignity as part of their healing process.

☐ We provide examples of how to make requests of patients to avoid making them feel pressured. For example, saying, "I'd love to come see you, but I'd rather visit when you feel up to it," rather than saying, "Would you like for me to come visit you?"

☐ We provide information about how visitors can discern if a patient desires a visit or not, and most importantly, we are ready to honor their choice if they decline a visit.

☐ We provide information about why some patients may decline for privacy reasons.

☐ We provide information about how to engage patients in conversations that are healthy and meaningful without intruding on personal health matters.

☐ We provide information about alternatives to hospital visits that patients can enjoy and be encouraged by.

☐ We provide information about questions to avoid asking patients and the importance of preserving their privacy.

☐ We provide information about the level of details the hospital visitor should report to the church about the patient.

☐ We provide information about how to give a patient some privacy even during a visit.

☐ We provide information about the people our members should not take with them on a visit, including children.

☐ We have rules about taking photos, recording videos, or using mobile phones during hospital visits.

Prayer Requests, Hospitalizations, and Funerals

 Tip: When a person is sick, their privacy is not sick. The person's privacy deserves respect. Ask the person how they prefer personal information be handled while they're sick. Create awareness about hospital visitation by instituting a checklist that members and clergy go over before visitation. Use the above checkboxes for ideas to create your own.

 Value: Taking extra steps to care about a patient's privacy creates confidence. People will always remember how you respected them when they were hospitalized.

 Action Steps: You've assessed what you're currently doing. Does your church already have rules in place for hospital visits and safeguarding patient information? The items you did not check are your action items to work on: list them. Have you designated someone within your church to handle this responsibility? Jot down your answers.

_____

_____

_____

What's your target date to assign someone to take this responsibility/when will you communicate this to members, volunteers, and other workers?

Day_____ Month_____ Year_____

What's your target date to complete these tasks?

Day_____ Month_____ Year_____

What questions would you ask me?

_____

_____

_____

_____

Privacy and Funerals

Privacy is for a living person. A dead person is not covered by privacy laws. They can't exercise their privacy rights. But, after a person dies, their surviving family can exercise their right to privacy against unjustifiable invasion of the dead relative's privacy—for example, accessing medical records, taking photos of the dead body, or visiting the scene where the person died. A most recent example is Vanessa Bryant, the wife of NBA legend Kobe Bryant. Mrs. Bryant sued the Los Angeles Sheriff's Department for leaking the photos of her husband's and daughter's bodies and the helicopter crash site where her husband, daughter, and other passengers died.[1] I'd be upset too. How would you feel? What was the impact on Kobe Bryant's surviving relatives? Emotional distress and violation of privacy, among other things. Kobe's surviving family claimed their privacy rights.

Let's talk about funerals. If the devil goes to prayer meetings, bachelor/bachelorette parties, weddings, and birthday parties, he also pencils in funerals. (He's the grinch of anything family or unity related.) Privacy issues can arise at any event. Depending on your culture, a lot of privacy issues can be in question during a funeral. The church is often in a position as the neutral party to help keep matters under control. A funeral is already a sad occasion; it's best not to add more sadness.

Eulogies, Remarks, and Speeches

Family feuds boil over at funerals, as emotional family members of the deceased are bound to disagree on a lot of issues. It's not right for the church to be standoffish like it doesn't concern them. For some individuals, the church community is really their family, so it's best to respect the relationship the deceased had with the church, even at their funeral. Words spoken about the deceased or their family members at the funeral should be kept general to preserve the family's privacy. Have you ever heard the saying "If you don't have anything good to say, don't say anything"? Thank heavens it's not just a saying; it's Scripture. We should say "only what is helpful for building others up according to their needs" (Ephesians 4:29).

Some funerals only grant immediate family members five minutes to make a statement or speech about the deceased. Everyone else is rightfully told to sit. Other funerals allow more people to speak—family and friends combined. Help the family keep matters under control because it's tough for the family to manage the occasion. This might mean reminding individuals to respect whatever your church's rules are and stick to great memories and humorous stories that can be told in three minutes max without violating privacy or creating an awkward feeling for the family. That means no provocative or eyebrow-raising private information about the deceased and no public remarks that might require an apology. Let people who want to make a remark know that if they don't know what to say, "I love you" or "I'm praying for you and your family" is perfectly fine to say to the family. A funeral is a very intimate, reflective, and private occasion. Minimize surprises.

Funeral Photos

Taking photos and posting them online should happen only if the family wants that. Whether they've made a statement requesting privacy or not, their privacy should be respected. The church should apply the wisdom of God without the family having to ask for privacy. If a funeral is happening under the roof of your sanctuary, the process should be peaceful, respectful, and private.

Other Funeral Matters

Stop funeral attendees who try to conduct business in the foyer. That isn't the time to pass out their business card to prospective clients.

That said, let's take a look at related privacy matters beyond the funeral that your church can help members navigate.

Personal finances are just that—personal. Members should rightfully keep them private. But raising awareness about the importance of planning or creating a will is important. I've seen some elderly members appoint a member of the clergy to step in to help manage their personal affairs and estate when the person becomes unable to do so. If that's the case, the member's privacy should be respected and protected. Also, even in churches, families split over unwritten and written wills alike after the funeral of a loved one. I've seen churches serve as mediators. The lesson in these scenarios is, privacy is great, but the church could help by letting people know they should plan ahead and communicate their wishes to a trusted person or an attorney. Some churches raise awareness on funeral planning, wills, and services, among other topics. They don't assume that everyone knows how to manage the affairs of an estate. Members need to know privacy is not absolute. Transparency with the right person about certain personal wishes helps.

I remember this quote from Angie Chatman's article in *Insider*: "My mother purchased her home on the south side of Chicago for $55,000 in 1986, the equivalent of $123,000 today. When she died without a will, court fees and fines left our family with just $40,500—a loss of over $80,000 on the purchase price of her house."[2]

Unfortunate. To me this was a reminder of the role that churches could play in the private lives and decisions of their members. That is, creating a sense of urgency about planning ahead while protecting members' privacy. The benefits of a will is obvious, but sometimes people shy away from planning in order to protect their privacy. I once heard a member of the clergy carelessly disclose information from a church member's will. Members knew it was an accidental disclosure but spread the information anyway. The clergyperson was supposed to be this person's power of attorney. This incident made some people lose confidence in the leadership. Having privacy awareness and resources for members that connect them to experts would help. Privacy rules for members of the clergy and church members would help also.

Assess What Your Church Is Doing about Will and Probate Seminars, Workshops, and Classes
Privacy is peace. The church is in a great position to help members achieve peace regardless of their circumstances. That means providing knowledge that makes it easier for people to handle their private decisions in a productive and beneficial way.

- ☐ Our church holds and/or points members to workshops about funeral planning, estate planning, and last will development.

- ☐ We address why privacy is important and how transparency with the person they select to implement the will is critical when they are creating their last will.

- ☐ We address aspects of estate planning and creating a will that individuals can share with a trusted loved one or attorney to ensure their wishes are carried out upon their death.

- ☐ We inform people of the importance of probate attorneys and related experts involved in estate and will planning.

Prayer Requests, Hospitalizations, and Funerals

- ☐ We strive to help our members plan and make decisions ahead of time about power of attorney and probate matters. "A good man leaves an inheritance to his children's children" (Proverbs 13:22 ESV).

- ☐ To increase members' confidence and transparency, we inform them that attorneys who handle probate matters have strict information security and privacy requirements from the state.

- ☐ As with any church seminar or workshop where people may share personal information during a discussion, participants understand they are not obligated to share more than is necessary during group discussions regarding their estate, funeral, and last will.

Assess What Your Church Is Doing about Funerals

- ☐ Our church has a policy that addresses privacy when conducting funerals at our facility.

- ☐ We have rules of behavior to help foster a peaceful, supportive, respectful, and private atmosphere.

- ☐ We have rules of behavior about taking photos and posting funeral photos online.

- ☐ We have rules of behavior about people's remarks or what they share with the audience during funerals.

Tip: Create rules for conducting a funeral at your church facility. Start with rules that will facilitate respecting members' and families' privacy. Even if a member of the clergy has the power of attorney, or is an attorney on probate matters, it doesn't mean the entire church is privy to that person's personal business. If you don't know what to do with all the details, this is a perfect time to make onion rings to help manage personal information. How much money someone's beneficiaries are getting or how much the church is getting is not information every member needs to know. For additional insights on this topic, also read the "Funeral" chapter in *Church Privacy 101*. Keep in mind, "By wisdom a house is built, and through understanding it is established" (Proverbs 24:3).

Church Privacy Team

Value: Overall, the church will earn trust and respect. Sound church privacy practices make the church become the hospital it should be. I'm reminded of this quote by Florence Nightingale: "The very first requirement in a hospital is that it should do the sick no harm."[3]

Action Steps: What progress has your church made with privacy related to funerals, wills, and probate matters? The items you did not check are your action items to work on: list them. Have you appointed someone within your church to handle this responsibility? Jot down your answers.

_____
_____
_____

What's your target date to assign someone to take this responsibility/when will you begin these tasks?
Day_____ Month_____ Year_____

What's your target date to complete these tasks?
Day_____ Month_____ Year_____

Think of the last funeral you attended. Can you identify privacy breaches that could have been avoided?

_____
_____
_____
_____
_____

What questions would you ask me?

_____
_____
_____
_____
_____

Apply your heart to instruction
and your ears to words of knowledge.
(Proverbs 23:12)

Part Four
Privacy Violations

Data Breach Costs

Anything that is measured and watched improves.
(Bob Parsons)

Regulators will unquestionably penalize a church for a data breach that management knew was likely and did little or nothing to prevent. "An ounce of prevention is worth a pound of cure" is an old proverb that still holds true. Doing your due diligence today, such as training your workers, improving processes, and hiring the right people in advance, will pay off. In reverse, disfavor with a regulator or a legal battle will cost you much more than you would have spent preventing the breach of personal information. Data breach planning and preparedness are underrated.

Preparedness

- Preparedness means your workers, contractors, vendors, volunteers, and members know what incidents and data breaches are and how they should respond.

- Preparedness means you can anticipate and spot a breach before it happens.

- Preparedness means you can reduce the negative impact that a breach would have had on people because you have the right tools and the right experts, and your staff can respond superfast. Timing is paramount. You need to respond without undue delay. That's what privacy authorities require.

Financial Risks and Assessment

By being prepared, you avoid financial risks such as the following:

- lawsuits
- opportunity costs—the loss of other opportunities you could have pursued with your money or time
- loss of your savings
- penalties
- regulatory fines
- cost of restoring the damage caused by a breach
- cost of replacing victims' credit cards if the breach involves financial information

Now, quickly, let's assess your church for data breach planning and data breach costs.

Assess Your Church's Data Breach Planning, Documentation, Training, and Communication

- ☐ Our incident and data breach response plans are updated periodically as necessary and align with data breach trends.
- ☐ We update our response plans to align with new risks.
- ☐ Our employees, contractors/vendors, freelancers, and volunteers are trained on incident and data breach responses.
- ☐ We hold periodic meetings to engage our staff and response team members.

Church Privacy Team

Assess Your Church's Awareness about and Readiness for Breach Response Costs

- ☐ We are aware of specific questions the state authorities will require us to answer in the event of a breach, and we have tools and experts to be able to address those questions within the required timeframe.

- ☐ We have an in-house privacy team or a service-level agreement with a privacy service to help analyze the impact of a data breach on victims, such as individuals, business partners, workers, and members.

- ☐ We are aware that state authorities require organizations to report when they are aware of a breach, in some cases even if the breach has not been confirmed. We have templates specific to these requirements.

- ☐ We have an internal IT team or tools or a service agreement with IT services to monitor our computer network after a breach to report any abnormal activities.

- ☐ We have a service agreement with a breach notification service company to handle sending notices of a breach to our members, donors, and visitors via email and postal mail.

- ☐ We have a service agreement with people such as forensics experts and crisis management experts to respond to data breach emergencies, including isolating the issue, fixing the problem, collecting evidence, and providing analysis.

- ☐ We have legal counsel with competence specific to information privacy and handling data breaches.

- ☐ We have a service agreement with a call center provider to handle questions/calls from members, donors, and visitors if there is a large number of people affected by a data breach.

- ☐ We have money set aside for compliance and liabilities should the victims of the breach decide to sue. We've transferred some of the costs to our data breach/cyber liability insurance company.

☐ We have applied the requirements of each state's privacy laws applicable to us.

☐ We have a plan for how to engage the media to preserve the trust and reputation of our church.

Tip: Hiring experts at the last minute to resolve a data breach will cost you more. Start building relationships early, and get agreements in place about expectations before you need experts. If you don't know anyone, don't worry about it. For starters, now you know one privacy expert—me. Through me, you'll meet other experts pretty soon. You're already ahead of most churches. Keep in mind, experienced experts are rare but can be secured. But you don't need to search hard and far if you know at least one expert who is already supporting churches. Leverage that person to connect with other experienced experts. When it comes to managing privacy risks, the network of people you know and their unique insights matter. If an experienced expert is willing to talk, schedule a get-to-know-you chat with them. You'll be glad you did.

Value: Good privacy planning saves you money in the long run. Relationships are better created when all is calm, so you can learn at your pace. A data breach is chaotic and emotional. You can overspend or get ripped off when you're desperate for help. Since you're starting early, you'll be better off.

Action Steps: You've assessed what your church knows and is doing about planning for a breach and the costs associated with a data breach. The boxes you didn't check are action items you'll work on going forward: list them below. Have you designated someone within your church to handle the responsibility of assessing data breach costs? Jot down your answers.

_____

_____

_____

What's your target date to assign someone to take this responsibility/when will you begin the tasks?
Day_____ Month_____ Year_____

What's your target date to complete these tasks?
Day_____ Month_____ Year_____

What questions would you ask me?

_____
_____
_____
_____
_____

Intelligent people are always ready to learn.
Their ears are open for knowledge.
(Proverbs 18:15 NLT)

15

Data Breach and Cyber Liability Insurance

Better to have, and not need, than to need, and not have.
(Franz Kafka)

Cyber liability insurance and data breach liability insurance make up a new insurance niche market. Fear is sold in bulk there. Shall I explain? By new, I mean it emerged between the mid-1990s and 2000 during the wide adoption of the Internet. That era is commonly referred to as the *dot-com bubble*. Regulators were hard at work cracking down on companies with no website privacy notices, those whose privacy notices were deceptive, and those who didn't provide adequate security protection for the personal data they collected. Because of the hefty penalties and fines, most online businesses reacted with fear and trembling. They secured insurance coverage. Today more businesses and organizations, including churches, have incorporated technology into their day-to-day processes. It's safe to say that almost every church has a web presence and conducts the bulk of its business online. With more use of technology, cyber risks have increased over the past twenty years; for example, there are more business interruptions, unauthorized activities, data losses, system malfunctions, human errors, and account compromises leading to identity theft. Cybercriminals have become more sophisticated, so legal and regulatory risks of data losses have increased. Many data breach laws have been passed, and lawsuits have soared. The good news is, insurance coverage has also evolved—in scope. But despite its expansion, there's a problem. Liability and data breach insurance language still sounds foreign and tricky for most buyers. It's intimidating—figuring out what's covered, what percentage is covered, what is excluded, and the buyers' obligations.

Don't think for a minute that buying insurance will cover all your liabilities. Negligence may be covered but not all types. Some could be excluded from the coverage you purchased or are considering. There are many wolves in sheep's clothing roaming the market for buyers who are scared and unwilling to handle personal information responsibly to preserve human dignity and privacy. These types of buyers want insurance to cover them when a breach strikes so they can continue doing nothing to adequately protect the privacy of their members.

It is acceptable to rely on your insurance company to cover any risks you can't anticipate or reduce by yourself. But data breach insurance is expensive. If you don't know what you're doing, you may get taken in. There's always confusing or hidden policy language. Regardless, you need insurance. Ready to get started?

Coverage

What personal information you collect from members, visitors, and donors and how you process or handle it is very unique to your church. Your cyber insurance policy should be as unique as your church. It needs to match your unique information collection processes and activities. To have a good insurance experience, the key is to get the coverage you need and cooperate with the insurance company about their requirements, including the time periods you should notify them should data be compromised or lost. Don't hide a data breach hoping it will go away. Remember, "Whoever conceals their sins does not prosper, but the one who confesses and renounces them finds mercy" (Proverbs 28:13). Concealing will only cost you your coverage and invite regulatory penalties and fines. Implement the safeguards that the insurance requires. Understand that although the policy may cover a list of items you need, the coverage of individual items is dependent on certain defined reporting time periods the insurance policy specifies for data breaches. It also depends on the maximum amount the policy will pay—if you meet or fail to meet certain obligations or conditions. What cyber liability insurance doesn't cover also varies. The good news is, cyber liability policies are evolving; there's plenty of room for negotiation with your insurance company. In the following section, I'll share examples of what a cyber liability insurance policy does cover and examples of what a policy does not cover, subject to possible changes in the future.

What's Covered by Most Insurance Policies

1. **Business interruption:** When your computer network is completely down due to a cyberattack or human error, this could mean that your workers are unable to send or receive emails. It could also mean you're paying your workers and vendors, but they can't get their work done because their devices are damaged or infected due to an incident. Or, in some cases, attendees of a paid event are unable to process payments or access your conference. In a nutshell, a cybersecurity incident that interrupts church operations and causes financial loss is covered.

2. **Data breach:** When your church has experienced a data breach, meaning that personal information such as employee records, credit cards, account numbers, personal contact information, or medical information has been accessed, lost, stolen, copied, altered, or publicized, an insurance policy will cover breach notification costs. Breach notification is required by law. It obliges organizations, upon being aware of a data breach, to inform individuals in a timely manner that their personal information or data has been compromised and could potentially cause harm. Sometimes authorized persons/employees compromise PI as well. Other data-breach-related efforts are also covered.

3. **Reputational damage:** The community associates the name of your church with feelings of safety, confidence, and integrity. But negative publicity can damage your credibility. Lost trust can result in a decline in membership, donors, visitors, or even event attendance. It can have a negative financial impact on the church. A policy covers this.

4. **Funds transfer fraud:** Let's say a criminal poses as your church's financial decision-maker in order to complete an unauthorized financial transaction that results in wiring funds to the criminal's account. In this case, the policy covers the losses and costs related to the unauthorized transaction.

5. **Defense and settlement:** This includes the costs of individual lawsuits as well as consumer class action processes. That means that both the defense and the settlement of claims are covered.

I've discussed five examples of items that are covered by most policies. Of course, there are conditions depending on the insurance company. Other items covered by cybersecurity liability policies may include coverage for law enforcement or government investigation, efforts made to respond to foreign law enforcement or foreign government inquiries, cyber extortion, regulatory fines and penalties, forensic investigations, credit monitoring for victims, cost of replacing electronic devices and software, and data recovery.

Most insurance companies say they'll cover you if, for instance, hackers hijack your entire website or network and ask that you pay them a ransom to recover your assets. This type of attack is known as a ransomware attack. Ask the insurance company if that coverage is the full ransom or a specific percentage. Let's say they'll pay 50 percent of a $5 million ransom, that still leaves you with a hefty amount to pay out of pocket. Some insurance policies may say they'll cover that ransom and also restore your website or help you rebuild. Another coverage may include investigation after a breach has been confirmed. Depending on how the breach occurred, you may need your own computer forensics done. Forensics experts are expensive. Read the fine print in the insurance policy and ask questions.

What's Not Covered by Most Insurance Policies

1. Potential long-term financial loss due to a data breach

2. A breach that occurs as a result of your church not implementing adequate policy-required privacy or cybersecurity safeguards—the protections the insurer indicated were your responsibility

3. A data breach that happens because your church failed to implement or appropriately apply information security and privacy best practices (safeguards, policies, system updates, and employee training) to prevent, detect, or correct the breach before it got worse

4. The cost of upgrading to more secure computer devices and software

5. A data breach due to insurrection or war

Now you have an idea what insurance does and does not cover. What if you're denied insurance coverage because of negligence or exclusions such as *failure to follow*? At a minimum, you would need to prove to the insurance carrier that you weren't negligent and that you maintained the required privacy and security safeguards. How do you redeem yourself? What evidence is acceptable? You may need to show the following:

- records of computer and network systems maintenance, including updates and patches/fixes
- system logs
- use of required encryption standard
- evidence of regular computer and network scans and monitoring
- employee training and awareness
- access control management
- information security, cybersecurity, and privacy plans
- policy documents, audit reports, and risk assessments, among others

Benefits

Insurance may pick up a large tab if you're not at fault. Earlier, we looked at a number of associated costs once you confirm a breach has occurred. For example, there are costs associated with notifying the victims and offering credit monitoring depending on whether the breach could result in identity theft or more. That could cost $180 to $300 per data-breached victim. But that doesn't mean those privacy-loving church folks won't sue you (that depends on your state's law). A significant amount of money may need to go into settlements when/if you lose your case in court or you realize you don't have a strong enough defense to win. Even if you lose, your lawyers get paid. And you need a public relations person to help prevent or clear any negative publicity. You need to get the word out to the media that you're taking responsibility and ownership of the breach, that you're doing your best under the circumstances to remediate the situation, and, most importantly, that your priority is protecting the people affected. These steps will help you rebuild trust. Otherwise, you could be raking in more liabilities and loss of credibility.

Don't Count on Your Savings

No church has money just sitting around to cover a bad situation such as a major data breach. If Target, Home Depot, and other giant retailers needed insurance to relieve their financial burden after a breach, it's a sign that all organizations, including churches, need data breach insurance. As I mentioned earlier, in some cases, the insurance is not enough. It only covers a portion of the losses. Can you cough up the difference and still pay your regular unrelated church bills? Can you avoid or afford closing down ministry projects? Or asking members for emergency contributions?

Read the policy's language. Make sure you understand your end of the bargain. What your church might be responsible for out of pocket could depend on several things: the nature of the breach, if it could have been avoided, or if it happened because of negligent conduct that your insurance coverage excludes. Every breach is different. So are insurance policies. Although this next example was in the commercial realm, this is how you learn from other organizations' misfortunes. It doesn't need to happen to a church to be applicable to you.

Sony was denied data breach coverage by its insurer's general liability insurance—based on the policy language. So was IBM's contractor who lost IBM's backup tapes that contained the personal information of 500,000 IBM employees. Ouch! Data breaches don't always happen online as some believe. These tapes fell off the contractor's truck and someone grabbed them from the side of the road. IBM recovered from the contractor the $6 million it spent to protect its employees from the negative impact of the breach. But the contractor could not recover the money from their own insurance due to policy language issues.[1] It can get complicated. Your church is not IBM, IBM Community Bible Church, IBM Presbyterian, or Sony Ministries. I get that. But again, these corporate examples shed important light on liability insurance in general. Imagine your church losing $6 million. The worst part? Not being able to recover it because of a silly jargonish sentence in the insurance policy that your church didn't ask the insurer to clarify. Learn from real-world examples.

Data Breach and Cyber Liability Insurance

Insurance Denial or Delay

Find out what could cause your church to be denied coverage. Let your insurer give you a few scenarios that will bar them from cutting you a check. Compare those scenarios to the information and exercises you're getting from this book. For example, having a privacy program, proper training, policies, procedures, security safeguards, compliance, vendor accountability, and access management and applying privacy principles (such as not collecting more personal information than is necessary). Insurers are not the only ones who want to see that you did all you could and should do. Based on my experience, regulators love that too. If you show you were diligent before a breach occurred, they may show you mercy by withholding hefty fines. You may endure a stern regulatory lecture and a consent decree or court order to improve in certain areas of privacy management, but that's by far better than fines. If you can demonstrate diligence in your practices, a court may cut you some slack and rule more favorably when you get sued.

This book is a practical reminder that you shouldn't snooze or lose. All the money your church will be paying the insurer should have a good return on investment. When your church is facing a data breach, it will need all the money its coverage can provide.

Ask your insurer about breach notification or reporting timeframe requirements—how quickly you should report to the insurer upon discovering a breach. Let me explain why. Depending on the nature of the breach, every minute the breach goes unreported could increase the risk or negative impact on the victims. That means it will also increase how much the insurance company spends. If you wait too long to report a breach, you may jeopardize your church's chances of getting coverage from the insurer. Most insurance companies, including Hiscox, have denied coverage to clients who were not upfront about data breaches. This happens a lot more than you realize to both small and large organizations. You should abide by the policy requirements.

General Liability

General liability insurance is great to have. But you need more. Don't let the word *general* fool you. I visualize general liability insurance as General Tso's chicken, rich flavor combination, but it always seems to be missing an ingredient. General liability does have an assortment of coverage. When

I work one-on-one with or coach someone such as yourself, I'm often asked, "Well, Grace, if it's not enough, what is the benefit of getting general liability?" Let me name a few benefits. General liability covers instances such as bodily injury and property damage that are caused at your church's physical building or on its property because your church was negligent. It covers injuries or damage caused by your products/services (including events). It also covers personal injury, which is a different type of injury from bodily injury. In Chapter 7, I detailed types of lawsuits alleging violation of privacy—libel, slander, and false light, among others. General liability insurance covers these types of claims. However, you still need specialty coverage for cybersecurity and data breaches.

It's best to understand the requirements, conditions, and obligations of your general policy and what the insurance covers so there are no surprises when you need help. Some churches have additional coverage for specific claims under the same insurer. Buy what you need. Prevent potential future disputes between you and your insurer. Disagreements will ensue when your coverage is denied or delayed. Churches experience this type of dispute more often than you think. It might even escalate to the insurer suing a church. What should you do? Leave no room for surprises. You should know what to expect when your insurer brings up out-of-pocket expenses. You should calculate these expenses from the onset before you buy the policy.

Pay close attention to what's covered so you'll know if you can afford the estimated out-of-pocket costs. Adding on specialty coverage for privacy breaches doesn't mean it will cost you an arm and a leg. But instead of assuming that a policy is automatically included in what you're paying for, ask, "Is data breach coverage an add-on? How much does that cost?" The insurer may tell you an amount from $650 to $1,000 a year, depending on the scale of personal data and the type of data, among other factors. So how do you prepare?

Insurance Terms

I could use this entire book to define insurance terms, and it still wouldn't be enough. Ask your prospective or current insurer to give you their definition of terms such as *data breach*, *cyber liability*, *cyber insurance*, *injury*, and *loss*. Find out whether your coverage includes business interruption and loss of data. Here are some sample questions you could ask:

- If hackers hijack our website and computer systems, then demand we pay a ransom to regain access to our website and church files, will our coverage pay the ransom?

- Will the church be covered if the offender is an employee or volunteer, such as the treasurer, versus external criminals or organized criminals from other countries or foreign governments?

- Will our church have coverage if a breach is caused by a contractor/vendor (as with IBM's data breach example I shared)?

- Will physical paper files, documents, tapes, CDs, thumb drives, website content, social media, and data processed by workers on-site and those who are working remotely be covered?

You want to know what's included before you pay and get your hopes up. What keeps you up at night about a possible data breach? Ask them about those concerns. Even if you're a novice, specific questions will push your insurer to offer you the right products and services.

Cyber Liability Insurance

There are two types of cyber liability insurance, first-party and third-party coverage. It's important to understand the difference between these and what your specific coverage will include or require.

First-Party Coverage

First-party coverage helps your church properly respond in the event that it experiences a data breach on its own computers, devices, systems, or network. It helps cover the costs of data breach investigations, including forensics, administrative efforts, expert guidance, development and delivery of notification to victims, credit report monitoring for victims, and the cost of public relations to preserve your church's reputation. That's a lot. So don't be bashful; ask your insurer to explain their specific first-party coverage and their policy terminology, which can be frightfully confusing and differ from one insurance company to another.

Third-Party Coverage

Think of the third party as a person, vendor, or company that provides products, systems, or services your church uses to process or handle members', visitors', and donors' personal information. Such third-party systems or services are necessary to help your church serve the ongoing needs of its community and perform its business operations. These include email services, cloud applications, web services, website hosting services, and credit card payment applications. Examples of these vendors or providers include Microsoft (365, Outlook, and Azure), Amazon Web Services, Google (Gmail and Google Drive), Salesforce Sales Cloud, IBM Cloud, and other tech vendors. Hired event teams, freelancers, and photographers are also third parties.

Church workers, members, contractors, or visitors may sue the church because of a data breach that negatively impacted them—though caused by a third party. Your church would need to have third-party coverage to cover the costs of claims or lawsuits associated with data breaches that happened because of or by a third party. This may include money to pay attorney's fees for lawsuits and settlements and the fines a regulator may levy on your church—your church needs to recover those costs. This will also include costs incurred for a data breach that did not happen on the church's own computers, devices, systems, or network but happened on a third-party's computers, devices, systems, or network.

Calculate Coverage

How do you calculate coverage? It can be a bit tricky. The rule of how much coverage you need is different for small, medium, and large churches. It might even be different for two small churches. The complication is in the details. What personal information you handle—how, why, who it belongs to—plays a part. It boils down to cutting your coat according to the size and complexity of the personal data you hold. Remember, I explained the costs of a data breach in Chapter 14. Should you get more coverage than the other church in your neighborhood? This is where you need to do the math. Your insurer is a pro at this. Estimate the scale—how many people's personal information you hold and what type of information components are in it, for example, contact information, financial information, health information, and identifying information including Social Security number, driver's license number, full name, birthdate, marital status, biometrics, and ethnicity. If you had to pay for people's credit monitoring after you experienced a breach and took care of all the potential expenses I mentioned under first-party costs, would $1 million in coverage be sufficient? Or would you need more like $5 million? Some insurers, such as AmTrust, offer coverage limits as low as $50,000.[2] That may be perfect for some small churches or churches with very limited data processing activities. Give the insurer enough accurate information so their estimation will be a close gauge of what you need.

Data Breach Insurance

If an insurer wants to sell you a data breach insurance policy, realize that you could be getting just the first-party coverage, not third-party coverage. Be sure to check that you are getting both. This way you get covered for risks that happen at your church and those that happen on the third-party vendor or contractor side that you have no control over but impact your church. Insurance makes it easier to afford lawsuits. Even if you're innocent, lawsuits cost money. Data breach insurance is a great add-on; not having it is like having a needle without thread, or soap without water.

Shop Around

Be ready to shop around until you find the coverage that's right for your church. Start with three quotes. Don't stop at three. Ideally, get as many quotes as you can manage. Compare the quotes side by side for pricing and quality. You need coverage that will meet your unique needs. Also, you don't want it to cost you more than it's worth. Nobody is impressed by who your insurer is—big names are not important. Go on insurers' websites and read about the data breach and cyber liability insurance they offer. Get comfortable with their terminology and your options. For example, you could start looking at The Hartford, Liberty Mutual, Hiscox, and Trimble, among others. These are just random examples, not endorsements. Expensive insurance doesn't mean good insurance, neither does inexpensive insurance. I've learned from insurance companies that you can't tell good and bad insurance apart based on pricing alone. Here's my take from a cybersecurity and privacy perspective: it boils down to the magnitude of your risks. Insurance is about risks, whether it's auto, home, boat, cyber, or data breach. All megachurches don't have the same risks, neither do all smaller churches. Make sure your insurance covers what you need it to cover. A good insurance is one that gives you the value you're looking for overall.

Before shopping for insurance, get a privacy expert and/or cybersecurity expert to chat with you about the data breaches and cyber risks you're planning on getting covered. Not all risks are covered by insurance. If you don't know what you're doing, you could spend money on insurance and still have a shipload of risks you assumed were covered, only to find out otherwise. It's funny that when I teach risk management, I get a few questions. But when I talk about liability insurance, everyone is on "stump the privacy expert" mode. It's all good. I'm glad the thought of insurance coverage gets everyone excited. But always consider all your risks. You don't go to your doctor and say, "Just give me the same medicine you prescribed to the last patient you just saw. He's in the waiting room raving about how good those meds are." No, you don't. Unless your doctor is a quack, your doctor will likely ask questions about your specific condition and symptoms. She'll give you a full examination before determining which medication you need, if any. Let a privacy and/or cybersecurity expert help you before you go shopping. Don't stress yourself. Share what concerns you before you settle on the options you have. They'll figure out a remedy.

That said, ready to get started with actionable steps? Let's go!

Assess What Your Church Is Doing to Assess Risks to Personal Information
Here's what you should evaluate in regard to the risks of losing personal information:

- What specific safeguards have you put in place to reduce risks—at the individual ministry level, for technologies used, and for employees, members' relationships, events, or services offered? Do you periodically check if those privacy safeguards are enough?

- Have you done what the law or regulations require regarding privacy? Are you following any particular standards to guide you or to help you measure how you're doing?

- What high risks are left that you can't find a solution for or can't control? What are you going to do? Say, "Whatever happens happens. We'll accept it"? That's called *risk acceptance*. In contrast, depending on the risk, you could work on getting insurance to cover the risks or remediate or mitigate the risks yourself.

Here are a few matters to keep in mind. How you handle risks is a choice. What happens when your church's computer system or network is broken into even after you did everything you could? Preparation can make insurance work well for you concerning those risks you couldn't possibly protect against. The three bullet points above help with preparing. Insurance companies look out for themselves also. In the event that personal information is breached, the insurance company will send experts to investigate your church. If computer related, the forensics specialists from your insurance provider will poke at your network and computers to find evidence of your own negligence so they can deny your claim. A data breach is just like an auto accident when it comes to insurance. At the end of the day the question will be, Who is responsible?

Don't Purchase More than You Need

Don't try to save money, then waste money. Take avocados as an example. Avocados are one of my favorite fruits. I read that avocado oil is healthy oil, but I love avocados for the taste. The problem is, avocados are expensive, and I'm relatively frugal. So I started buying them in bulk at Costco to save money. Eight avocados in a bag. I learned online that you can trick fruits into not ripening in unison. So I separated and hid the avocados in different parts of the kitchen so they wouldn't talk to each other. But somehow when I checked, they'd gotten ripe at the same time. I was bewildered. Those hardheaded avocadoes had betrayed me.

Then I realized this technique only works with bananas. Too late. I ate as many avocados as possible, but I still ended up wasting a few. That was how I figured out it was better to buy avocados individually than to buy them in bulk and waste money. The moral of my avocado story? Don't rush and overspend on insurance to get protection. Liabilities are expensive, but overspending or wasting money is not a solution. You can have a privacy and/or security expert join you when you speak with an insurance agent. Why not? They can help you come up with a strategy and determine what insurance can do for your church's unique situation and how much coverage you need. That way, you pay for and get just what you need. You will avoid spending more money to save a little money. You need to be calculated about your decisions.

Assess What Your Church Is Doing to Prepare for Insurance Coverage

☐ We have a privacy risk management plan.

☐ Our risk management is strategic (i.e., it considers the resources we have and our unique information collection activities to come up with approaches and decisions to reduce or find appropriate remedies to privacy risks).

☐ We identify privacy risks.

☐ We assess privacy risks.

☐ Our risk assessment is cyclical.

☐ We monitor risks, then prioritize, remediate (correct the issue), or mitigate them (reduce the risk).

☐ We identify and evaluate the privacy threats we're up against (employees, vendors/contractors/freelancers, technology, and external threats including cyberpunks, cyber terrorists, and hacktivists).

☐ We've taken as many risks as possible into account.

☐ We've determined that the remaining/uncertain risks we cannot resolve or reduce will be transferred to an insurance company.

☐ We've identified and labeled those remaining risks as *residual risks*.

☐ We are considering or shopping for data breach liability insurance to cover the residual risks.

With that said, even with insurance, by law, you still have responsibilities. Insurance companies take Proverbs 22:26 literally. That is, they don't promise to pay for someone else's mistake or debt—

Data Breach and Cyber Liability Insurance

especially as they have no clue what they're up against. To cover themselves, they'll ask questions to get to know which risks your church has, what you're doing about them, and what the insurer is up against. The insurance company won't just sign papers to take all your risks off your hands. *No.*

 Tip: Don't approach insurance companies because you just want to transfer your responsibilities elsewhere. Be strategic. Know which risks you want to transfer to insurance. If prospective insurance companies allow you to skip your homework or don't even mention that you need to complete a few action items on your own before coverage begins, they're taking you to the cleaners. Nix that relationship! Don't do it! Realize that, like any insurance, should you experience a breach, cyber liability and/or data breach, insurance companies will investigate you first to see if the data breach occurred due to your negligence. Insurance is not a way to help you avoid all your privacy and cybersecurity responsibilities. The law will hold your church accountable.

 Value: Insurance coverage is a lifesaver. The risks you can't possibly avoid are what you hand over to the insurance company. Sophisticated hackers are perpetually ahead of the game and can hack even the strongest networks and establishments. You can't avoid or plan enough to prevent that. It's a question of *when* they'll break in, not *if* they will. Great insurance providers can cover your church's related expenses when it does happen. They're the good angels.

 Action Steps: You've assessed what your church is doing to identify areas where privacy and security are vulnerable and the threats to those vulnerabilities, and you've assessed the risks. The boxes you did not check are your action items moving forward: list them below. Have you designated someone within your church to handle this responsibility? Jot down your answers.

_____

_____

_____

Church Privacy Team

What's your target date to assign someone to take this responsibility/when will you begin the tasks?
Day_____ Month_____ Year_____

What's your target date to complete these tasks?
Day_____ Month_____ Year_____

List questions you would like to ask insurance companies when you call to get a quote:
_____
_____
_____
_____
_____

What questions would you ask me?
_____
_____
_____
_____
_____

A static hero is a public liability.
Progress grows out of motion.
(Richard E. Byrd)

Conclusion
You Can Take a Deep Breath Now

Faith is not jumping to conclusions. It is concluding to jump.
(W. T. Purkiser)

Was this helpful? Thank you for going on this privacy journey with me. I hope you are more reassured, excited, aware, and prepared than you were when you first started reading. Now it's time to think about the strategies that will help you achieve your goals. Be proud of yourself. What's more? *Church Privacy 101* is a great prelude to this book. For a short and quick read, you'll also enjoy *Church Privacy Who Cares? You!* It's the eye-opener that sets everything in motion; it will help you understand why you're taking the steps in this book, instead of just feeling like there is a set of tasks you *have to do* without grasping the big picture. Grab *Church Privacy 101*, and enjoy what God says about privacy and how privacy unfolds in the Bible in the lives of many, for instance, in David's, Joseph's, Esther's, and Jesus' lives. More importantly, you'll also find some thought-provoking modern accounts of privacy concerns in and out of church.

In *Church Privacy Team*, I've defined privacy and personal information, the law, privacy notices, and policies. I've looked at many church activities through different traditional and modern processes for collecting and using members' personal information. And I covered health, counseling, employees, volunteers, technology, e-commerce, events, data breach costs, prayer requests, you name it. But there's more.

Remember, privacy practices are ongoing. So these three books are just the tip of the iceberg. Training is a must-have. Update your policy as it applies to your church's business situation and needs, which will always evolve with time. Don't just go through this book once and then let it collect physical or virtual dust. Make a habit of going over this book quarterly or at least once every six months. That's the prescription I'm writing you today. You have the power to make whatever privacy moves work best for you with the help of a professional who can help you make the right business decisions. If you need more information, do not hesitate to contact me—I can make this even easier for you. Going through this book makes you and your church a part of my thriving church privacy community. Stay connected. Sign up if you haven't already at www.ChurchPrivacyBookSeries.com to make it official. I am always ready to help wrangle difficult privacy questions. Connect with me if you have questions. You can also find me on Twitter or Instagram.

Are you undecided about what will work best for your church? What's overwhelming you? I can help you figure out a strategy and provide the help you need—whether it's coaching for your administrators or leaders, periodic training for your workers, or privacy speakers for all members to get them on the same page. What if you could get that for free? Well, ask! Reach out to me anytime. Let's talk. As a church, you're already the most humanitarian organization on earth. If you're people-centric, you must be privacy-centric. Sensitivity to church members' privacy needs will result in trust and compliance with privacy laws and regulations.

Remember, your world is ever changing. This book will change with it. Sometimes books can't get updated quickly enough on the latest developments in privacy. That's why knowing a real expert you can speak with or get a refresher from is key. Still, look out for *Church Privacy Team 2.0* in the near future. COVID-19 has been a significant change agent impacting how you communicate going forward. Technology is moving at a faster pace than ever. And as more churches, including yours, have evolved to online campuses, virtual services, and hybrid worship services, the human need for privacy has grown with it. But don't focus all your attention on how technology is problematic for privacy. Technology is not the only reason you and your members have privacy needs. Your privacy needs transcend technology, dating as far back as the Garden of Eden where Adam argued that he couldn't attend to God's unannounced visit because he wasn't dressed (Genesis 3:10). Likewise, regulators are authorities appointed by God who often show up unannounced. What will your argument be? So lead by example. Lead by obedience. Foster an irresistible privacy culture at your church by taking on one chapter of this book at a time.

By the way, I'm so proud of you for making this effort to start great privacy practices at your church. You'll be so excited about what you discover in your church. Do me a favor and pray about the

Conclusion

steps you'll be taking. Pray for your church and its members. Not only that, help the Mrs. Lindqvist in your church and the fellow churchgoers who would sue for privacy violation. You're not sure how? Download your free privacy prayer poster at www.ChurchPrivacyBookSeries.com because you should approach privacy decisions with an attitude of prayer. Every church has a potential privacy malpractice or conflict brewing. It's just a matter of time before it spills over. Don't be caught unprepared. And now comes the best part . . . watch a video of me making the crunchiest onion rings ever. I'll share it in my newsletter.

You only learn who has been swimming naked when the tide goes out.
(Warren Buffet)

Christian leaders are called to be change agents for Christ, bringing healing and restoration into the brokenness of their communities and workplaces.

(Richard Stearns)

Appendices

Appendix A: Sample Privacy Job Descriptions

Appendix B: US Federal and State Privacy Laws

Appendix C: International Privacy Laws and Regulations

Appendix D: Other International Privacy Guidelines

Appendix E: Major Retailers' Data Breaches

Appendix F: Mrs. Lindqvist's Story

Appendix G: Additional Church Data Breaches and Invasion of Privacy Lawsuits

Appendix H: Onion Rings Template

Appendix I: Great Privacy and Cybersecurity Books

Appendix A
Sample Privacy Job Descriptions

Privacy coordinators carry out most of the inventory and assessment activities and get everyone in line. Going through this book will evoke questions. The coordinator can organize those questions.

Next, and an absolute must, is consulting with a privacy expert for an hour to ask questions. If you don't have specific questions, you're wasting your money. It costs from $100–$500 per hour.

Assuming your church already has legal counsel, if your counsel only has experience in other areas of law and is not familiar with data privacy or has never implemented privacy compliance requirements, you're throwing money away. Your data privacy expert should have experience in privacy application and implementation. They should be well versed in information security, skilled in cyber security, and experienced with existing and emerging information technology. Make sure they're certified. Certifications include Certified Information Privacy Manager (CIPM) and Certified Information Systems Security Professional (CISSP). These are available to lawyers and nonlawyers. Certifications show their commitment. When creating a job description or consulting an expert, require certification. It's better to start a relationship with one or two privacy experts before you have an emergency. Have your legal counsel participate in your discussions with a privacy expert. Not all privacy experts are lawyers and not all lawyers are privacy experts. Remember this: a great privacy expert is very passionate about their work. They're excited about solving privacy problems.

An expert who can offer training, awareness, webinars, and seminars to the entire church is critical. They should be able to teach you as they help you. How you evaluate an expert is by how well they break down complex concepts into ways you can understand them. They are few, and they stay booked. According to the industry association (International Association of Privacy Professionals or IAPP), in 2021 there were a little over eighteen thousand certified privacy professionals in the world. I said "certified," but be sure to find one with the expertise I've described above. Starting and building a relationship with an expert early, long before you need them, is good business. Your church should have privacy training at least twice annually, with workshops and informal discussions every quarter.

Your privacy coordinator can communicate and schedule defined timeframes for training that align with your policies. Consult, but there's no need to retain, a lawyer for information privacy at this point if you're just starting out. Again, in 2024 it costs from $100–$500 per hour.

Hurry and start to get your house in order, and bring in an expert as needed. I've included (below) two job descriptions that show you there's more to be done than just consulting a privacy lawyer and calling it a day. These are the people who will work on the day-to-day privacy activities for you. It doesn't matter if they're full-time, part-time, or consultants. Pay attention to their responsibilities. These are activities you should begin regardless of the title you give the people in your church who take on these positions. Both sample job descriptions are modified from job descriptions developed and previously used by the University of Toronto (https://ischool.utoronto.ca/about-us/). They've been modified and repurposed with permission.

Position: Privacy Advisor

This is a more experienced role than the privacy coordinator.

Department: Privacy, Information Access, and Policy Management

The Privacy, Information Access, and Policy Management Office is looking for a regular, full-time privacy advisor. This position provides expertise in the areas of information and privacy management and supports access and privacy strategies and activities that enable [church name] to fulfill its obligations under local, state, federal, and international laws and related access and privacy legislation.

The advisor, as a member of the Privacy, Information Access, and Policy Management team, and under the direction of the privacy director, works in partnership with departmental and program managers and leaders within [church name] to implement information access, privacy policies, and processes. This position participates in the development and delivery of training and workshops, conducts research on a wide range of privacy-related matters, and is responsible for monitoring, reporting, and escalating any risks to privacy to ensure that appropriate actions are taken.

Specific Responsibilities:

- Support the director; the Privacy, Information Access, and Policy Management Department; and the designated head of the public body about strategic, tactical, and administrative privacy activities.

- Investigate concerns and complaints and take appropriate action regarding the collection, use, and disclosure of personal information and allegations into breaches of privacy; escalate to the director any reputational, legal, or regulatory risk.

- Provide reports and recommendations for improving access and privacy procedures and practices and increasing administrative and operational productivity.

- Ensure that notifications, forms, procedures, and processes for collecting personal information and obtaining authorization/consent for the use and disclosure of personal information are regularly reviewed for compliance with privacy requirements and related regulatory authorities.

- Liaise with legal counsel, administrators, faculty, and staff on privacy matters, complaints, investigations, and appeals.

- Participate in Privacy, Information Access, and Policy Management strategic planning, program, policy, and service.

- Conduct policy analysis and research and prepare reports and recommendations for the development and implementation of institute policies involving the collection and use/disclosure of personal information.

- Participate in reviews of policies and practices of the church to assess risks to privacy. Provide strategic input from an information access and privacy and compliance perspective for [church name] policies and guidelines involving personal information.

- Respond to inquiries and requests for access to information received by the Privacy, Information Access, and Policy Management Office that are subject to the law; provide advice and guidance in the application of law/regulation and resolve issues that may arise.

- Analyze information requests and work with staff and leadership across [church name] to identify and produce records responsive to data requests.

- Research and analyze case law and precedents and consult with stakeholders to ensure their views and concerns are considered in the application of discretion.

- Assist with privacy breach investigations.

- Support the privacy director in managing data breaches and significant privacy matters, including interaction with third-party service providers, legal counsel, and the privacy team; breach notification; liaison; and providing reports to the director and leadership.

- Author Privacy Impact Assessments (PIAs) for projects and initiatives to determine privacy and security issues and gaps in policy procedures and technologies, identify risk mitigation strategies, and ensure adherence to legal, regulatory, and contractual privacy.

- Determine the needs for Information Sharing Agreements (ISAs). May participate in the negotiation and execution of ISAs and other agreements between [church name] and a third party involving the collection and disclosure of personal information/data.

- As assigned by the privacy director, assist with the development of operations, plans, proposals, business cases, and cost-benefit analysis.

- Assist with the planning, development, delivery, and evaluation of employee privacy awareness training, education sessions, and materials; actively participate in training initiatives, new employee orientation, and offers advice.

- As assigned by the privacy director, prepare and update Privacy, Information Access, and Policy Management communications to raise awareness of specific privacy issues and risks within the [church name] community and to ensure that employees, volunteers, vendors, partners, donors, visitors, members, and the public understand their respective rights, obligations, and responsibilities in relation to privacy.

- Support the development and delivery of privacy tools and resources to promote privacy awareness and support compliance including creating website content for [church name]'s Privacy, Information Access, and Policy Management intranet.

Qualifications:

- Bachelor's degree or diploma in an appropriate discipline and a minimum of five years related experience in a public sector environment. CIPP designation an asset. An equivalent combination of education/training.

- Demonstrated in-depth experience in planning, developing, and implementing access and privacy-related projects.

- Team player with superb analytical, facilitation, leadership, advisory, and supervisory skills.

- Excellent verbal, written, and interpersonal communication.

- Well-developed planning, organizing, decision-making, implementation, problem-solving, and conflict-resolution skills.

- Proven ability to deal tactfully and decisively with sensitive members' issues while maintaining the highest level of customer service and confidentiality. Demonstrated ability to work under pressure, meet tight deadlines, and handle changing priorities.

- Proficiency in MS Office products and records management.

Position: Privacy Coordinator

Department: Privacy, Information Access, and Policy Management

The Privacy, Information Access, and Policy Management Office is looking for a regular, full-time privacy coordinator. This position coordinates the administrative aspects of information access and privacy processes and programs. The coordinator assists the privacy director and privacy advisor in ensuring that legal, regulatory, and contractual obligations are met. As a member of the privacy program team, this position provides specialized and technical administrative support; recommends and implements improvements to records management systems, processes, and procedures; and promotes and supports departmental initiatives and organizational information access and privacy strategies.

Specific Responsibilities:

- Serve as the first point of contact for inquiries and requests for access to information, assess privacy needs and escalate as appropriate, and provide general assistance to privacy programs.

- Provide administrative support concerned with ensuring compliance as it pertains to local, state, industry, federal, and international laws.

- Receive and track all information access requests, including consultations from other public bodies.

- Continuously review all relevant processes to ensure the highest level of business ethics and contractual terms and conditions.

- Design, develop, implement, and maintain the records management system, and ensure confidentiality is maintained.

- Ensure that all information relating to an inquiry or complaint is documented in the records management system, including electronic storage of all paper-based documents.

- Ensure that files are secured, retained, and disposed of in accordance with records management policies.

- Support the ongoing development, implementation, and improvement of the privacy program, policies, and procedures.

- Streamline processes for seamless coordination of programs and services, maintain related records and materials, and assist in developing and preparing presentations.

- Update privacy policies and procedures, privacy plans, and printed/electronic staff training materials as assigned by the privacy director and advisor.

- Draft correspondence, reports, privacy impact assessments, and other relevant documentation on behalf of the privacy director and privacy advisor.

- Coordinate privacy awareness training delivery by organizing schedules; handle invitations, registrations, room bookings, and set up; maintain training and workshop calendars; and other related duties. Attend and assist in training sessions as required; take notes and support attendees.

- Assist in designing, developing, and maintaining data reports on the effectiveness of training strategies, and bring areas of concern to the privacy director and privacy advisor.

- Assist in the coordination and publishing of web-based announcements and other information related to Privacy, Information Access, and Policy Management initiatives, programs, and updates under the guidance of the privacy director, advisor, and privacy and information management. Ensure that website notices are current and make necessary updates.

- Monitor the departmental budget and provide report summaries to the associate director at regular intervals. Prepare a variety of financial forms and work with the finance department to resolve any anomalies in the budget.

- Maintain a reference library of relevant communications, research, and programs.

- Assist the privacy director with completion of special privacy assignments and projects.

- Exercise sound, independent, professional judgment. Demonstrate initiative and take responsible action. Decisions involving unfamiliar circumstances are made in consultation with the privacy director, privacy advisor, or external privacy sources.

Qualifications:

- Bachelor's degree from an accredited institution plus completion of up to two years of postsecondary education in a related field, including studies in business, office administration, legal, or paralegal, and supplemented with relevant privacy training.

- Two to four years of experience in administrative systems and business practices through which a working knowledge of administering records management systems was developed.

- A combination of education and experience may be considered.

- Basic knowledge and understanding of information access and privacy principles and the ability to exercise resourcefulness in dealing with new situations.

- Ability to prepare, maintain, update, and retrieve related materials, search records, and compile information.

- Demonstrated skills in administrative and coordination support to a wide range of programs and services with strong ability to manage multiple tasks and deadlines.

- Exemplary communication, interpersonal, and customer service skills, acting as the first point of contact. This role will be able to explain policies and procedures, conduct research, and provide information on programs and services, while maintaining the highest level of confidentiality.

- Sound analytical and problem-solving skills to review and assess inquiries, requests, and documents. Experience in Internet navigation, developing content for the web, and project management/tracking software.

- Advanced skills in MS Office products, with knowledge and experience working with databases.

This book and this example offer an overview of job descriptions. The companion course offers additional resources and job descriptions you can tailor to your church environment.

Appendix B
US Federal and State Privacy Laws

US Federal Laws

Don't despair. This appendix is more fun than you think. The US has sectorial privacy laws. *Sectorial* means US privacy laws and regulations address very specific privacy concerns and industries. A comprehensive privacy law/regulation is one that would apply to both private and public sectors. On a state level, the approach to privacy law has begun to lean toward a comprehensive approach. Not so with US federal law. Here's a handful of examples of privacy laws the feds have had for a while now. There are more.

The US Constitution doesn't mention the word *privacy*, but it protects people's right to privacy in the First, Fourth, Ninth, and Fourteenth Amendments.

The Privacy Act restricts how the feds handle, access, and use your personal information and records.

Health Insurance Portability and Accountability Act (HIPAA) protects personal health information including medical records.

The Fair Credit Reporting Act (FCRA) protects your rights against those annoying credit offers. You can decline receipt of these offers. Plus, the FCRA makes sure you get at least one free credit report from each of the major credit reporting agencies every year. It's great to encourage your church members to get their free credit reports. Members use their cards and accounts for offerings, tithes, events, etc., which means the church (and its giving apps) serves as an access point for criminals to intercept those transactions either physically or remotely. Because credit/debit cards and financial accounts are exposed every time and anywhere people conduct transactions, the church should encourage members to take advantage of their free credit reports.

The Electronic Communications Privacy Act (ECPA) makes it illegal for anyone to intercept, disclose, or use wire, oral, or electronic communication without consent.

Children's Online Privacy Protection Act (COPPA) requires organizations whose websites target young kids (under the age of thirteen) to obtain consent from parents before asking children to divulge personal information.

Protection of Pupil Rights Amendment (PPRA) gives parents the right to protect their children against schools and school contractors deceptively collecting personal information from their children. Such rights allow parents to prevent school surveys from collecting information from children that reveal parents' or families' religious beliefs, relationships, psychological issues, and political affiliations. Keep in mind, states have their own unique privacy requirements. If your church is running a school, check state requirements for surveys.

Other US Federal and State Laws

Some laws are not typically called privacy laws, but they touch on unique privacy concerns and implications. Here are a few:

- Americans with Disabilities Act (ADA)

- Cable Communications Policy Act of 1984 (Cable Act)

- California Consumer Privacy Act (CCPA) 2018

- Children's Internet Protection Act of 2001 (CIPA)

- Children's Online Privacy Protection Act of 1998 (COPPA)

- Communications Assistance for Law Enforcement Act 1994 (CALEA)

- Computer Fraud and Abuse Act of 1986 (CFAA)

- Federal Information Security Management Act (FISMA)

- Consumer Credit Reporting Reform Act of 1996 (CCRRA)

- Fair Credit Reporting Act (FCRA) 1970

- Controlling the Assault of Non-Solicited Pornography and Marketing (CAN-SPAM) Act of 2003

- Electronic Fund Transfer Act (EFTA) 1978

- Equal Employment Opportunity Commission (EEOC) 1965

- Employee Retirement Income Security Act of 1974 (ERISA)

- Fair and Accurate Credit Transactions Act of 2003 (FACTA)

- Fair Credit Reporting Act (FCRA) 1970

- Federal Information Security Management Act of 2002 (FISMA)

- Federal Trade Commission Act of 1914 (FTCA)

- Driver's Privacy Protection Act of 1994

- Driver Privacy Act of 2015

- Electronic Communications Privacy Act of 1986 (ECPA)

- Electronic Freedom of Information Act of 1996 (E-FOIA)

- Fair Credit Reporting Act of 1999 (FCRA)

- Family Education Rights and Privacy Act of 1974 (FERPA; also known as the Buckley Amendment)

- Gramm-Leach-Bliley Financial Services Modernization Act of 1999 (GLBA)

- Privacy Act of 1974—including US Department of Justice Overview

- Privacy Protection Act of 1980 (PPA)

- Right to Financial Privacy Act of 1978 (RFPA)

- Stored Communication Act (SCA) 1986

- Telecommunications Act of 1996

- Telephone Consumer Protection Act of 1991 (TCPA)

- Uniting and Strengthening America by Providing Appropriate Tools Required to Intercept and Obstruct Terrorism Act of 2001 (USA PATRIOT Act)

- Video Privacy Protection Act of 1988[1]

Consumer advocates suggest that these laws are not enough and that the US should do what the European Union and California are famous for doing: have a law that covers the government and private companies; give consumers more privacy rights; get strict with and levy hefty fines and other penalties on offenders; hold organizations accountable for mishandling, misusing, selling, deceiving, or stealing personal info from people; and give consumers the right to sue. There may not be a comprehensive law, but guess what? State privacy laws are working harder on doing all of the above.

On November 26, 2019, when the Consumer Online Privacy Rights Act (COPRA) was introduced to the US Senate, the feds were debating over whether we were going to adopt a comprehensive law. This will apply to any entity or individual processing data or information that's personal in nature. The draft law is loaded with consumer rights but hasn't become a law yet.

How will you know if you'll be affected? Are small businesses off the hook? How small exactly? Everyone wants to be a nonprofit or small business to skip accountability. We'll delve into COPRA in *Church Privacy Team 2.0*. Prayerfully, by then, the Senate will have decided.

More on US State Privacy Laws

In California, if you're not bringing in $25 million per year as a business, the California Consumer Privacy Act (CCPA) doesn't apply. If you're processing personal data of less than one hundred thousand people, households, or devices, the law doesn't apply. If you're not receiving 50 percent of your total revenue from selling (or sharing) personal information with other entities, you're free to go. Wait! If you're in a heavily regulated industry, such as the financial, credit reporting, health, or education sectors, other strict privacy and security rules apply. You're already held accountable to other stringent standards and requirements. But get legal advice before you relax.

Appendix C
International Privacy Laws and Regulations

Let's go global. Most churches now have an international résumé. Back in 2018 and earlier, there were churches that weren't online. Going global via Zoom and other platforms that you're using means you have members, partners, donors, supporters, and followers abroad. Congrats! I'm really happy for you. But to whom much is given, much is expected (Luke 12:48). I didn't quote the law; that's Scripture. But that is the approach of many privacy laws/regulations, including General Data Protection Regulation (GDPR) and other international laws, that come with that expanded territory you have been praying for.

"Oh, that you would bless me and enlarge my territory!" (1 Chronicles 4:10.) This is one prayer that got mass answers from heaven. The purpose of this book is to remind you of your responsibilities and the penalties for not accepting them. "From everyone who has been given much, much will be demanded; and from the one who has been entrusted with much, much more will be asked" (Luke 12:48). I almost typed "much more will be hacked." God forbid. That's not Scripture. But you get the point.

You can't have your cake and eat it too. Your church is not getting off easy even if it is seen as a nonprofit or faith organization. Remember Mrs. Lindqvist in Sweden? It's about respecting the humanity and dignity of others by lawfully collecting and handling their personal information.

If you have donors, subscribers, supporters, or long-distance members living in jurisdictions that extend the privacy rights of their residents across borders, the laws apply to your church. Just because your church is physically located in Cleveland, Ohio, doesn't mean anything to privacy authorities in France or Germany. Think about this: You're not just dealing with the national law in that particular country or jurisdiction where you have an international member. States and provinces within that country may have unique privacy requirements that apply to you too. Make sense?

Here's a caravan of international privacy laws. If you're curious, poke around as many of these laws as you'd like. You have a lot of insight to gain.

International privacy laws include but are not limited to the following list. (Note: Laws and regulations provided in this book are offered to provide you with additional insight into different jurisdictions. However, these laws, regulations, and frameworks are subject to amendments, name changes, revisions, and sometimes invalidation by the courts of law. We recommend you research and stay up to date with changes to the specific jurisdiction that's of interest to you.)

- Argentina: Personal Data Protection Act (a.k.a. Habeas Data) 2000

- Algeria: Law No. 18-07 of June 10, 2018

- Angola: Data Protection Law (Law no. 22/11, June, 17 2011)

- Australia: Privacy Act of 1988

- Austria: Data Protection Act 2000, Austrian Federal Law Gazette part I No. 165/1999 (Datenschutzgesetz 2000 or DSG 2000)

- Belgium: Belgium Data Protection Law and Belgian Data Privacy Commission

- Benin: Data Protection Act, 2009

- Botswana: Data Protection Act of 2018

- Brazil: Privacy currently governed by Article 5 of the 1988 Constitution

- Bulgaria: The Bulgarian Personal Data Protection Act, January 1, 2002. Bulgarian Data Protection Authority

- Burkina Faso: Law No. 010-2004/AN on the Protection of Personal Data

- Canada: The Privacy Act – July 1983, and the Personal Information Protection and Electronic Data Act (PIPEDA) of 2000 (Bill C-6)

- Cape Verde: Law 133-V-2001 on the Protection of Personal Data, 2001

- Chad: Law No. 007/PR/2015 on the Protection of Personal Data

- Chile: Act on the Protection of Personal Data, August 1998

- Colombia: Law 1266 of 2008 and Law 1273 of 2009.

- Congo: Law 29-2019 on the Protection of Personal Data, October 10, 2019

- Côte d'Ivoire: June 19, 2013

- Czech Republic: Act on Protection of Personal Data (April 2000) No. 101

- Denmark: Act on Processing of Personal Data, Act No. 429, May 2000

- Egypt: The Law on the Protection of Personal Data issued under Resolution No. 151 of 2020

- Estonia: Personal Data Protection Act of 2003, June 1996, consolidated July 2002

- European Union: European Union Data Protection Directive of 1998, EU Internet Privacy Law of 2002 (DIRECTIVE 2002/58/EC), and General Data Protection Regulation (GDPR) 2016

- Finland: Act on the Amendment of the Personal Data Act (986), 2000

- France: Data Protection Act of 1978 (revised in 2004)

- Gabon: Data Protection Law adopted in 2011

- Germany: Federal Data Protection Act of 2001

- Ghana: Data Protection Act, 2012

- Greece: Law No. 2472 on the Protection of Individuals with Regard to the Processing of Personal Data, April 1997

- Guernsey: Data Protection (Bailiwick of Guernsey) Law of 2001

- Guinea: Data Protection Act, 2016; Equatorial Guinea enacted, by means of a general legal framework for data protection matters, its Law No. 1/2016, of July 22, 2016 ("the Data Protection Law").

- Hong Kong: Personal Data Ordinance (the "Ordinance"), 1995

- Hungary: Act LXIII of 1992 on the Protection of Personal Data and the Publicity of Data of Public Interests (excerpts in English)

- Iceland: Act of Protection of Individual and the Processing of Personal Data, January 2000

- India: Information Technology Act of 2000

- Ireland: Data Protection (Amendment) Act, Number 6 of 2003

- Italy: Data Protection Code of 2003, Legislative Decree 196/2003 (the "Code")

- Japan: The Act on the Protection of Personal Information (APPI) (Act No. 57 of 2003 as amended in 2015)

- Kenya: Data Protection Act of 2019

- Korea: Personal Information Protection Act (PIPA), Act on the Promotion of Information and Communications Network Utilization and Information Protection (Network Act), and Credit Information Use and Protection Act (Credit Information Act)

- Latvia: Personal Data Protection Law, March 23, 2000

- Lesotho: Data Protection Act, 2013

- Lithuania: Law on Legal Protection of Personal Data, June 1996

- Luxembourg: The Data Protection Act, 2018

- Madagascar: Law No. 2014-038 relating to protection of personal data is the main regulatory framework in Madagascar (the Data Protection Law).

- Malaysia: The Malaysia Personal Data Protection Act, 2010

- Mali: The Constitution of Mali; Law No. 2013/015; Law No. 2013-015 of May 21, 2013, on the Protection of Personal Data; and Law No. 2019-056 of December 5, 2019, on the Repression of Cybercrime

- Malta: Data Protection Act (Act XXVI of 2001), Amended March 22, 2002, November 15, 2002, and July 15, 2003

- Mauritania: Draft Law No. 2017 – 020 on the protection of personal data. Regulator Personal Data Protection Authority

- Mauritius: Mauritius Data Protection Act, 2017

- Mexico: Federal Law for the Protection of Personal Data Possessed by Private Persons: the regulation deals with data subject rights, security, and breach notification provisions, cloud computing, consent and notice requirements, and data transfers.

- Morocco: The Moroccan Data Protection Act (Act 09-08)

- Netherlands: Dutch Personal Data Protection Act 2000 as amended by Acts dated April 5, 2001, Bulletin of Acts, Orders and Decrees 180, December 6, 2001

- New Zealand: Privacy Act, May 1993; Privacy Amendment Act, 1993; and Privacy Amendment Act, 1994

- Niger: Law No. 2017-28 of May, 3 2017, on the Protection of Personal Data ("the Law"). Niger has recently enacted the Law.

- Nigeria: Data Protection Regulation, 2019

- Norway: Personal Data Act, April 2000 – Act of 14 April 2000 No. 31 relating to the processing of personal data (Personal Data Act)

- Philippines: Data Privacy Act of 2011; recognized right of privacy in civil law and a model data protection code

- Poland: Act of the Protection of Personal Data, August 1997

- Portugal: Act on the Protection of Personal Data (Law 67/98 of 26 October)

- Romania: Law No. 677/2001 for the Protection of Persons concerning the Processing of Personal Data and the Free Circulation of Such Data

- Rwanda: Data Protection Bill, 2021, Law No. 058/2021

- São Tomé and Príncipe: Law No. 03/2016. Data Protection Law, 2016

- Senegal: Data Protection Act, 2008

- Seychelles: The Data Protection Act (the "Act") was enacted in 2003 (Act No. 9 of 2003)

- Singapore: The E-commerce Code for the Protection of Personal Information and Communications of Consumers of Internet Commerce

- Slovak Republic: Act No. 428 of 3 July 2002, on Personal Data Protection

- Slovenia: Personal Data Protection Act, RS No. 55/99

- South Africa: Protection of Personal Information Act, 2013, and Electronic Communications and Transactions Act, 2002 (ECTA), regulating the electronic collection of personal information

- South Korea: The Act on Promotion of Information and Communications Network Utilization and Data Protection of 2000

- Spain: Organic Law 15/1999 of 13 December on the Protection of Personal Data

- Sweden: Personal Data Protection Act (1998:204), October 24, 1998

- Switzerland: The Federal Act on Data Protection of 1992

- Taiwan: Computer Processed Personal Data Protection Law—only applies to public institutions

- Thailand: Official Information Act, B.E. 2540 (1997) for state agencies and Personal Data Protection bill under consideration

- Togo: Law No. 2019-014 Relating to the Protection of Personal Data ("the Law") 29 October 2019, in the Official Gazette of the Togolese Republic

- Tunisia: Tunisia's request to accede to the Convention for the Protection of Individuals with Regard to Automatic Processing of Personal Data, 2015

- Uganda: The Data Protection and Privacy Act, 2019

- United Kingdom: UK Data Protection Act, 1998

- Vietnam: The Law on Electronic Transactions, 2008

- Zambia: The Electronic Communications and Transactions Act, No. 4, 2021, and Data Protection Act, No. 3, 2021

- Zimbabwe: Cybersecurity and Data Protection Bill, 2021, and Consumer Protection Act, 2019

Examples of African Countries with Draft Comprehensive Privacy Bills:

- Burundi: Data Protection Draft Law of 27 Nov 2004

- Eswatini: Constitution of Swaziland Act No. 1 of 2015 and Swaziland Consumer Protection Regulation, 2016

- Ethiopia: 1995 Constitution of the Federal Democratic Republic of Ethiopia, the 2005 Criminal Code of the Federal Democratic Republic of Ethiopia, the 1960 Civil Code, the Computer Crime Proclamation No. 958/2016, and the Freedom of the Mass Media and Access to Information Proclamation No. 590/2008

- Tanzania: The Cybercrimes Act, 2015, and the Constitution of the United Republic of Tanzania

Never underestimate these jurisdictions. Just like the US, while some jurisdictions may not yet have a comprehensive privacy-specific law, they have a collection of legal mechanisms, including a constitution and several sectoral regulations and laws that directly or indirectly address confidentiality and personal information in numerous contexts, including online/cyberspace activities, electronic communication, health, innovation, telecommunication services/products, employment, education, finance/banking, and children. Such provisions generally require covered entities to maintain the confidentiality of personal information. I've stated one or two examples for all the countries listed, but they have other laws and regulations. Be mindful of privacy in your church mission work in any jurisdiction across the globe.

Appendix D
Other International Privacy Guidelines

The Electronic Frontier Foundation (EFF) has a comprehensive list that I love to reference. Here you have a list to browse but not to get overwhelmed by. The EFF has been around since 1990, advocating for civil liberties in the digital space. One benefit of reviewing these documents is, they help you see the critical need for privacy and that privacy protection is not new; the medium is new. The bonus is that you can glean the rationale for unique policy approaches in various parts of the world. Happy browsing!

- Article 12 from The Universal Declaration on Human Rights 1948

- Article 17 from The International Covenant on Civil and Political Rights 1966

- Article 16 from The Convention on the Rights of the Child 1989

- E/CN.4/1990/72: Guidelines for the regulation of computerized personal data files 1990

- Article 8 from the Convention for the Protection of Human Rights and Fundamental Freedoms 1950

- Council of Europe: Recommendations and Resolutions of the Committee of Ministers

- Council of Europe: Recommendation No. R(99) 5 for the protection of privacy on the Internet 1999

- OECD Guidance on Policy and Practice: Privacy Online (book)

- OECD Guidelines on Cross-Border Privacy Law Enforcement, 2006 – ongoing

- OECD Guidelines for the Security of Information Systems and Networks: Towards a Culture of Security 2002

- Article 18 from The Cairo Declaration on Human Rights in Islam 1990

- Article 4.3 from the Declaration of Principles on Freedom of Expression in Africa 2002

- Article 5 from the American Declaration of the Rights and Duties of Man[1]

When you get a chance, look up, hang out, and peruse the above guidelines directly at the EFF website (https://www.eff.org/issues/international-privacy-standards). All the articles are included there to give you additional information and awareness of why privacy is so important in the world around you and in the church you serve. Privacy is not a fad.

Appendix E
Major Retailers' Data Breaches

I'm aware your church is not a retail store, but data breaches have a universal impact. It doesn't matter where the breach happens or the root cause; how it happens is typically very similar, and the impact is negative and wounds the victims' confidence in a number of ways. Here I share data breaches that reveal lessons you should learn about the privacy risks associated with your vendors or contractors. Check out the articles.

Target

In 2013, Target stores lost personal data from 40 million credit and debit cards to hackers and paid a multistate settlement of $18.5 million. The hackers gained access through one of the retail giant's vendors.

Vendor Risk Perspective:

- https://www.zdnet.com/article/anatomy-of-the-target-data-breach-missed-opportunities-and-lessons-learned/

Costs:

- https://www.breitbart.com/tech/2017/05/28/cost-targets-data-breach-nearing-300-million/

- https://www.usatoday.com/story/money/2017/05/23/target-pay-185m-2013-data-breach-affected-consumers/102063932/

Regulators:

- https://www.usnews.com/news/articles/2014/03/26/ftc-investigates-target-data-breach

Home Depot

In 2014, Home Depot experienced a data breach that affected more than 40 million customers' financial information. The retailer paid $17.5 in a multistate settlement. The perpetrators gained access to the data by stealing credentials from the retailer's third-party vendor.

Vendor Risk Perspective:

- https://www.infosecurity-magazine.com/news/home-depot-breach-third-party/

Costs:

- https://www.eweek.com/security/home-depot-security-breach-affects-56m-credit-card-holders
- https://fortune.com/2017/03/09/home-depot-data-breach-banks/

Regulators/Investigation:

- https://www.infosecurity-magazine.com/news/home-depot-to-pay-2725m/

Goodwill

In 2013, Goodwill experienced a data breach of its point-of-sale system compromising 800,000 payment cards. Hackers gained access to the nonprofit's payment system by breaching its third-party vendor.

Vendor Risk Perspective:

- https://www.crn.com/news/security/300073911/goodwill-malware-at-third-party-payment-processor-caused-breach.htm
- https://www.esecurityplanet.com/networks/goodwill-data-breach-linked-to-third-party-vendor/

Costs:

- At the time of publication, information was not available on the monetary costs that Goodwill incurred as a result of the data breach.

Regulators/Investigation:

- https://krebsonsecurity.com/2014/07/banks-card-breach-at-goodwill-industries/

- https://news.softpedia.com/news/GoodWill-Completes-Breach-Investigation-330-Stores-Affected-457850.shtml

Appendix F
Mrs. Lindqvist's Story

So you don't miss the deep privacy implications, I suggest you read this sad but true story. I also share this story in Chapter 1 of *Church Privacy 101*, but I don't mind retelling it because of its importance.

How a Church Lady Became a Criminal
Who knew that one simple photo would evolve into an expensive lawsuit and inspire my book. The story began in autumn 1998. Mrs. Lindqvist posted a photo of church volunteers to a website. The events that followed ignited a legal fire. Sadly, she did *not* obtain consent from the people in the photo and was ordered by the courts to pay hefty fines for her transgression. Lindqvist appealed and pled her innocence, to no avail. The case wrapped up roughly five years later and left the church and Mrs. Lindqvist with many lessons to learn and share.[1]

Again, I detail this case in the companion book, *Church Privacy 101*. Information on how to order *Church Privacy 101* is a few pages away.

Why is this story important?
Mrs. Lindqvist's case is a significant lesson for the church, that some of the seemingly innocuous behaviors or activities of churchgoers could violate privacy and could lead to costly legal actions and negative publicity. They can divide a church community and destroy longstanding relationships. How do you prevent this from happening? Read all the companion books in the Church Privacy Book Series for a holistic understanding of privacy. You can't protect or prevent what you don't know.

Appendix G
Additional Church Data Breaches and Invasion of Privacy Lawsuits

Here are a few more church-related breaches or lawsuits, which weren't covered in this book.

St. Wenceslaus Catholic Church, Omaha

A sinister email scam asked members of the church to buy Apple iTunes cards for a parishioner in the hospital. Thousands of dollars were taken from the generous congregants.

Our Lady of Grace Church, Greensboro

The scam involved impersonating the parish priest and asking people for money. Reports indicated approximately ten pastors in the Diocese of Charlotte were impersonated within a four-month period.

First Presbyterian Church of Nashville

The email of the executive pastor was hacked, and the criminals obtained the email addresses of church members, impersonated the pastor, and made solicitations to members.

Lakewood Church, Houston

In 2014, robbers got physical by cracking the safe and making away with $600,000. That was one weekend's collection money, including cash, checks, and credit card information from Lakewood Church, Houston. Pastor Joel Osteen urged members to monitor their bank and credit card accounts for any suspicious activity. Fortunately, in December of 2021 a plumber found the stolen money stashed in a wall in the church, per a CNN report. Notwithstanding, Pastor Joel and the leadership had made the right move by focusing on protecting church members' privacy.

Arizona Court on Minister's Liabilities

An Arizona court ruled that a pastor and his church could be sued based on malpractice and other grounds as a result of the pastor's disclosure of confidential information shared with him by a church member. The key point here being, ministers who disclose confidential information obtained during counseling sessions may be exposing themselves, as well as their church, to legal liability on the basis of a number of grounds, including malpractice, invasion of privacy, defamation, and infliction of emotional distress.[1]

More Cases: Members Suing Churches Over Privacy

I mentioned before that it doesn't matter who wins or loses in court. Having to go to court at all and the negative publicity that comes with it is bad news for any church. Keep in mind that, recently, privacy laws and regulations have changed drastically. Individuals have more legal rights now under different laws than they had ten or twenty years ago. Organizations have been more regulated, penalized, and fined in the past six years than ever before. The prevalence of Internet use also helps spread the word on offenders. Here are a few cases where members sued their church or pastors for violating privacy:

1. *Duncan v. Peterson*: a minister, Richard Duncan, and Moody Church sued Erwin Lutzer, the senior pastor of the church, and Bervin Peterson, the chairman of the board of elders, for false light invasion of privacy.[2]

2. *Snyder v. Evangelical Orthodox Church*: this case involved the public dissemination of private information to a congregation, despite a church official's promise not to do so.[3]

3. *Guinn v. Church of Christ of Collinsville*: a case that involved the question of whether tort damages could be awarded as a result of a church's public humiliation of an individual who had already withdrawn from church membership.[4]

4. *Smith v. Calvary Christian Church*: the Michigan Supreme Court examined whether an individual having withdrawn from a church would make the church potentially liable for having publicly divulged private facts about the individual, namely, that he had consorted with prostitutes.[5]

5. *Westbrook v. Penley*: the Texas Supreme Court addressed whether a pastor, who was also a licensed professional marriage counselor, was liable for revealing information learned from a former congregant during secular counseling.[6]

Appendix H
Onion Rings Template

From my website, www.ChurchPrivacyBookSeries.com, you can download an editable and printable copy of an onion anytime of the day you want to make Onion Rings—that is, when you brainstorm who you're considering sharing important personal information with, how much you should share, and who to tell first. You'll have an option of a small or large onion to meet your privacy needs. Remember, you can have onions for different decisions or information you're thinking about sharing. Give your onion a name so you know what it's for and, if you wish, give it a little description.

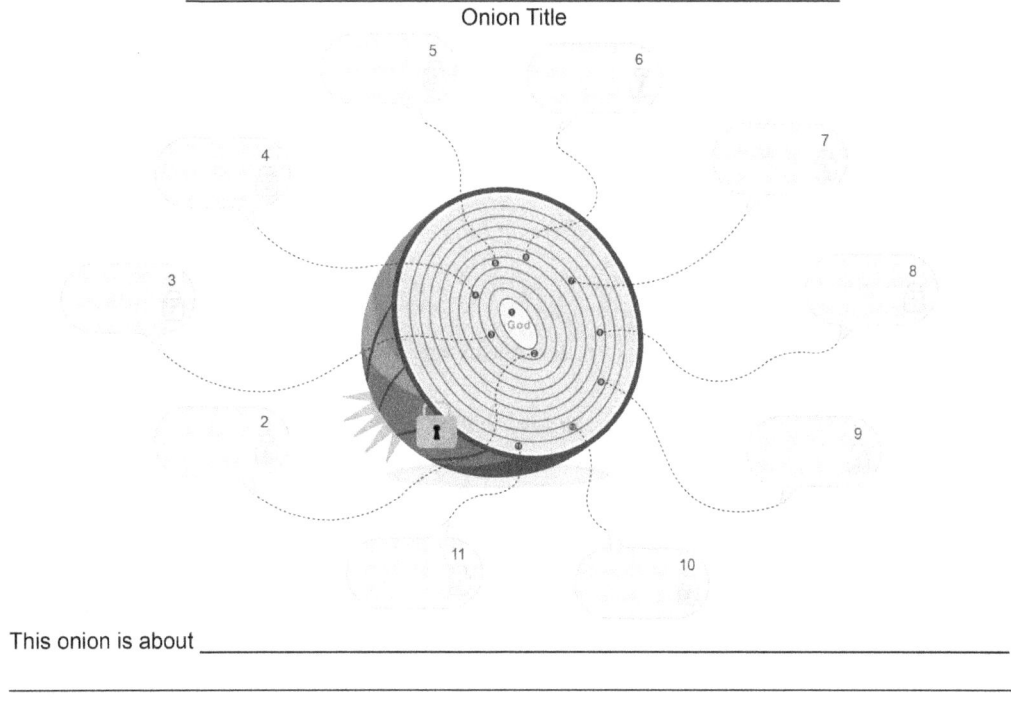

Figure 7. Privacy onion rings template

Appendix I
Great Privacy and Cybersecurity Books

These books are not church-specific privacy books, but they offer insights about privacy and data protection concerns that can be applied in your church. Visit www.ChurchPrivacyBookSeries.com and sign up for more updates, suggested readings, tools, and evolving privacy guidelines.

1. *The Permission Seeker's Guide Through the Legal Jungle: Clearing Copyrights, Trademarks and Other Rights for Entertainment and Media Productions* by Joy R. Butler

2. *Unpopular Privacy: What Must We Hide?* by Anita Allen

3. *Privacy and Freedom* by Alan F. Westin

4. *Nothing to Hide: The False Tradeoff between Privacy and Security* by Daniel J. Solove

5. *The Art of Invisibility: The World's Most Famous Hacker Teaches You How to Be Safe in the Age of Big Brother and Big Data* by Kevin Mitnick

6. *Privacy Law and Society* by Anita L. Allen and Marc Rotenberg

7. *Social Engineering: The Science of Human Hacking* by Christopher Hadnagy

8. *Cyber Security: Threats and Responses for Government and Business* by Jack Caravelli and Nigel Jones

9. *Ghost in the Wires: My Adventures as the World's Most Wanted Hacker* by Kevin Mitnick with William L. Simon

10. *Social Engineering: The Art of Human Hacking* by Christopher Hadnagy

11. *Zoom for Teachers: The 2020 Screen By Screen Guide To Use Zoom At Its Best. A Fool-Proof Approach To Meetings, Webinars & Online Lessons. Privacy Tips Included!* by Emma Bradley

12. *Cybersecurity for Beginners* by Raef Meeuwisse

13. *Cyber Security: Law and Guidance* by Helen Wong

14. *Cyber Security for Seniors* by Steve Krantz

15. *Cybersecurity: What You Need to Know About Computer and Cyber Security, Social Engineering, The Internet of Things + An Essential Guide to Ethical Hacking for Beginners* by Lester Evans

16. *Cyber Privacy: Who Has Your Data and Why You Should Care* by April Falcon Doss

More Recent Privacy-Related Book Releases

1. *Unmasking AI: My Mission to Protect What Is Human in a World of Machines* by Joy Buolamwini

2. *Privacy Is Power: Why and How You Should Take Back Control of Your Data* by Carissa Véliz

3. *Data Privacy Deception & Abuse: Uncovering the Misuse of Personal Information by the Tech Giants* by James Goldmann

4. *GDPR and Your Role as the Data Protection Officer: Mastering Compliance; Navigating the GDPR Landscape as a DPO* by Alexander P. Clarke

5. *Privacy and Data Recovery in Cloud Computing* by Ameer M. Shariff

6. *AI Powered Data Privacy & Data Protection for Small Businesses* by Sabira Arefin

Connect with Grace beyond the Page

While Grace partners with organizations to achieve legal and regulatory compliance, train employees, and develop content, she is also available for the following favorites:

Keynotes, Talks, and Workshops

Grace delivers targeted content for groups and breakout workshop sessions that speak to church members, employees, and anyone in a ministry facilitator or other leadership role. Perfect for conferences, retreats, conventions, and meetings.

Leadership Privacy Development Training

In this lecture, Grace uncovers the potential of leaders and teaches them how to recognize and minimize privacy risks. She unravels the key principles that align their vision and mission to help leaders grow in how they care for people.

Church Privacy Team

Organizational Privacy Consulting

Grace gives churches and ministries the tools, strategic direction, and tailored and customized solutions to help them reach their full privacy potential.

Divinity Schools, Colleges, Universities, Seminaries, and Associations

Grace gives talks under different types of budgets and programs including Training and Development, Learning Materials, Continuing Education, and Speaker Budgets.

Privacy Concierge Coaching

Grace maintains a select portfolio for leaders who need one-on-one coaching to maintain their own privacy balance while leading their church organizations.

See What Grace Is Up To

Request Grace to speak at your next event or for a media interview.
Visit www.GraceBuckler.com/Speaking.

Connect with Grace beyond the Page

"Absolutely wonderful. I didn't realize how much I didn't know about privacy in the church! It's amazing as well as warm, educational, empowering, and relatable. Her humor keeps it interesting."

"She's practical, candid, affirming, and on point with biblical and life applications. Where was Grace when I was in seminary? It's never too late to unlearn the harmful practices I've learned for many years. I definitely wouldn't have thought about privacy in this way."

"Brilliant illustrations and thought-provoking real-world examples. I felt closer to our mission as a church thanks to her passion for fostering more trust, lasting relationships, and genuine fellowship in the church."

Scan this QR code for more information on courses.

About Grace

Grace Buckler is a recognized privacy, data protection, cybersecurity, and in-demand global privacy author, advisor, expert, and speaker. She has presented numerous topics on privacy for corporations, associations, business groups, colleges, universities, governments, and youth organizations worldwide. Grace is the founder of The Privacy Advocate, a data privacy consulting firm. Her fifteen-year career budded in the federal market where she served as a consultant and subject-matter expert both in the US and overseas. As an award-winning consultant for the United States Secret Service, Grace also served numerous federal entities with acknowledged excellence, including the Department of Health and Human Services (HHS), the Transportation Security Administration (TSA), the Defense Information Security Agency (DISA), the Department of Justice (DOJ), the Department of Homeland Security (DHS), the Department of Defense (DoD), and the Defense Counterintelligence and Security Agency (DCSA). Seven years of her career have been spent serving diverse markets, including Fortune 500 companies, startups, and nonprofits. She has authored articles for industry journals, functioned as an expert reviewer for US and European books in her industry, and served as faculty and an advisory board member for the largest global privacy association, the

International Association of Privacy Professionals. Grace speaks regularly as a privacy subject matter expert for Startup Law 101 Series.

Grace is a go-to privacy advisor, coach, and instructor for many leading organizations, law firms, churches, educational institutions, religious organizations, and clergy who desire to improve or master privacy risk management, gain members' trust, and achieve legal and regulatory compliance. In addition to her experience in cybersecurity, data privacy, and technical communication, Grace graduated summa cum laude from Albany Law School and holds a wealth of industry certifications including the Certified Information Systems Security Professional (CISSP), Certified Information Systems Auditor (CISA), Certification in Risk and Information Systems Control (CRISC), Project Management Professional (PMP), Certified Information Privacy Professional (European Data Protection Law & Practice), Certified Information Privacy Professional (US Corporate Privacy Law), Certified Information Privacy Professional (Government), Certified Information Privacy Manager (CIPM), and Certified Data Privacy Solutions Engineer (CDPSE).

When not wrangling privacy issues, Grace is a foodie! Some of her favorite street foods include Puerto Rican elote, West African boiled peanuts and roasted maize with plums, and Belgian waffles with strawberries and cream. She enjoys theater, traveling, discovering quaint towns, and trying new recipes from all parts of the world.

Ways You Can Engage with Grace throughout the Year

Speaking and Consulting Programs

7 Distorted Privacy Beliefs

Take Grace to Work Day

Take Grace to Church Day

Leadership Privacy Makeover

Grace, Teach My Parents Privacy

Single and Private

Privacy and Purity

Married and Private

Privacy with Kids and Teens

Senior and Private

Privacy That Heals

Startup and Small Business Privacy

Beyond Privacy

Tough Questions, Tough Conversations

For information, visit www.GraceBuckler.com/Speaking.

Stay in the Loop: Subscribe to Grace's emails for more spicy church privacy musings and for a chance to receive a free virtual privacy course ($699 value). Visit www.ChurchPrivacyBookSeries.com.

When you sign up, you'll also receive

- up-to-date info on her latest releases,

- downloads and other freebies when available (e.g., the world's first Privacy Prayer Poster), and

- information about when she's at a conference or church near you discussing privacy matters.

Get a Free 15-Minute Live Privacy Breakfast with Grace: This is a custom offer with a Q&A session ($499 value). It's for your church, your leadership, or individual ministry groups (singles, couples, teens, men, women, and seniors). This free gift is subject to availability. Send us your request via www.GraceBuckler.com/Speaking.

Take Grace to Church Day: You can take Grace to your church any day of the week. There's no place she'd rather be. Grace is available for your church's

- business meetings,

- employee retreats,

- organizational and operational consulting,

- leadership coaching,

- privacy courses, and

- privacy orientation for new employees.

Book Grace at www.GraceBuckler.com/Speaking.

Tough Questions, Tough Conversations: Got embarrassing, burning, frustrating, and tough privacy questions? We can relate. Send questions to grace@gracebuckler.com with the subject "Tough Questions." Limited to two questions per person and also subject to availability.

Available Anywhere Books and E-books Are Sold

Bulk Orders: You can purchase *Church Privacy: Who Cares? You!*; *Church Privacy 101*; and *Church Privacy Team* for church leadership and for different ministries in your church. Let your church and church bookstore know you need copies. You'll receive a discounted rate for bulk orders of 10 or more if you order at www.NADPublishing.com. You can also scan this QR code to save 30–40% on our books.

Thoughts: Did you enjoy this book? Was it helpful? Great, let's hear about it. One of your first steps in making a privacy difference starts here. That is, helping other people enjoy and learn from this content. Grace would appreciate you taking just a few minutes of your precious time to leave a review of this book—let Grace and other readers know what you enjoyed most, how it helped, and how you're applying or planning to apply your newfound knowledge. Imagine how many people you'd help by leaving a review on Amazon (even if you bought your book elsewhere).

Your Bright Ideas: Did you know you could email Grace and let her know your thoughts and the bright privacy ideas you've come up with that have helped you personally and at church? Also, if you'd like for Grace to feature your thoughts, experiences, and ideas in her next release or post, let us know, and we'll consider them based on availability.

Send emails to grace@gracebuckler.com.

Special FREE Bonus Gift for You

To help you achieve more success, there are extra BONUS GIFTS for you at www.ChurchPrivacyBookSeries.com.

Bonus Gifts:

Privacy Prayer

Onion Rings Privacy Template

7 Responses to Privacy Invaders

Secure your spot for a free virtual course.
Scan the QR code below.

Additional Training Resources

Privacy Success for Church Volunteers and Employees

This resource provides secrets to turning volunteers into privacy allies who can protect your church and ministry from privacy violations and regulatory and legal issues. To access these quarterly tips, subscribe to the newsletter at www.ChurchPrivacyBookSeries.com.

Photo Credit: The Climate Reality Project

NEW Church Privacy Team Course

Now that you've read *Church Privacy Team*, you probably have lots of questions and tough church privacy decisions to make, and you'd love to have Grace on your side for your church's privacy journey. Don't wait, friend. This course is the best news since *Church Privacy Team* was penned. Join Grace in this fun and simple course. Let yourself be a beginner. Let Grace show you how to get it down every step of the way. Secure your spot at www.LearnChurchPrivacy.com or scan the QR code.

NEW Expert Resources

Attend Grace's Church Privacy On Demand live privacy coaching. Wrangle privacy in church like a pro. And if your church would love to hack her caravan of phenomenal privacy experts, data protection specialists, and privacy lawyers in your area (including proven and trusted cybersecurity and insurance gurus), we'll provide suggestions to attendees.

Scan the QR code for more information on courses.

Connect with Grace Online

Find Grace online and on social media. Help her protect privacy and spread love. Visit www.ChurchPrivacyBookSeries.com and GraceBuckler.com. Better yet, scan this QR code so you don't need to type. Get there quicker!

Notes

* Links provided in this book other than those owned by NAD Publishing are offered to provide our readers with additional information. These links might be unavailable, relocated, or re-indexed by the website owners at any time. We have no control over the availability of these resources.

Preface

1. Scott Berkun, "The Truth about Choosing Book Titles," Scottberkun.com, December 4, 2012, https://scottberkun.com/2012/the-truth-about-picking-book-titles/.

Introduction

1. Sam Bocetta, "How Hackers Emptied Church Coffers with a Simple Phishing Scam," Dark Reading, June 19, 2019, https://www.darkreading.com/network-and-perimeter-security/how-hackers-emptied-church-coffers-with-a-simple-phishing-scam/a/d-id/1334971.

2. Lindsey O'Donnell, "BEC Hack Cons Catholic Church Out of $1.75 Million," Threat Post, April 30, 2019, https://threatpost.com/bec-hack-cons-catholic-church/144212.

3. Sam Bocetta, "How Hackers Emptied Church Coffers with a Simple Phishing Scam."

4. Armen Keteyian, "Hackers Hit Church's Collection Plate," *CBS News*, June 30, 2011, https://www.cbsnews.com/news/hackers-hit-churchs-collection-plate/.

5. Bob Allen, "Southern Baptist Mission Board Reports Data Breach," Baptist News Global, August 1, 2018, https://baptistnews.com/article/southern-baptist-mission-board-reports-data-breach/.

6. Mark Huffman, "Hackers Increasingly Target the Church Collection Plate," ConsumerAffairs, January 26, 2015, https://www.consumeraffairs.com/news/hackers-increasingly-target-the-church-collection-plate-012615.html.

7. Adaure Achumba, "Triad Church Warns of Phishing Scam Asking for Gift Card Purchase," *WFMY News 2*, August 2, 2018, https://www.wfmynews2.com/article/news/local/triad-church-warns-of-phishing-scam-asking-for-gift-card-purchase/83-579667892.

8. Michigan Catholic Conference, "Information about Recent Cyber Attack and Data Breach," Michigan Catholic Conference, n.d., https://www.micatholic.org/benefits/data-breach/.

9. Armen Keteyian, "Hackers Hit Church's Collection Plate."

10. Zachary Ignoffo, "Dark Web Price Index 2021," Privacy Affairs, August 8, 2022, https://www.privacyaffairs.com/dark-web-price-index-2021/.

11. Dee Parsons, "Pastors Ignoring Confidentiality: Having Gospel Gossip Authority?" *The Wartburg Watch*, February 27, 2012, http://thewartburgwatch.com/2012/02/27/pastors-ignoring-confidentiality-having-gospel-gossip-authority/.

12. Steve Gardner, "Church of Christ on Trial and Donahue: Fornication Publicly Disclosed in the Disfellowship Process," Authentic Theology, January 8, 2020, https://authentictheology.com/2020/01/08/church-of-christ-on-trial-and-donahue-fornication-publicly-disclosed-in-the-disfellowship-process/.

13. Foo, Yun Chee, "EU Court Says Jehovah's Witnesses Must Comply with Data Privacy Laws in Door-to-Door Preaching," Reuters, July 10, 2018, https://www.reuters.com/article/idUSKBN1K01LJ.

14. United Nations Conference of Trade and Development, "Data Protection and Privacy Legislation Worldwide," UNCTAD, December 14, 2021, https://unctad.org/page/data-protection-and-privacy-legislation-worldwide.

Chapter 1

1. Lyle Daly and Jack Caporal, "Identity Theft and Credit Card Fraud Statistics," The Ascent, updated March 9, 2023, https://www.fool.com/the-ascent/research/identity-theft-credit-card-fraud-statistics/.

2. Erin Duffin, "Number of Reported Cases of Identity Theft, by State U.S. 2020," Statista, February 9, 2021, https://www.statista.com/statistics/587690/identity-theft-complaints-victims-by-state-in-the-us.

3. WTHR, "Goodwill Caught Selling Donors' Personal Information," WTHR, November 4, 2013, https://www.wthr.com/article/news/local/goodwill-caught-selling-donors-personal-information/531-a7b20d7f-aa7c-4417-8c73-1c1fa30989b5.

Chapter 3

1. National Institute of Standards and Technology, "NIST SP 800-53," NIST, n.d., https://www.nist.gov/privacy-framework/nist-sp-800-53.

Notes

Chapter 4

1. The University of Washington, "Privacy & Security," University Book Store, The University of Washington, n.d., https://www.ubookstore.com/privacy.

2. Edinburgh Napier University, event banner, https://www.napier.ac.uk.

3. Tara John, "California Woman Sues Chipotle for $2.2 Billion Over Using Her Photograph," *Fortune*, January 9, 2017, https://fortune.com/2017/01/09/california-woman-sues-chipotle-for-2-2-billion-over-using-her-photograph.

Chapter 5

1. Brian Krebs, "Target Hackers Broke in Via HVAC Company," Krebs on Security, February 5, 2014, https://krebsonsecurity.com/2014/02/target-hackers-broke-in-via-hvac-company.

2. Web Titan, "Cost of a Retail Data Breach: $179 Million for Home Depot," Web Titan, Titan HQ, March 14, 2017, https://www.webtitan.com/blog/cost-retail-data-breach-179-million-home-depot/.

3. CNBC, "Saudi Aramco Facing $50 Million Cyber Extortion over Leaked Data," CNBC, July 22, 2021, https://www.cnbc.com/2021/07/22/saudi-aramco-facing-50m-cyber-extortion-over-leaked-data.html.

4. Federal Trade Commission, "Eli Lilly Settles FTC Charges Concerning Security Breach," FTC, January 8, 2002, https://www.ftc.gov/news-events/press-releases/2002/01/eli-lilly-settles-ftc-charges-concerning-security-breach.

5. Upwork and Freelancers Union, "Freelancing in America: 2019," Upwork and Freelancers Union, September 23, 2019, https://www.slideshare.net/upwork/freelancing-in-america-2019/1.

6. What To Become, "36 Fascinating Gig Economy Statistics [2023 Update]," What To Become, October 21, 2021, https://whattobecome.com/blog/gig-economy-statistics/.

Chapter 6

1. PCI Compliance Guide, "PCI FAQs," PCI Compliance Guide, n.d., https://www.pcicomplianceguide.org/faq.

2. U.S. Department of Health and Human Services, "Health Information Privacy," HHS, n.d., https://www.hhs.gov/hipaa/index.html.

Chapter 7

1. Roger Barrier, "Can I Sue My Pastor?" Crosswalk, Salem Web Network, January 14, 2014, https://www.crosswalk.com/church/pastors-or-leadership/ask-roger/can-i-sue-my-pastor.html.

2. David Middlebrook, "Pastoral Confidentiality: An Ethical and Legal Responsibility," Assemblies of God, February 2, 2010, https://news.ag.org/features/pastoral-confidentiality-an-ethical-and-legal-responsibility.

3. Ken Behr and Dale Hudson, "Church Confidentiality Policy: What's Appropriate in Children's Ministry," Church Leaders, October 25, 2021, https://churchleaders.com/children/childrens-ministry-articles/150808-appropriate-confidentiality-in-ministry.html.

Chapter 8

1. Karl Vaters, "Small Churches Are Not a Problem, a Virtue or an Excuse," Church Leaders, March 10, 2022, https://churchleaders.com/pastors/pastor-articles/373661-small-churches-not-problem-virtue-excuse.html.

2. Alisyn Camerota, "Little People Accuse Reich of Critical Shortcoming," *Fox News*, May 20, 2015, https://www.foxnews.com/story/little-people-accuse-reich-of-critical-shortcoming.

3. Karl Vaters, "7 Reasons Small Churches Are an Essential Part of the Body of Christ," Pivot, August 6, 2019, https://www.christianitytoday.com/karl-vaters/2019/august/7-reasons-small-churches-are-essential.html.

4. Karl Vaters, "How an Unspoken Justin Bieber Joke Taught Me to Treat Everyone as an Image-Bearer," KarlVaters.com, February 12, 2021, https://karlvaters.com/justin-bieber/.

Chapter 9

1. Louise Matsakis, "FTC Hits TikTok with Record $5.7 Million Fine over Children's Privacy," *Wired*, February 27, 2019, https://www.wired.com/story/tiktok-ftc-record-fine-childrens-privacy/.

2. Russell Brandom, "YouTube Will Pay up to $200 Million after Allegedly Violating Children's Privacy," The Verge, August 30, 2019, https://www.theverge.com/2019/8/30/20841055/youtube-kids-ftc-fine-200-million-privacy-violations.

3. Federal Trade Commission, "Children's Online Privacy Protection Rule: A Six-Step Compliance Plan for Your Business," FTC, n.d., https://www.ftc.gov/tips-advice/business-center/guidance/childrens-online-privacy-protection-rule-six-step-compliance.

Chapter 10

1. Negar Mojtahedi, "Popular Free Apps Compromise Your Personal Information and Security," *Global News*, December 9, 2015, https://globalnews.ca/news/2391430/popular-free-apps-compromise-your-personal-information-and-security/.

2. Information Commissioner's Office, "What Is Personal Data?" ICO, n.d., https://ico.org.uk/for-organisations/guide-to-data-protection/guide-to-the-general-data-protection-regulation-gdpr/key-definitions/what-is-personal-data/.

3. Federal Trade Commission, "Protecting Personal Information: A Guide for Business," FTC, October 2016, https://www.ftc.gov/tips-advice/business-center/guidance/protecting-personal-information-guide-business.

4. Jason Aten, "Apple Is Outing Apps That Snoop on Your Personal Information: In iOS 14, Apps that Look at Your Clipboard Are Getting Flagged," Inc., June 30, 2020, https://www.inc.com/jason-aten/apple-is-outing-apps-that-snoop-on-your-personal-information.html.

Chapter 11

1. Paul Roberts, "2017 Data Breach Report Finds Phishing, Email Attacks Still Potent," Digital Insider, Digital Guardian, August 6, 2021, https://www.digitalguardian.com/blog/2017-data-breach-report-finds-phishing-email-attacks-still-potent.

2. Federal Trade Commission, "FTC Imposes $5 Billion Penalty and Sweeping New Privacy Restrictions on Facebook," FTC, July 24, 2019, https://www.ftc.gov/news-events/news/press-releases/2019/07/ftc-imposes-5-billion-penalty-sweeping-new-privacy-restrictions-facebook.

3. Katie Collins, "Facebook Fined $11.4M in Italy over Data Misuse" CNET, December 7, 2018, https://www.cnet.com/tech/services-and-software/facebook-fined-11-4m-in-italy-over-data-misuse/.

4. Adam Satariano, "Facebook's WhatsApp Is Fined for Breaking the E.U.'s Data Privacy Law," *New York Times*, updated October 4, 2021, https://www.nytimes.com/2021/09/02/business/facebook-whatsapp-privacy-fine.html.

5. Federal Trade Commission, "Google and YouTube Will Pay Record $170 Million for Alleged Violations of Children's Privacy Law," FTC, September 4, 2019, https://www.ftc.gov/news-events/news/press-releases/2019/09/google-youtube-will-pay-record-170-million-alleged-violations-childrens-privacy-law.

6. Jon Porter, "Twitter Hit with €450,000 GDPR Fine Nearly Two Years after Disclosing Data Breach," The Verge, December 15, 2020, https://www.theverge.com/2020/12/15/22176008/twitter-gdpr-fine-protected-tweets-ireland-data-protection-commission.

7. Jacob Kastrenakes, "Twitter faces $250 Million FTC Fine for Misusing Emails and Phone Numbers," The Verge, August 3, 2020, https://www.theverge.com/2020/8/3/21353232/twitter-ftc-fine-misused-email-phone-advertising-2011-settlement.

8. Brian Fung, "Lawmakers Say TikTok Is a National Security Threat, but Evidence Remains Unclear," CNN, March 21, 2023, https://www.cnn.com/2023/03/21/tech/tiktok-national-security-concerns/index.html.

9. Matsakis, "FTC Hits TikTok with Record $5.7 Million Fine."

10. Dan Goodin, "WhatsApp Gives Users an Ultimatum: Share Data with Facebook or Stop Using the App," Ars Technica, January 6, 2021, https://arstechnica.com/tech-policy/2021/01/whatsapp-users-must-share-their-data-with-facebook-or-stop-using-the-app/.

Chapter 13

1. Stella Chan, "Kobe Bryant's Widow Sues LA County Sheriff and the Department for Crash Photo Leak," CNN, September 22, 2020, https://www.cnn.com/2020/09/22/us/kobe-bryant-widow-lawsuit-los-angeles-sheriff/index.html.

2. Angie Chatman, "When My Mother Died without a Will, I Learned a Big Lesson about Money Management as an African American," *Insider*, September 9, 2019, https://www.businessinsider.com/personal-finance/what-mothers-death-taught-me-about-money-as-african-american-2019-9.

3. Florence Nightingale, "Florence Nightingale Quotes," Goodreads, accessed April 25, 2023, https://www.goodreads.com/quotes/487512-the-very-first-requirement-in-a-hospital-is-that-it.

Chapter 15

1. Joshua D. Rogaczewski, "Data Breach Insurance: Does Your Policy Have You Covered?" Of Digital Interest, McDermott Will & Emery, May 26, 2015, www.ofdigitalinterest.com/2015/05/data-breach-insurance-does-your-policy-have-you-covered.

2. Kat Tretina, "Best Cyber Insurance Companies," Investopedia, updated March 31, 2023, https://www.investopedia.com/best-cyber-insurance-5069694.

Appendix B

1. Information Shield, "United States Privacy Laws," Information Shield, n.d., accessed April 27, 2023, https://informationshield.com/free-security-policy-tools/us-data-privacy-laws/.

Appendix D

1. Electronic Frontier Foundation, "International Privacy Standards," EFF, n.d., accessed April 27, 2023, https://www.eff.org/issues/international-privacy-standards.

Appendix F

1. Criminal Proceedings against Bodil Lindqvist, Case C-101/01 (Court of Sweden, 2002), https://eur-lex.europa.eu/legal-content/EN/TXT/?uri=CELEX:62001CJ0101.

Appendix G

1. Church Law & Tax, "Pastor, Church & Law," *Christianity Today*, accessed May 17, 2023, https://www.churchlawandtax.com/pastor-church-law/liabilities-limitations-and-restrictions/clergy-malpractice/.

2. Richard Duncan and Hope Church v. Bervin Peterson, Erwin Lutzer, and The Moody Church, No. 2-04-0911, 408 Ill.App.3d 911, 947 N.E.2d 305, 349 Ill.Dec. 668 (2010), https://caselaw.findlaw.com/court/il-court-of-appeals/1181795.html.

3. Claudia Lenore Snyder v. Evangelical Orthodox Church, Nos. H003864, H003647 (1989) https://caselaw.findlaw.com/ca-court-of-appeal/1769364.html.

4. Guinn v. Church of Christ of Collinsville, No. 62154, 1989 OK 8, 775 P.2d 766, 60 OBJ 144 (1989), https://law.justia.com/cases/oklahoma/supreme-court/1989/10494.html.

5. David Orion Smith v. Calvary Christian Church and Mark Byers, No. 114287, (2000), https://caselaw.findlaw.com/mi-supreme-court/1275616.html.

6. C.L. Westbrook Jr. v. Peggy Lee Penley, No. 04-0838 (2007), https://caselaw.findlaw.com/tx-supreme-court/1068336.html.

Index

Page numbers in *italics* indicate figures or tables.

A

access to personal information
    approval process for, 98–102
    assessment of privacy practices with, 24, 30–31, 169
    criteria for, 99
    for freelancers, 115–121, *118–119*
    management plan for, 221
    by owner, 41, 42, 82
    tips, values, and action steps for, 99–100, 101–102
    training and, 135
    website permission options for, 117–*119*
    See also disclosure of personal information

accountability
    in church culture, 11–13, 175–183, 221
    for personal information, 30–32, 42, 160
    with privacy roles, 43
    to regulators, 205–206, 288

accuracy of personal information, 41, 42, 82

Acts 9:10-15 (Saul of Tarsus), 197

administrative access on online platforms, 112, 118, 123–124

advertisements on websites and apps, 233–234

age and birthdate, 25, 91, 212, 265, 267, 268

age verification requirements, 149

altar call (invitation) in worship services, 255, 256–258

altar counselors (volunteers), 254, 255, 256

analytics, website, 84

announcements in churches, 269, 270

antivirus software, 220, 241

Apple IOS, 223

Apple's App Store, 223, 231, 234–235

apps, 222–238
    assessment of privacy practices with, 230–231, 235–237
    Bible, 233–238
    for church management, 227–232
    deletion of nonessential, 223, 231
    of external workers, 224–225
    inventory and evaluation of, *226–227*, 231, 237
    privacy concerns with, 222–225, 232, 233–235
    seven steps of security with, 225–226
    tips, values, and actions steps for, 231–232, 237–238

attorneys, privacy, 77, 201, 290, 314, 315

audit teams, 46

B

banner privacy notices for events, 90, 92

baptisms, 27, 258

Behr, Ken, 183

Bible apps, 233–238

Bible Gateway, 233, 234

Bible Hub, 233

Bible studies, cameras at, 253

BigScoots, 83

birthdates, 91, 212, 265, 267, 268

bookstores/gift shops
    example privacy statement for, 87–*88*
    implied consent with records of, 63
    patron records of, 28
    secure shopping at, 145–162 (*see also* financial transactions, security of)
    training of staff at, 149–150

Bryant, Vanessa, 280

Buckler, Grace, 3–5, 198–199, 309–311, 347–358

bulletins, church, 28, 257, 261–264, *263*, 266–268, 270

business interruptions, 239, 295

C

cameras in churches, 252–260
    See also photos/videos

CCPA (California Consumer Privacy Act), 12, 323, 325

certifications for privacy experts, 200–201, 314

chief privacy officers (CPOs), 44, 136

children, 211–216
    childcare for, 27, 213, 214, 216
    online privacy protection for, 94, 211–212, 213–215, 247, 323
    parental/guardian consent for, 94, 212, 213, 214–215, 244, 247, 323
    privacy notices and, 73, 79, 84, 213, 214
    social media violations against, 244, 247, 250

Children's Online Privacy Protection Act (COPPA), 149, 211, 215, 247, 323

"Childrens Online Privacy Protection Rule" (FTC), 215

China, 249–250

choice of church members, 252–260, 261, 268–270, 276–279

church bulletins, 28, 257, 261–264, *263*, 266–268, 270

church clinics, 163–164, 167–168

"Church Confidentiality Policy: What's Appropriate in Children's Ministry" (Behr and Hudson), 183

church culture
    accountability in, 11–13, 175–183, 221
    complaints of sexual misconduct in, 179–184

    criticism and disagreements in, 175–176, 182
    mental health privacy in, 188–195
    of privacy, 54, 207, 209, 221, 237, 259, 310
    of trust, 32, 48–51, 53–54, 71, 74, 157, 169, 194

church decision-making structures, 100–101

church directories, 264–266, 268–269, 270

church management apps, 227–232

church meetings, cameras at, 253

church members
    credit/debit cards of, 117, 149, 151
    from other countries, 12, 60, 61, 167, 243, 326–335
    personal data collected from, 24–26, 28
    privacy training for, 67–68
    trust of, 32, 48–51, 53–54, 71, 74, 157, 169, 194
    See also choice of church members

church operations, 103–216
    of bookstores, 145–162
    and children, 211–216
    and counseling, 171–174, 184–188
    employees in, 124–127, 131–135, 142–144
    freelancers and vendors in, 104–124, 127–131
    of gyms, 162–163, 165–167, 169
    of health clinics and fairs, 163–165, 167–170
    leadership/clergy in, 171–184
    and mental health, 188–195
    of small churches, 196–210
    See also specific topics, e.g. bookstores

church policies. *See* privacy policies

church privacy
    introduction to, 6–16
    basics of, 17–102, 309–310 (*see also* privacy basics)
    in church operations, 103–216
    with communication and technology, 217–285 (*see also* communications; technology)
    designating leaders for (*see* privacy team)
    violations of, 287–308 (*see also* privacy violations)

Index

Church Privacy 101 (Buckler), 4–5, 15, 48–49, 134, 208, 283, 309, 339

church privacy notices. *See* privacy notices

Church Privacy: Who Cares? You! (Buckler), 309

church services. *See* worship services

clergy. *See* leadership/clergy

collection limitation, 41, 42, 212, 213, 273

collection of personal information, 23–29, 73, 80, 81, 145–146, 212

communications, 261–285
    announcements, 269
    assessment of privacy practices with, 266–269, 273–274, 277–278, 282–283
    church bulletins, 28, 257, 261–264, *263*, 266–268, 270
    directories, 264–266, 268–269, 270
    during funerals and estate planning, 280–284
    during hospitalizations, 276–279
    for prayer announcements and requests, 28, 96, 258, 261–264, *263*, 272–276
    tips, values, and action steps for, 269–271, 275–276, 279, 283–285
    See also email; technology

complaints, handling
    importance of, 14–15
    privacy advisors and coordinators for, 316, 319
    with privacy notices, 73, 79, 83
    of sexual misconduct in church, 179–184

compliance, privacy, 128–131, 165, 167, 168, 177

computer networks, 218, 220, 239–240, 241, 290, 295

computers, securing, 202–203, 208

See also devices

conferences. *See* events

confidentiality, 119–121, 182–183

congregants. *See* church members

consent for children by parent/guardian, 94, 212, 213, 214–215, 244, 247, 323

consent for data collection
    avoiding lawsuits with, 62–64
    children and, 211–212, 213, 214, 215, 323
    at events, 89, 90, 93, 94–95
    with health information, 166
    as privacy principle, 41, 42
    types of, 62–64
    withdrawal of, 94

consent for information sharing
    in church communications, 93, 94–95, 261, 262, 268, 269–270
    in counseling situations, 172–174

contact information
    in privacy notices, 73, 79, 80–81, 84, 93
    for privacy roles, *136*

contract workers. *See* external workers

cookies, website, 85, 229–230, 234, 236–237

COPPA (Children's Online Privacy Protection Act), 149, 211, 215, 247, 323

COPRA (Consumer Online Privacy Rights Act), 325

costs
    of data breaches, 9–11, 24, 106, 139, 289–291
    of insurance policies, 300, 302–307
    of privacy management, 12

counseling
    assessment of privacy practices with, 172–173, 185–186
    data-collection from, 27
    examples of lawsuits over, 341, 342
    informal advice as, 172, 173
    with leadership/clergy, 171–174, 341, 342
    with professionals or volunteers, 172, 184–188
    safety and legal concerns in, 174, 186
    tips, values, and action steps for, 177–178, 186–188

court proceedings (records), 22

COVID-19 pandemic, 107–108

CPOs (chief privacy officers), 44, 136

credibility, establishing, 32, 48–51, 53–54, 71, 157, 169, 194, 208

credit/debit cards
    of church, 146
    of church members, 117, 149, 151
    in data breaches, 9, 289, 336
    free credit reports for, 322
    PCI DSS for, 147–150, *148*, 158
    vendor payment systems for, 146–147

credit monitoring, 296, 297, 303

customer care and service teams, 46

customer service for apps, 228–229

cyberattacks, 6–9, 298, 336–338, 340
    See also data breaches

cyber liability insurance, 149, 290, 293, 294–296, 301–302, 307
    See also insurance policies

cybersecurity, 218–222
    assessment of, 155, 220, 221–222
    versus data privacy, 218
    definition of, 155, 218–219
    liability policy coverage for, 296, 300, 304
    resources on, 344–345

D

dark web, personal information on, 9

data breaches
    assessment of privacy practices with, 289–291
    costs/consequences of, 9–11, 24, 106, 139, 289–291, 295, 297–298, 301
    examples of, 6–9, 298, 336–338, 340
    insurance for, 294–299, 301–308
    lawsuits over, 57, 66–67, 290
    logging, 135, *137–138*
    negligence and, 57, 66–67, 206, 290, 296, 297, 298–299, 305, 307
    preparedness for, 288–292
    prevention of, 9, 13–16
    responding to, 135, *136–138*, 288–292, 295, 297–298
    risks from, 139, 269, 289
    tip, value, and action steps for, 291–292
    by vendors, 105–106, 128–129, 336–337

data breach insurance, 293–294, 298, 303, 307
    See also insurance policies

data protection officers (DPOs), 44

data retention policies
    for health-care information, 166, 168, 169
    for personal information, 33, 36, 141
    for worker information, 125, 127

David's repentance (Psalm 51:13), 179

death records, 27
    See also funerals

debit cards. *See* credit/debit cards

defamation, 10, 57, 64–66, 300, 341

devices
    apps for (*see* apps)
    donation of, 37–38
    of external workers, 105, 128–129, 302
    insurance coverage for, 296
    limiting access to, 202, 203
    network connections of, 218, 220, 239–240, 241, 290, 295
    physical security for, 96, 221
    storage of personal information on, 30, 96
    See also cybersecurity

digital and paper information, 36, 42, 167, 185, 219, 301

direct marketing, 82

directories, church, 264–266, 268–269, 270

disclosure of personal information

as basis for lawsuits, 10, 57, 245, 341–342
as choice of church members, 261, 268–270
in counseling situations, 171–174, 185–188
health-related, 164–165, 166–169
legal obligation for, 82, 186
nondisclosure agreements and, 119–120
Onion Model for management of, 47–55
in prayer requests, 272–276
privacy policies and, 125, 127
risks of, 139, 269
role of privacy advisors in, 316

disposal policies, 36–39, 82, 221

divorce example (Matthew 19:8-9), 234

documents, creating, 143, 206, 221

donations as security risks, 34–35, 37–38

DPOs (data protection officers), 44

driver's license numbers, 9, 120, 202

due diligence, evidence for, 36, 43, 66–67, 132, 135, 240, 297, 299, 304–305

Duncan v. Peterson, 9, 341

E

e-commerce sites, 149, 158, 160
See also bookstores/gift shops

ECPA (Electronic Communications Privacy Act), 142, 322, 324

education. *See* training

EFF (Electronic Frontier Foundation), 225, 334, 335

electronic and paper information, 36, 42, 167, 185, 219, 301

email, 239–243
accounts, protection of, 30, 274
attachments, 8, 84, 239–240
with events and marketing, 92, 93–94
as preferred mode for discussions, 169
security with, 84, 240–242
vulnerabilities with, 8, 239–240, 340

employees
for childcare, 213, 214, 216
exit interviews for, 13
personal data collected from, 24–26, 27
privacy notices for, 78, 88–89
privacy policies for, 124–127
salary negotiations with, 142–144
tips, values, and action steps for, 126–127, 143–144
training for, 131–135, 289

employment privacy, 142

encryption
for cybersecurity, 220–221
for due diligence, 96, 297
of email with TLS, 84
PCI compliance with, 151
with SSL, 157, 158, 166

estate planning, 281–283, 284

evangelism/outreach, 11, 28

events, privacy notices for, 89–95, 168–169

exit interviews, 13

external workers
contracts with, 107, 115, 119, 129–130, 147
insurance coverage for, 302, 303
privacy policies with, 104–105, 106–107, 122, 127–131, 224–225
security with devices and apps of, 105, 128–129, 147, 224–225, 302
timeframes for jobs of, 119, 129
training of, 289
See also freelancers; third-party services; vendors

F

Facebook, 244–246

fairness, 181, 274

false light and defamation, 10, 57, 64–66, 300, 341

FBI (Federal Bureau of Investigation), 6, 8
FCRA (Fair Credit Reporting Act), 142, 322, 323, 324
Federal Trade Commission (FTC), 35, 215, 224, 245, 247, 324
fellowship, value of, 188
filming worship services, 252–260
finance teams, 46
financial impacts of data breaches, 9–11, 24, 106, 139, 289–291
financial transactions, security of, 146–162
    assessment of privacy practices with, 149, 151, 153, 155, 156, 160
    with payment processors, 151–154
    with PCI DSS compliance, 147–150, *148*, 158
    privacy laws regulating, 58
    with SSL online, 155–158
    tips, values, and action steps for, 150, 153–154, 156–157, 161–162
    vendor payment systems and, 146–147, 153
    with website privacy notices, 158–159
financial transactions, unauthorized, 295
first-party insurance coverage, 301
frameworks (guidelines), 60–62
fraud, 224, 295
freelancers, 107–124, 127–131
    access permissions for, 115–121, *118–119*
    avoiding scams with, 108, 109–117, 121–122, 128–129
    communicating with, 114, 116, 121, 123
    compliance of, 128–131
    direct-hiring of, 106–107
    disruptions with, 114–115
    guidelines for working with, 112–117, 121–124, 224–225
    paying, 112, 123–124
    platforms for, 107, 111, 113, 115, 121–122

    prevalence of, 108
    privacy policies for, 104–105, 106–107, 122, 127–131, 224–225
    services provided by, 109–110, 116–118
    for websites, 112, 116–121
    See also external workers
FTC (Federal Trade Commission), 35, 215, 224, 245, 247, 324
funerals, 280–281, 283–284

G

gateways/platforms (for payments), 151–154
GDPR (General Data Protection Regulation), 57, 149, 166–167, 211, 213, 326
general liability insurance, 298, 299–300
gift shops. *See* bookstores/gift shops
gig workers, 107–110
    See also freelancers
Goodwill Industries, 34–35, 337–338
Google Play, 223
government data, 21–22
Guinn v. Church of Christ of Collinsville, 341
gym services, 162–163, 165–167, 169

H

hacking, 6–9, 159, 202–203
healings at worship services, 253–254
health-care compliance, 165, 167, 168
health clinics, 163–164, 167–168
health fairs, 164–165, 168–169, 170
health information
    collecting, 163, 164, 168
    privacy laws regulating, 57–58, 163–165, 166–167, 322
    protecting, 162–170

Index

social media and, 96

health insurance, 163, 166

HIPAA (Health Insurance Portability and Accountability Act), 163, 164, 165, 166–167, 322

hoarding information, 33

Home Depot, 106, 337

hospitalizations, 276–279

hotlines for mental health challenges, 192

Hudson, Dale, 183

human resources teams, 45

I

IBM data breach, 298

identity theft, 7, 34–35, 295

illnesses and hospitalizations, 261–264, *263*, 276–279

implied consent, 63–64

incidents, privacy, 135–139, *137*

industry codes and regulations, 59, 147–150, 322–325, 327–333

information security, 45, 61, 155, 219, 220–222

information technology (IT), 45, 218, 219, 290

insurance policies, 293–308
    introduction to, 293–295
    asking questions about, 298–301
    assessment of risks and need for, 304–307
    benefits versus denials, 297–299
    for bookstore websites, 149
    cost and risk calculations with, 300, 302–307
    coverage commonly in, 294–297
    cyber liability, 294–296, 301–302, 307
    general liability, 299–300
    negligence and, 296, 297, 298–299, 305, 307
    timely reporting of losses to, 294, 295, 299
    tip, value, and action steps for, 307–308

internal audit teams, 46

internal privacy notices, 88–89

internal privacy policies, 96–102

international standards/laws, 60, 61, 167, 243, 326–335

interviews, privacy rights in, 142–144

intrusion lawsuits, 10, 56, 62–64

inventory of personal information, 23–32

investigations into misconduct, 181–184

invitation (altar call) in worship services, 255, 256–258

IT (information technology), 45, 218, 219, 290

J

job descriptions for privacy roles, 44–45, 314–321

job interviews, privacy rights in, 142–144

jobs, privacy. *See* privacy roles; privacy team

John 3:1-21 (Nicodemus), 255, 257

John 19:38 (Joseph of Arimathea), 255, 257

Joshua 2:14 (Rahab and Israel's spies), 197

K

kindness, 176, 182, 193, 204, 280

L

language use in notices, 76, 77

laptops. *See* devices

laws and regulations
    children-related, 211–212, 213, 215
    church-related, 57–60, 67, 105, 291
    compliance through training, 66–68
    four categories of, 154–155
    frameworks as guides for, 60–62
    health-care related, 162–165

industry codes and regulations, 59, 147–150
international, 60, 61, 167, 243, 326–335
US federal and state, 322–325

lawsuits, 56–69
introduction to, 9–11
assessments and actions for avoiding, 57–62, 63–68
awareness of laws and, 57–62, 66–69
data breach/negligence, 57, 66–67, 290
disclosure of private facts, 10, 57, 245, 341–342
examples of, 9, 245, 341, 342
false light/defamation, 10, 57, 64–66, 341
insurance coverage for, 296, 300
intrusion/privacy invasion, 10, 56, 62–64
over online photos, 91, 95, 339
privacy violations leading to, 10, 56–57, 245, 341–342
by regulators, 9, 62

lawyers, privacy, 77, 201, 290, 314, 315

layered privacy notices, 75–76, 77, 85–86

leaders, designating. *See* privacy team

leadership/clergy, 171–184
assessment of privacy practices of, 172–173, 176–177, 181–183, 185–186
in counseling role, 171–174, 341, 342
misuse of privileges by, 174–175
as power of attorney, 282, 283
sermons by, 173, 174–178, 204, 208
sexual misconduct and, 179–184
tip, value, and action steps for, 177–178, 182–184

legal teams, 45

libel, 66, 97, 300

limitation on collecting personal information, 41, 42, 91, 167, 212, 213, 273

Lindqvist, Bodil, 91, 95, 339

location information, 96–97

logs of incidents and data breaches, 135, *137–138*

loyalty (false) versus privacy, 179–180

Luke 15:4 (parable of lost sheep), 14–15

M

Mailchimp, 83

marketing privacy, 93–94

Matthew 19:8-9 (divorce example), 234

media responses to data breaches, 291, 297–298

media team responsibilities, 256

members. *See* church members

mental health privacy concerns, 188–195

microphone misuse, 174–178

Microsoft Windows, 223

Middlebrook, David, 182

MOU (memorandum of understanding), 129

N

NDA (nondisclosure agreement), 119–121

negligence
insurance policies and, 296, 297, 298–299, 305, 307
lawsuits, 57, 66–67, 290
regulators and, 205–206, 288

networks, computer, 218, 220, 239–240, 241, 290, 295

Nicodemus (John 3:1-21), 255, 257

NIH (National Institution of Health) website example, 85–*86*

NIST (National Institute of Science and Technology) 800 series, 61

nonprofit organizations, 57–58

notices. *See* privacy notices

Index

O

Onion Model for sharing information
    assessment of privacy practices with, 51–54, 343
    about counseling situations, 171–172
    examples of, 47–51, *50, 51*
    about mental health, 193
    Onion Rings template for, 54, *343*
    when handling complaints, 182

opportunity costs, 289

outreach/evangelism, 11, 28

over-accommodation of people, 206

oversharing, 48, 185, 264

P

PAP (prayer and privacy), 264, 275

paper and electronic information, 36, 42, 167, 185, 219, 301

parable of lost sheep (Luke 15:4), 14–15

parental/guardian consent for children, 94, 212, 213, 214–215, 244, 247, 323

passwords, 36, 112, 220

"Pastoral Confidentiality: An Ethical and Legal Responsibility" (Middlebrook), 182

pastors. *See* leadership/clergy

payment platforms, 151–154

PCI Compliance Guide, *148*

PCI DSS (Payment Card Industry Data Security Standard), 147–150, *148,* 158

permission options for freelancers, 115–121, *118–119*

personal identifiable information (PII), 224, 225

personal information, 18–39
    introduction to privacy and, 7–9, 13–15
    access to (*see* access to personal information)
    assessment of privacy practices with, 30–31, 36–37, 51–54, 304
    of children, 212–215
    collecting, 23–29, 73, 80, 81, 145–146, 212
    collection limitations with, 41, 42, 91, 167, 212, 213, 273
    definition of, 18–19, 21–23, 120
    disclosure of (*see* disclosure of personal information)
    disposal policies for, 36–39, 82, 221
    example with "Eden," 20–22
    hoarding, 33
    inventory of, 23–32
    privacy principles with, 41–42
    privacy rights with, 81–82
    protection of (*see* protection of personal information)
    risk reduction and risk acceptance with, 304–305
    sale of, 9, 34–35, 81, 97
    sample privacy notice and, 78–85
    sensitive, 20–21, 23, 26, 162
    sharing (with Onion Model), 47–55
    social media and, 96–97
    storage of (*see* storage of personal information)
    tips, values, and action steps for, 31–32, 38–39, 54–55
    types of, 19–20, 24–26
    See also data breaches

Personal Information Protection and Electronic Data Act (PIPEDA), 57, 327

PHI (Protected Health Information), 162–164, 165, 166–168

photos/videos
    of children, 214
    at events, 90–91, 92–93, 94–95, 281
    lawsuits over, 91, 95, 339
    release forms needed for, 90–91, 93, 94–95, 339
    on social media, 90–91, 93, 94–95
    of worship services, 252–260

physical security, 221

PII (personal identifiable information), 224, 225

PIPEDA (Personal Information Protection and Electronic Data Act), 57, 327

Planning Center app, 228–229

policy management teams, 46

posters, privacy prayer, 242, 311

power of attorney appointment, 283

PPRA (Protection of Pupil Rights Amendment), 323

prayer categories, 274

prayer requests, 28, 96, 258, 261–264, *263*, 272–276

preparedness for data breaches, 288–292

privacy, 40, 50, 56, 155
   See also church privacy

privacy advisors, 315–318

privacy analysts, 44

privacy basics, 17–102, 309–310
   and laws, 56–69
   for personal information, 18–39
   privacy notices and policies, 70–102
   privacy principles, 40–55

privacy books and resources, 344–346

privacy by default, 159–162

privacy by design, 159–162

privacy certification, 200–201, 314

privacy consciousness, 204

privacy coordinators/office managers, 43–44, 45, 47, 100, 136, 314, 315, 318–321

privacy courses/seminars, 15, 67, 134, 353

privacy directors, 315, 317, 318, 319–320

privacy engineers, 44

privacy experts/consultants
   definition/description of, 44, 314
   for analysis of laws, 58, 61–62
   certification for, 200–201, 314
   consultation with, 310, 314
   for health-care compliance, 167, 168
   for insurance decisions, 304, 305–306
   limited number of, 134, 291, 314
   for privacy notices, 77
   relationships with, 291, 310, 314
   in small churches, 200–201, 208
   for trainings, 42–43, 67, 132, 314

privacy incidents, 135–139, *137*

privacy jobs. *See* privacy roles

privacy managers, 44, 314

privacy notices, 70–95
   children and, 73, 79, 84, 213, 214
   definition of, 41, 70–71, 72, 77
   for events, 89–95, 168–169
   examples of, 78–88
   guidelines for creating, 72–77
   internal, 88–89
   layered, 75–76, 77, 85–*86*
   as legal statement, 77–78
   as privacy principle, 41, 42
   sections of, 79–85
   tips, values, and action steps for, 77, 94–95
   uniqueness of, 71–72, 77–78, 158–159
   updating, 73, 83
   usability tips for, 75–77

privacy policies
   assessment of privacy practices with, 125–128, 129–130
   for counseling, 185–186
   for data/device disposal, 38
   definition and purpose of, 70–71, 104–105
   for employees, 124–127
   for external workers, 104–105, 106–107, 122, 127–131, 224–225

for granting access to personal data, 98–102
for protection of personal data, 30–32
for storage of personal data, 96–98
for technology, 221
tips, values, and actions steps for, 123–124, 126–127, 130–131

privacy principles, 40–55
as basis for laws and regulations, 57
golden rules of, 41–43
with Onion Model for sharing information, 47–55, *50, 51, 343*
roles for implementing, 43–45
team contributions to, 45–47

privacy project managers, 44

privacy rights
definition of, 56
during investigations of misconduct, 181–182
list of, 81–82
of mentally ill, 189–195
privacy notices and, 73, 81–82

privacy risks. *See* risk(s)

privacy roles, 43–47
accountability with, 43
contact information for, *136*
descriptions of, 43–45, 314–321
student internships with, 54, 201
teams collaborating with, 45–46
See also privacy experts

privacy settings, 159–162

privacy statements, 71, *86, 87–88*

privacy team, designating leaders for
for apps, 232, 237–238
for bulletins and directories, 270
for camera use, 259
for children's privacy, 212, 215
for complying with laws and regulations, 68
for counseling privacy, 177–178, 187–188
for cybersecurity, 222
for data breach responses, 291–292
for data disposal and device donations, 38
for email privacy, 242–243
for event privacy, 95
for funeral and estate planning, 284
for handling complaints, 183–184
for health privacy considerations, 169
for hospital visitations, 279
for insurance coverage, 307–308
for inventory of personal information, 31–32
for leadership/clergy situations, 177–178, 183–184
for managing privacy risks, 141–142
for mental health awareness, 194
for policies on storage and access, 98, 101–102
for prayer request privacy, 275
for privacy notices, 74, 77
for privacy policies, 126, 130
for secure financial transactions, 150, 154, 156–157, 161–162
for sharing of personal information, 54–55
at small churches, 206–207, 208–209
for social media privacy, 251
for trainings, 134, 150

privacy versus false loyalty, 179–180

privacy violations
identification of, 31
insurance as protection against, 293–308
by social media companies, 243–250
types of, 10, 56–57
See also data breaches; laws and regulations

probate, wills, and estate planning, 281–283, 284

product development teams, 45

Protected Health Information (PHI), 162–164, 165, 166–168

protection of personal information
accountability for, 30–32, 42, 160
in church communications, 261–270

with freelancers, 112, 115, 117, 123–124, 224–225
in health-related settings, 162–170
importance of, 22–23
with physical security, 42
with technical privacy settings, 21, 160–161

Psalm 51:13 (David's repentance), 179

publicity, negative, 10–11, 139, 291, 295, 297–298, 301

publicity materials, consent with, 93, 94–95

publicly available information, 22

public record data, 21–22

purpose limitation, 41, 42, 91, 167, 212

Q

quality control with personal information, 41, 42, 82

R

Rahab and Israel's spies (Joshua 2:14), 197

ransomware attacks, 8, 296, 301

reading level of notices, 76, 77

receptionists as gatekeepers, 265–266

registration for events, 28, 89, 91–92, 94–95

regulators
    accountability to, 205–206, 288
    avoiding penalties from, 36, 43, 66–67, 132, 135, 240, 299
    basis for fines by, 24, 132, 211, 215, 240, 288, 293
    examples of investigations by, 336, 337, 338
    lawsuits by, 9, 62
    on PII definition, 224
    privacy notices and, 75, 85
    social media concerns of, 243–244, 250

Reich, Robert, 198

release forms for photos, 90–91, 93, 94

religious beliefs, 21, 323

reputational damage
    of churches from data breaches, 10–11, 139, 291, 295, 297–298, 301
    of individuals from privacy breaches, 57, 66, 97, 139, 204

responsible parties. *See* accountability

retention policies. *See* data retention policies

risk(s)
    acceptance, 304–305
    assessments of, 129, 139–141, 166, 304–307
    from data breaches, 139, 269, 289
    management of, 140–141, 304–307
    residual, 306

role-based training, 132

S

safe places for deep sharing, 49

safety reasons for disclosing information, 174, 186, 257

salary negotiations and guides, 142–144

sale of personal information, 9, 34–35, 81, 97

sanctuary volunteers (altar counselors), 254, 255, 256

Saul of Tarsus (Acts 9:10-15), 197

Saxton, Jo, 180

scams with freelancers, avoiding, 108, 109–117, 121–122, 128–129

search engines, 85, 158

secretaries, 29, 265

Secure Sockets Layer (SSL), 155–158, 166

sensitive personal information, 20–21, 23, 26, 162

sermons, 173, 174–178, 204, 208

Servant Keeper app, 229–230

sexual harassment policies, 181

Index

sexual misconduct, 179–184

sharing information, Onion Model for, 47–55
See also disclosure of personal information

shredding of papers, 36, 221

slander, 65, 66, 97, 300

small churches, 196–210
action plan for, 200–202, 203–204, 206–210
assessment of privacy practices at, 207–210
prevalence of, 200
privacy as concern for, 196–198, 199, 202–206
tip, value, and action steps for, 208–210

"Small Church Finances" (Vaters), 203

Smith v. Calvary Christian Church, 341

Snyder v. Evangelical Orthodox Church, 9, 341

social media, 243–251
assessment of privacy practices with, 93, 244–250
children's privacy on, 211, 214–215
permission options for builders of, 117–119, *118–119*
personal information and, 96–97, 243
photos on, 90–91, 93, 94–95
in privacy notices, 84
as publicly available information, 22
violations by companies in, 243–244, 245–246, 247, 248–249, 250

Social Security numbers, 112, 202

software updates/patches, 160–161, 220

spiritual expressions and decisions, 252, 253–255, 256–258

SSL (Secure Sockets Layer), 155–158, 166

St. Ambrose Catholic Parish Church (Ohio), 6

stigma of mental illness, 190–191

storage of personal information
assessment of privacy practices with, 24, 29–31, 96–97
internal rules for, 96–98

privacy notices and, 80
with retention and disposal policies, 33, 36
tip, value, and action steps for, 97–98
training on, 97

streaming worship services, 246, 252–260

Strickland, Danielle, 180

Stripe, 83

student internships, 54, 201

suicide, 189, 192

Sunday school, 213, 216

Sunday services. *See* worship services

T

Target, 106, 128–129, 336

team, privacy. *See* privacy team

team support for privacy practices, 45–47

technology, 217–286
apps, 222–238 (*see also* apps)
assessment of privacy practices with, 155, 220, 221–222, 230–231, 235–237, 240–242, 244–250, 256–258
cameras, 252–260
cybersecurity, 218–222
email, 239–243 (*see also* email)
and prayer requests, 96, 272–273
social media, 243–251 (*see also* social media)
tips, values, and action steps for, 221–222, 231–232, 237–238, 242–243, 250–251, 258–260
updates with, 160–161, 230, 241

testimonies, 274

third-party insurance coverage, 302, 303

third-party services
data breaches through, 105–106, 128–129, 336–338
data storage through, 30, 82
for deleting data from devices, 37

for disposal of personal information, 36
examples of, 83, 85
of gig workers/freelancers, 109–110
implied consent with, 63
insurance for, 302, 303
privacy notices and, 73, 80, 81
for processing payments, 146–147, 151, 153
for websites, 84–85, 112, 116–121
See also external workers

TikTok, 211, 249–250

timeframe for sharing information, 50, 53

tithing/offering records, 28

TLS (Transport Layer Security), 84

tracking, online, 229–230, 233–235

training
assessment of, 133–135
avoiding lawsuits with, 57–62, 66–68
for awareness, 42–43, 47, 97, 132, 237, 317–318
as best place to start, 47, 66–68
of bookstore staff, 149–150
on children's privacy, 213, 214, 216
for counseling privacy, 185, 186
with courses and seminars, 15, 67, 134, 353
with creative engagement, 54, 67–68, 99, 131–132, 237
customized, 131
on data breach responses, 289
for employees, 131–135, 289
for events, 92
of external workers, 289
for healthcare privacy, 166
for mental health awareness, 192, 193
with posters, 242, 311
privacy experts for, 42–43, 67, 132, 314
privacy policies as, 126
as proof of due diligence, 67–68, 132, 134
resources for, 347, 357–358
in small churches, 207

for technology-related security, 220, 221, 230, 237, 240, 241–242
types of, 132
updates and timeframes for, 133–134
for volunteers, 101, 289

training department, 46

transparency
building trust with, 74
in funeral and estate planning, 282–283
as privacy principle, 41, 42
about sharing of counseling information, 171–172, 173

Transport Layer Security (TLS), 84

trust, building, 32, 48–51, 53–54, 71, 74, 157, 169, 194

trust, misplaced, 202–203

Twitter, 248–249

U

University of Toronto, 315

updating technology products, 160–161, 230, 241

usability tips for notices, 75–77, 85–87, *86*

US Constitution, 322

ushers in worship services, 253, 258, 259

V

Vanderbloemen's Guide, 143

Vaters, Karl, 196, 200, 203

vendors
bookstore payment systems by, 146–147, 151, 153
data breaches by, 105–106, 128–129, 336–338
definition of, 128
privacy policies for, 104–105, 106–107, 122, 127–131, 153, 224–225
See also freelancers

Index

verbal consent, 62–64

Verizon Data Breach Investigation Report (2017), 239

violations. *See* privacy violations

viruses, computer, 240

visiting during hospitalizations, 276–279

volunteers
    altar counselors, 254, 255, 256
    childcare, 213, 214, 216
    collection of data from, 28
    for evaluating apps, 231
    exit interviews for, 13
    privacy example with, 19–21
    sensitivity during worship services by, 253–255
    student internships, 54, 201
    training for, 101, 289

VPN (virtual private network), 241

W

Watson, Emily, 34–35

websites
    Bible, 235–236
    blocking, 241
    bookstore privacy notices for, 158–159
    children's privacy on, 211–212, 213, 214–215
    cookies on, 85, 229–230, 234, 236–237
    examples of privacy notices for, 78–88
    freelancers for, 112, 116–121
    https:// versus http://, 157
    and links to other websites, 83
    permission options for builders of, 117–119, *118–119*
    prayer requests on, 272–273
    privacy notices for, 70, 72–77, 213
    search engines for, 85, 158
    security/performance of, 85, 156
    SSL for secure shopping on, 155–158
    usability of, 75–77, 85–87, *86*

Westbrook v. Penley, 342

WhatsApp, 244, 245, 250

whistleblowers, 180–181

wills, probate, and estate planning, 281–283, 284

WordPress, 83

worship services
    altar call (invitation) in, 255, 256–258
    apps for management of, 227–228
    privacy choices with cameras in, 252–259
    YouTube for streaming, 246

written consent, 62–64

Y

YouTube, 211, 246–247

www.ingramcontent.com/pod-product-compliance
Lightning Source LLC
Chambersburg PA
CBHW082149070526
44585CB00020B/2140